Oxford AQA History

A LEVEL AND AS

D1650842

Democracy and Nazism: Germany 1918–1945

REVISION GUIDE

 RECAP   APPLY   REVIEW   SUCCEED

Robert Whitfield

Kirsty Taylor

OXFORD

OXFORD
UNIVERSITY PRESS

Great Clarendon Street, Oxford, OX2 6DP, United Kingdom

Oxford University Press is a department of the University of Oxford.
It furthers the University's objective of excellence in research,
scholarship, and education by publishing worldwide. Oxford is a
registered trade mark of Oxford University Press in the UK and in
certain other countries

British Library Cataloguing in Publication Data
Data available

978-0-19-842142-9

1 3 5 7 9 10 8 6 4 2

Kindle edition: 978-019-842143-6

Paper used in the production of this book is a natural, recyclable
product made from wood grown in sustainable forests.
The manufacturing process conforms to the environmental
regulations of the country of origin.

Printed in Great Britain by Bell and Bain Ltd., Glasgow

Acknowledgements

The publisher would like to thank Sally Waller for her work on
the Student Book on which this Revision Guide is based and Judith
Daniels for reviewing this Revision Guide.

The publishers would like to thank the following for permissions to
use copyright material:

I. Aicher-Scholl: *The White Rose: Munich 1942-1943*, (Wesleyan
University Press, 1983). © 1983 by Inge Aicher-Scholl. Reproduced
with permission from Wesleyan University Press.

A. Kitson: *Germany, 1858–1990: Hope, Terror and Revival*, (Oxford
University Press, 2001). Reproduced with permission from Oxford
University Press.

F. von Papen: *Memoirs*, Translated by Brian Connell, (Andre
Deutsch, 1952). Reproduced with permission from Andre Deutsch/
Carlton Books.

Although we have made every effort to trace and contact all
copyright holders before publication this has not been possible in all
cases. If notified, the publisher will rectify any errors or omissions at
the earliest opportunity.

Cover illustrations: Sueddeutsche Zeitung Photo/Mary Evans

Artwork: Aptara

Links to third party websites are provided by Oxford in good faith
and for information only. Oxford disclaims any responsibility for
the materials contained in any third party website referenced in this
work.

Contents

PART ONE   AS AND A LEVEL

The Weimar Republic 1918–33

| RECAP | APPLY | REVIEW |

Contents *continued*

PART TWO   A LEVEL
Nazi Germany 1933–45

| | | RECAP | APPLY | REVIEW |

Introduction

The *Oxford AQA History for A Level* textbook series has been developed by a team of expert teachers and examiners led by Sally Waller. This matching revision guide offers well-researched, targeted revision and exam practice advice on the new AQA exams.

This guide offers you step-by-step strategies to master your AQA History exam skills, and the structured revision approach of **Recap**, **Apply** and **Review** to prepare you for exam success. Use the progress checklists on pages 3–4 as you work through the guide to keep track of your progress. Other exam practice and revision features include the '**How to...' guides** for each AQA question type on pages 6–7 and a **Timeline** of key events to help you see the themes.

 **RECAP**

Each chapter recaps key events and developments through a variety of concise points and visual diagrams. **Key terms** appear in bold and red; they are defined in the glossary.

SUMMARY highlights the most important points at the end of each chapter.

 Key Chronology provides a short list of dates to help you remember key events.

APPLY

Carefully designed revision activities help drill your grasp of knowledge and understanding, and help you apply your knowledge towards exam-style questions.

Apply Your Knowledge activity tests your basic comprehension, then helps apply your knowledge to exam questions.

Plan Your Essay activity prepares you for essay exam questions with practical essay plans and techniques.

Improve an Answer activity shows you one or more sample student answers, and helps you to evaluate how the answers could be improved.

To What Extent or **Assess the Validity of This View** is an extension activity to help you practise the A level essay question.

Revision Skills provides different revision techniques. Research shows that using a variety of revision styles can help cement your revision.

Examiner Tip highlights key parts of an exam question, and gives you hints on how to avoid common mistakes in exams.

Source Analysis activity helps you practise evaluating sources and prepares you for the sources exam question.

Key Concept covers the concepts which are strongly linked to the essay questions you might find in your exams. This activity helps to drill your understanding of the key Democracy and Nazism concepts:

- 'Right' and 'Left'
- Liberalism
- Nationalism
- Racialism
- Anti-Semitism
- Social Darwinism

REVIEW

Throughout each chapter, there will be opportunities to reflect on the work you have done, and support on where to go for further revision to refresh your knowledge. You can tick off the Review column from the progress checklist once you've completed this. **Activity Answers Guidance** and the **Exam Practice** sections with full sample student answers also help you review your own work. Also, don't forget to refer to the **Top Revision Tips for A Level History** on page 143 to help you organise your revision successfully.

The topic Democracy and Nazism: Germany is a **Component 2: Depth Study**, which means you will have studied key concepts and primary sources relating to the topic.

The **AS LEVEL** exam lasts 1.5 hours (90 minutes), and you have to answer two questions.

The **A LEVEL** exam lasts 2.5 hours (150 minutes), and you have to answer three questions.

On these pages, you will find guidance on how to tackle each type of question in your exam.

How to master the AQA sources question

In **Section A** of your Democracy and Nazism: Germany exam, you will encounter one sources question that you must answer. Here are the steps to consider when tackling the sources question:

1 **Look at the question posed**
Note (underline) the focus of the question.

EXAMINER TIP

AS LEVEL You have to answer one sources question on **two** primary sources (worth 25 marks). Try to spend about 50 minutes on this question.

A LEVEL You have to answer one sources question on **three** primary sources (worth 30 marks). Try to spend about 60 minutes on this question.

2 **Read the first source (including the provenance) carefully**
Keep the focus in mind. Underline or highlight the parts of the source that offer a view relevant to the focus of the question. This will give you the author's 'overall' view.

EXAMINER TIP

If you're aiming for top grades, look again at the source: see if there are any sub-arguments or views. Underline or highlight these in a different colour.

3 **Begin your evaluation**
Analyse the provenance, as well as the content and argument of the source. Use your own knowledge where appropriate to support your evaluation. You should consider the following (where relevant) in relation to the focus of the question:

❏ Author (as an individual and as a representative figure; position and intent)

❏ Date and context

❏ Target and actual audience

❏ Tone and emphasis (tone can add to or detract from value; emphasis shows the author's key concerns, which may affect value).

EXAMINER TIP

You should begin your answer with the overall view of the source, and cite material which both supports and challenges this. Remember to comment clearly on the source's value for the focus of the question. To achieve top grades, repeat step 3 for any sub-arguments.

4 **Make a judgement**
Consider how valuable the source is in relation to the focus of the question.

5 **Follow the same steps 2–4 for the next source or sources**
At **AS LEVEL** you will need a further paragraph in which you **compare** the two sources directly and give a judgement on the more valuable.

At **A LEVEL** you **don't** need to make any comparative judgements and there is no need for an overall conclusion.

REVIEW

Take a look at the Exam Practice sections on pages 63 and 85 of this guide to reflect on sample answers to the sources question.

How to master the AQA essay question

In **Section B** of your Democracy and Nazism: Germany exam, you will encounter a choice of essay questions. Here are the steps to consider when tackling an essay question:

1 Read the question carefully
Note (underline) key words and dates.

EXAMINER TIP

AS LEVEL You have to answer one essay question (worth 25 marks) from a choice of two questions. Try to spend about 40 minutes on this question.

A LEVEL You have to answer two essay questions (each worth 25 marks) from a choice of three questions. Try to spend about 45 minutes on each answer.

2 Plan your essay and form a judgement
Use whichever approach will best enable you to answer the question – this may be chronological or thematic.

EXAMINER TIP

Plans can be in the form of columns, spider diagrams, mind-maps, flow charts and other styles, but should both help you to form a judgement and to devise a coherent structure for your answer.

3 Introduce your argument
Having made a judgement, advance this in your introduction. The introduction should also be used to show your understanding of the question, particularly key terms and dates, and to acknowledge alternative views and factors.

4 Develop your argument
The essay should proceed logically, supporting your balanced argument through the opening statements of the paragraphs. Remember: comment first, followed by specific and precise supporting information.

EXAMINER TIP

Don't forget to write analytically. Your job is to argue a case and evaluate events, developments and ideas, rather than simply describing what happened in a story-telling (narrative) fashion.

EXAMINER TIP

To achieve top grades, remember that a good argument will have balance. You should examine alternative ideas and factors, and explain why they are less convincing than those you are supporting.

5 Conclude your argument
Your conclusion should repeat the judgement given in the introduction and summarise your argument. A good conclusion will not include any new information and will flow naturally from what has gone before.

REVIEW

In the Exam Practice sections on pages 27 and 82, you will find sample answers and helpful examiner tips to the essay exam question.

AQA AS and A Level History mark schemes

Below are simplified versions of the AQA mark schemes, to help you understand the marking criteria for your **Component 2: Depth Study** History exam paper.

AS LEVEL	Section A: Extracts	Section B: Essay
5	Good understanding of provenance and tone of the sources. Very good knowledge, with argument linked to the question. Comparison contains a substantiated judgment. [21–25 marks]	Good understanding of the question. Range of knowledge, with specific supporting information. Analytical, well-argued answer. Structured effectively. Substantiated judgement. [21–25 marks]
4	Good understanding of provenance and tone of the sources. Good knowledge, with argument linked to the question. Comparison partly substantiated. [16–20 marks]	Good understanding of the question. Range of knowledge. Analytical, balanced answer. Structured effectively. Limited judgement. [16–20 marks]
3	Reasonable understanding of provenance and tone of the sources. Shows awareness of knowledge, with argument linked to the question. Partial comparison. [11–15 marks]	Reasonable understanding of the question. Some knowledge, with limited scope. Answer contains some balance or is one-sided. Structured adequately. Partial judgement. [11–15 marks]
2	Partial understanding of provenance and tone of the sources. Some knowledge, with limited link to the question. Undeveloped comparison. [6–10 marks]	Partial understanding of the question. Some knowledge, with very limited scope. Answer contains limited balance, or is descriptive. There is some structure. Undeveloped judgement. [6–10 marks]
1	Little understanding of provenance and tone of the sources. Limited knowledge, not all linked to the question. Comparison is vague or too general. [1–5 marks]	Limited understanding of the question. Limited knowledge. Answer is vague or too general. Structure is limited. Unsupported judgement. [1–5 marks]

A LEVEL	Section A: Sources	Section B: Essays
5	Very good understanding of provenance and content of the sources. Balanced argument, substantiated judgement. Very good knowledge, linked to question. [25–30 marks]	Very good understanding of the question and of the issues/concepts. Range of knowledge, with specific and precise supporting information. Full analytical, balanced answer. Good organisation, structured effectively. Well-substantiated judgement. [21–25 marks]
4	Good understanding of provenance and content of the sources. Partial or limited judgement. Good knowledge, linked to question. [19–24 marks]	Good understanding of the question and of the issues/concepts. Range of knowledge, with specific and precise supporting information. Analytical, balanced answer. Good organisation, structured effectively. Some judgement. [16–20 marks]
3	Some understanding of provenance and content of the sources, may contain imbalance. Judgement is not fully convincing. Awareness of knowledge, linked to question. [13–18 marks]	Reasonable understanding of the question, with some awareness of the issues/concepts. Range of knowledge, may contain imprecise supporting information. Answer links to the question and contains some balance. Structured effectively. Partial judgement. [11–15 marks]
2	Partial understanding of provenance and/or content of the sources (accurate for 1–2 sources or provenance or content only). Unconvincing judgement. Some knowledge is present, may contain limited link to question. [7–12 marks]	Partial understanding of the question, with some awareness of the issues/concepts (may contain generalisations). Some knowledge, with limited scope. Answer contains limited balance, or is descriptive. There is some structure. Undeveloped judgement. [6–10 marks]
1	Partial understanding of provenance and/or content of the sources (accurate for at least one source, may be inaccurate). Judgement is lacking. Limited knowledge is present, not all linked to question. [1–6 marks]	Limited understanding of the question, with inaccurate or irrelevant understanding of issues/concepts. Limited knowledge. Answer is vague or too general. Structure is limited. Unsupported judgement. [1–5 marks]

Timeline

The colours represent different types of event as follows:

● Blue: economic events   ● Red: political events
● Black: international events (including foreign policy)   ● Yellow: social events   ● Green: religious events

1918
- ● **Nov** – Kaiser Wilhelm II abdicates and new republic established
- ● **Nov** – New German government signs armistice

1919
- ● **Jan** – Communist (Spartacist) uprising in Berlin, suppressed by army and Freikorps
- ● **June** – Germany forced to accept Treaty of Versailles
- ● **July** – Constitution of the new German Republic approved by Reichstag

1920
- ● Kapp Putsch in Berlin

1923
- ● German economy hit by hyperinflation
- ● **Jan** – French and Belgian troops occupy the Ruhr industrial area
- ● **Nov** – Hitler and Nazis attempt to seize power in Beer Hall Putsch in Munich

1924
- ● **April** – Dawes Plan introduced to ease reparations payments

1926
- ● Germany accepted into League of Nations

1929
- ● **June** – Young Plan
- ● **Oct** – Wall Street Crash leads to mass unemployment

1930
- ● **March** – Collapse of coalition government led by Müller; replaced by Brüning who needs to rule by presidential decree
- ● **Sept** – NSDAP gain support in Reichstag election

1932
- ● **July** – NSDAP becomes largest party in Reichstag after election

1933
- ● **Jan** – Hindenburg appoints Hitler Chancellor, in coalition with other parties
- ● **Feb** – Reichstag fire leads to Decree for Protection of the People and the State
- ● **March** – Enabling Act gives Hitler dictatorial power
- ● **April** – Law for the Re-establishment of a Professional Civil Service
- ● **May** – Trade unions banned and replaced with German Labour Front
- ● **July** – All non-Nazi parties either banned or voluntarily disbanded
- ● Nazi regime and Catholic Church sign a concordat

1934
- ● Protestant Confessional Church established
- ● **June** – SA purged in Night of Long Knives
- ● **Aug** – Death of Hindenburg. Hitler becomes President and Chancellor with title of Führer

1935
- ● **Sept** The Nuremberg Laws

1936
- ● Olympic Games held in Berlin
- ● Four Year Plan introduced led by Goering

1937
- ● Encyclical letter from the Pope criticises repression of Catholic Church in Germany

1938
- ● **Feb** – Hitler purges army leadership
- ● **March** – Austrian *Anschluss*
- ● **Nov** Jewish property and synagogues attacked on Reichkristallnacht

1939
- ● **Aug** – Nazi-Soviet Pact agreed to divide Poland between the two powers
- ● **Aug** – Rationing of some key foodstuffs
- ● **Sept** – German forces invade Poland, leading to start of Second World War
- ● Start of ghettoisation in Poland
- ● **Oct** – Euthanasia programme approved

1940
- ● **Jan** – First euthanasia of mentally ill by gas

1941
- ● **June** – German forces invade the USSR
- ● *Einsatzgruppen* deployed behind Eastern Front
- ● **Aug** – Euthanasia programme halted

1942
- ● **Jan** – Wannsee Conference
- ● Germany adopts 'Total War' measures

1943
- ● **Jan** – Defeat of German army at Stalingrad marks the decisive turning point in the war
- ● Sustained bombing against German cities by British and Americans

1944
- ● **July** – Attempt to assassinate Hitler by army officers in Bomb Plot fails

1945
- ● Liberation of Auschwitz and other camps
- ● **April** – Hitler commits suicide
- ● **May** – Germany concedes defeat with unconditional surrender

1 The establishment and early years of the Weimar Republic, 1918–24

1 Impact of war, the political crises of October to November 1918, and the establishment of the Weimar Constitution

RECAP

Germany's defeat in World War One led to the abdication of Kaiser Wilhelm II in November 1918 and ushered in a period of political instability and upheaval in Germany. The struggle for power that followed resulted in a new Constitution in July 1919 which confirmed that Germany was to be a democratic republic. The establishment of the new Constitution, however, did not resolve all of the tensions and conflicts that had divided Germany in the immediate aftermath of its defeat.

The abdication of the Kaiser

KEY CHRONOLOGY	
1918	
29 September	Ludendorff called for armistice negotiations
30 September	**Kaiser** promised political reform
1 October	Prince Max of Baden formed new government
28 October	Kaiser introduced further reforms making the **Chancellor** accountable to the **Reichstag**
30 October	Naval mutiny at Wilhelmshaven
3 November	Naval mutiny spread to Kiel
8 November	Revolt in Bavaria led to declaration of Bavarian Socialist Republic
9 November	Declaration of a German Republic in Berlin and abdication of the Kaiser

Kaiser Wilhelm II was forced to abdicate because of the events of Autumn 1918.

- By the end of September 1918, the German army on the Western Front was on the brink of defeat and its High Command, led by General Ludendorff, wanted to negotiate an **armistice** with the Allies.
- Ludendorff understood that the Allied leaders, especially President Wilson of the USA, would not negotiate with an autocratic monarch. There were attempts in early October to reform the German political system by giving the Reichstag more power, but these reforms did not go far enough to satisfy the Allies.
- News that Germany was on the brink of defeat shattered the morale of the German people, adding to the discontent that had resulted from years of hardship due to the war effort. Workers in large cities began to threaten strike action and, in Munich on 8 November, a Bavarian Republic was declared.
- There was discontent, too, among the German armed forces, as soldiers and sailors lost respect for their officers. On 3 November there was a **mutiny** at the main naval base in Kiel.
- Workers' and Soldiers' Councils, similar to those of the **Soviets** that had been set up in Russia during its 1917 revolution, were established in parts of Germany.
- The threat of a general strike in Berlin led to the collapse of the Kaiser's government on 9 November. The Chancellor, Prince Max, resigned and the head of the Social Democratic Party (SPD), Friedrich Ebert, became the leader of a new government.
- Later, on 9 November, General Groener told the Kaiser that the army would not fight for him. The Kaiser had little choice but to abdicate.

The struggle for power

KEY CHRONOLOGY

1918		1919	
10 November	Ebert–Groener Pact	6 January	Spartacist revolt suppressed by army and **Freikorps**
11 November	Armistice signed with Allies		
6 December	Spartacist demonstrations in Berlin	19 January	Elections for the Constituent Assembly
23–24 December	Sailors' revolt in Berlin put down by the army	July	Constitution of the new German Republic approved by Reichstag

Following the abdication of the Kaiser, a struggle for power ensued, in which different political groups vied for control to shape the future political, economic and social structure of Germany.

- Friedrich Ebert, leader of the moderate socialist SPD, did not believe in violent revolution. He wanted to build a democratic, parliamentary system of government, and his first priority was to organise elections for a **Constituent Assembly** which would draw up a new Constitution.
- In Berlin and other major cities, there was ongoing disorder as unemployed ex-soldiers and discontented workers became embroiled in demonstrations, strikes and violent clashes with the police and army.
- Workers' and Soldiers' Councils regarded themselves as rival sources of power and demanded radical and immediate change, including the confiscation of land from the aristocracy, the nationalisation of important industries, and democratic control over the army, the civil service and the judicial system. **Left-wing** political groups, such as the USPD and the Spartacists, supported these demands.
- The role of the army was crucial in the struggle for power. The army's new leader, General Groener, valued order and discipline and was determined to defeat any attempt at a **communist** revolution. To this end, he agreed a Pact with Ebert to support the government as long as the Chancellor promised to resist radical change to the army.
- In December 1918 the army intervened to stop a Spartacist demonstration in Berlin and then crushed a sailors' anti-government revolt.
- In January 1919 the Spartacists attempted an armed uprising against the government in Berlin. Led by Karl Liebknecht and Rosa Luxemburg, the insurgents occupied public buildings and newspaper offices. With limited support, the rising was defeated by the army and the Freikorps (**paramilitary** organisations made up of former soldiers) in brutal street fighting. Both Liebknecht and Luxemburg were killed after being captured.

The defeat of the Spartacists paved the way for elections to the Constituent Assembly later in January. The Constituent Assembly chose Ebert as President of the new German Republic and a coalition government was formed by the SPD, Centre and German Democratic parties. The way was clear for the Assembly to draw up a new Constitution.

	Spartacist League	USPD	Social Democratic Party (SPD)
Founded	1916. A revolutionary and anti-war breakaway group from the SPD, led by Karl Liebknecht and Rosa Luxemburg.	1918. A radical and anti-war breakaway group from the SPD, led by Hugo Hasse.	1875. A mass socialist party led by Friedrich Ebert and Philipp Scheidemann.
Aims	A republic controlled by workers' and soldiers councils, nationalisation of industry and replacement of army by workers' militias.	A republic ruled by Reichstag but cooperating with workers' and soldiers councils, nationalisation of industry, reform of army.	A republic ruled by Reichstag, with democratic freedoms and welfare rights. Some nationalisation of industry.
Support in 1918	Some workers joined their rallies and demonstrations but membership was very small c5000.	Growing in strength, their membership was c300,000.	Had been the largest party in the Reichstag in 1912 and, with c1 million members in 1918 still appealed to many working-class voters.

The main left-wing groups in 1918

The establishment of the Weimar Constitution in 1919

President – Head of State

- Elected every seven years
- Appointed and dismissed ministers and could dissolve the Reichstag and call new elections
- Supreme commander of the armed forces
- Had reserve powers (Article 48) to rule without the Reichstag's consent in an emergency

Appoints

Chancellor

- Had to have the support of at least half the Reichstag
- Proposed new laws to the Reichstag

Provides advice

Needs 50% majority before appointed

Drafts laws for the Reichstag to debate

The Reichsrat

- The second chamber, made up of representatives from the separate states **(Länder)**
- Each state represented in proportion to its population, but no state to have more than 40 per cent of the seats
- Could provide advice on laws but could be overridden by the Reichstag

The Constitution of the new German Republic was very democratic and had several strengths:

- All German men and women over the age of 20, had the right to vote in elections for the President, the Reichstag and in local elections
- Seats in the Reichstag were allocated by **proportional representation** – each party was allocated a share of deputies in the Reichstag in line with its share of the popular vote
- The Constitution guaranteed important individual rights, including equality before the law and the rights of free speech, conscience and to belong to trade unions and political parties
- Important issues could be put to a popular vote in a referendum

The Reichstag

- Elected every four years
- The Chancellor and ministers were responsible to the Reichstag
- Voted on the budget; new laws required the approval of a majority of Reichstag deputies

There were, however, a number of problems with the Constitution:

- Proportional representation led to the proliferation of small parties and made it very difficult for one party alone to form a government with a majority in the Reichstag; all governments in the Weimar Republic were coalition governments
- Article 48 of the Constitution gave the President emergency powers to rule the country by decree, i.e. without the need for a Reichstag majority; most constitutions give emergency powers to the Head of State – what matters is how often these powers are used and in what circumstances
- The main weakness of the Constitution was that the army, the civil service and the judiciary were not reformed and remained under the control of the old aristocracy; key institutions of the state were, therefore, controlled by people who did not support the democratic values of its new constitution

SUMMARY

- Defeat in war brought about major political changes in Germany, which satisfied many of those who had long called for a more democratic system of government.
- Many others, however, were not satisfied. Radicals on the left felt that the changes did not go far enough and that the revolution of November 1918 had been betrayed, while on the **right** there were many who believed that the Republic should not have been established in the first place.

APPLY

APPLY YOUR KNOWLEDGE

Number the following events of 1918 in the correct order. Add dates where you can.

Order	Date	Event
		The Kaiser appointed Prince Max of Baden Chancellor, and he formed a government.
		Prince Max said the Kaiser had abdicated. He resigned and made Friedrich Ebert the new leader of Germany.
		The armistice was signed.
		General Groener informed the Kaiser that the army no longer supported him so Kaiser Wilhelm II abdicated.
		Mutiny in the navy spread to the main base in Kiel.
		General Ludendorff suggested the Kaiser made political reforms and requested an armistice.
		Bavaria was declared a republic.

EXAMINER TIP

A detailed knowledge of chronology is one of the things examiners will be looking for. Knowing the complex order of events that led up to the Kaiser's abdication and the armistice will be essential in answering exam questions on the political crises of Autumn 1918.

APPLY YOUR KNOWLEDGE

In the table below are some features of the Weimar Constitution. Decide whether each feature was a strength or a weakness (you may decide some could be both!), and give a reason for your decision.

	Strength	Weakness	Reason
All men and women over 20 had the vote.			
Proportional representation meant coalition governments were highly likely.			
The armed forces, civil service and judiciary remained unchanged.			
Electorate could decide important issues through referendums.			
No state was allowed to dominate the Reichsrat.			
Some human rights were written into the constitution.			
President had emergency powers to rule by decree in emergencies.			
Chancellor and all ministers were responsible to the Reichstag.			

EXAMINER TIP

This activity will help you revise the different points of the Weimar Constitution as well as its strengths and weaknesses. This will be useful in answering many different exam questions on topics such as why Weimar eventually failed, as well as those directly concerned with the constitution itself.

HOW IMPORTANT?

A LEVEL **How important was the defeat of the Spartacists in the establishment of the new Weimar government in Germany in 1919?**

a Copy and complete the following table to help you recall information and assess the Spartacists' defeat and think of other factors that allowed the new government to be established.

Ways in which the defeat of the Spartacists was important	Ways in which the defeat of the Spartacists was not important	Other factors that allowed the Weimar government to be established

b Place the factors you listed in the third column of part **a** – including defeat of the Spartacists – in order of importance. For each one, include a qualifier such as 'highly', 'very', or 'quite', for example.

c Use your answers to parts **a** and **b** to help you write an answer to the exam question.

EXAMINER TIP

This question requires an analysis of the importance of the different factors that enabled the new constitution of the Weimar Republic to be set up in July 1919.

PLAN YOUR ESSAY

AS LEVEL **'The main reason the Kaiser was forced to abdicate was because he had lost the support of soldiers and sailors.' Explain why you agree or disagree with this view.**

a Decide whether each statement below could be used to support or challenge the view in the exam question.

	Support	Challenge
1 The refusal of two crews to obey orders to attack British ships was the start of unrest in the navy and led to mutinies elsewhere.		
2 The Kaiser's attempted reforms to end his autocracy did not satisfy the Allies. President Wilson still demanded his abdication before they would grant an armistice.		
3 On 3 November, sailors in the main naval base at Kiel mutinied and took control of the base. The navy was no longer being commanded by the Kaiser.		
4 German civilians were suffering badly from shortages of food and other essentials because of the war effort. News that the army was about to be defeated led to strike action and unrest on the streets.		
5 On 9 November, Prince Max claimed the Kaiser had abdicated, resigned as chancellor and declared Friedrich Ebert, leader of the SPD, as the new Chancellor.		
6 General Groener informed the Kaiser on 9 November of the army's refusal to continue the war with Wilhelm II as leader.		

b Write at least one more statement that could be used to support the judgement in the exam question, and at least one more statement that challenges it.

c Use your answers to parts **a** and **b** to plan your essay to answer the question above.

EXAMINER TIP

Planning your exam answers is essential so it's important to practise writing essay plans. There are lots of different ways to write essay plans. Find one that works for you.

2 The Impact of the Versailles Settlement on Germany

The peace treaty to end the war between Germany and the Allies was signed on 28 June 1919 in the Palace of Versailles outside Paris. It punished Germany for its role in starting World War One and for the damage to life and property caused by the war. The Treaty had a profound impact on German politics throughout the lifetime of the Weimar Republic.

The Peace Settlement of Versailles, 1919

Germans from across the political spectrum hated the Treaty of Versailles. Most had expected a negotiated peace settlement based on President Wilson's Fourteen Points, but instead were presented with what they saw as an unjust and 'dictated peace':

- The German delegation to the Peace Conference was not allowed to participate in the discussions about the terms of the Treaty.
- Once the **Allies** had agreed on the terms of the Treaty, the German government was allowed to suggest only minor changes.
- The German government was given seven days to accept or reject the Treaty. Rejection would have led to a resumption of the fighting. The German army High Command advised that military resistance would be futile.
- Divisions in Germany over whether to sign the Treaty led to a political crisis and the fall of the Scheidemann government.

The terms of the Treaty

Germany lost land to France, Belgium, Denmark, Poland and Lithuania; all of its overseas colonies were confiscated

There were severe restrictions on the German armed forces; the army was limited to 100,000 men, the navy was allowed only 6 battleships and no submarines, and Germany was forbidden from having an air force

Germany would have to pay reparations to the Allies for damage caused by the war

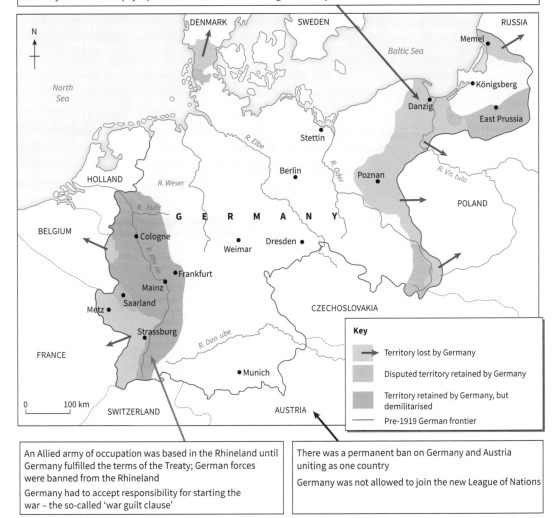

Key

→ Territory lost by Germany

Disputed territory retained by Germany

Territory retained by Germany, but demilitarised

— Pre-1919 German frontier

An Allied army of occupation was based in the Rhineland until Germany fulfilled the terms of the Treaty; German forces were banned from the Rhineland

Germany had to accept responsibility for starting the war – the so-called 'war guilt clause'

There was a permanent ban on Germany and Austria uniting as one country

Germany was not allowed to join the new League of Nations

The political impact of the Versailles Treaty in Germany

The Treaty both united and divided German opinion. Most Germans agreed that:

- The Treaty was a 'dictated peace' which had humiliated a proud and powerful country.
- The 'war guilt clause' was unfair because Germans had believed that they were fighting a just war.
- The reparations were too harsh and would cause severe economic problems.
- They had been denied their right to **national self-determination**, while that of smaller nations such as the Poles and the Czechs had been respected.

On the other hand, the deep political divisions in Germany were made worse by the signing of the Treaty.

For pro-republican parties of the left and centre (SPD, DDP, and Centre):	For anti-republican parties on the right (DVP, DNVP), and the ex-soldiers who joined the Freikorps:
There was no alternative to signing the Treaty, as Germany was too weak to resist.	Signing the Treaty was another act in a series of betrayals that included the November Revolution of 1918 and the signing of the armistice. Those involved in these events were labelled the 'November Criminals', and the signing of the armistice was called the 'stab in the back'.
The policy of 'fulfilment', adopted as a pragmatic response, meant that Germany would outwardly comply with the terms of the Treaty while trying to find ways to modify it or get around it.	Anti-republican parties and para-military groups were committed to the overthrow of the republic.

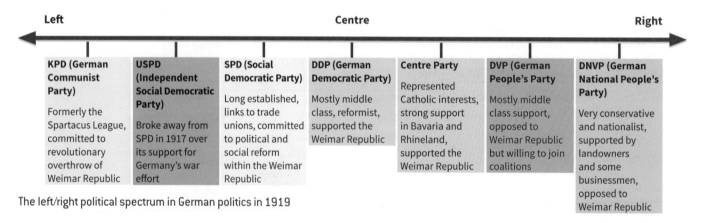

The left/right political spectrum in German politics in 1919

Reactions to the Treaty from abroad

The Treaty was drawn up by the Allied powers, but they did not agree about its impact.

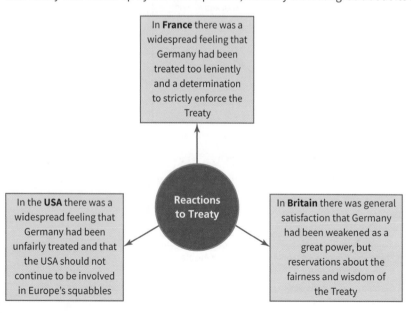

In **France** there was a widespread feeling that Germany had been treated too leniently and a determination to strictly enforce the Treaty

In the **USA** there was a widespread feeling that Germany had been unfairly treated and that the USA should not continue to be involved in Europe's squabbles

In **Britain** there was general satisfaction that Germany had been weakened as a great power, but reservations about the fairness and wisdom of the Treaty

SUMMARY

- The signing of the Treaty of Versailles was accepted by some as the inevitable consequence of Germany's defeat.
- For those who did not believe that the German army had ever been defeated, the signing of the Treaty was yet another act of betrayal that further undermined the legitimacy of the republic.

APPLY

APPLY YOUR KNOWLEDGE

a   Create a mind-map of reasons why Germans hated the Treaty of Versailles, including a short explanation for each one. Try to include at least nine reasons and remember to include links between reasons.

War guilt

Many resented having to accept blame for starting the war, as they didn't believe that was the case

Reasons why Germans hated the Treaty of Versailles

EXAMINER TIP

The first part of this activity will help you to answer questions on reactions to the Treaty of Versailles, while the second part will help you to evaluate reactions to the different aspects of the Treaty.

b   Choose nine reasons from your completed mind-map. Write each of the nine reasons on a separate card and arrange the cards into a diamond-9 formation, with the most important at the top and the least important at the bottom. Write a paragraph explaining why you have arranged the cards as you have.

EXAMINER TIP

Remember that not all Germans would have felt the same way. For example, Germans living in territory that would no longer be part of Germany would probably have particularly hated that aspect of the Treaty. The better answers will consider things from different people's points of view.

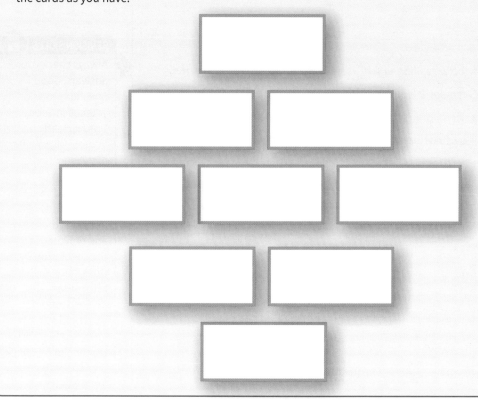

KEY CONCEPT

The political 'right' and 'left', nationalism and liberalism are key concepts for the study of modern Germany.

a Define the following terms:

- Left-wing
- Right-wing
- Nationalism
- Liberalism

b Which groups in society are likely to adopt left-wing views or right-wing views?

EXAMINER TIP

Key concepts run throughout the whole course, so knowledge of them across different topics will be useful for a huge number of exam questions.

IMPROVE AN ANSWER

Below are two introductions to answers on this question:

A LEVEL 'The Treaty of Versailles failed to live up to the expectations of the Germans and shattered the Weimar government's hopes for stability.' Assess the validity of this view.

Answer 1

The Treaty of Versailles did fail to live up to the expectations of the Germans, however, it did not totally shatter the Weimar government's hopes for stability. Although many Germans had expected the peace settlement to be based on President Wilson's Fourteen Points and the principle of selfdetermination, the actual settlement largely ignored these and was regarded as being extremely harsh and unfair. The way in which the Treaty had been imposed as a diktat on Germany was deeply resented and this affected the Weimar government's hopes for stability as many associated the new government with that treaty. Although there were some prepared to work with the treaty in the hope of change in the future, there is no doubt that for most Germans the Treaty meant disillusionment and bred resentment, directed towards the Weimar government.

Answer 2

The Germans hated the Treaty of Versailles which was signed in June 1919 in the Hall of Mirrors at Versailles. The German delegates only arrived after the treaty had been drawn up by their old enemies, Britain, France and the USA and they really had no choice except to sign it. If they had not done so, Germany would have been threatened with invasion and the German army was in no state to continue the war. The Germans hated the war guilt clause which was used to justify a demand for reparations. They also resented the loss of territory, such as Alsace–Lorraine and the Polish Corridor in Europe and all their overseas colonies. They did not like having their army reduced to 100,000 men and the fact they could have no U–boats, no airforce and only six battleships. All this created problems in Germany and meant that people were opposed to the Weimar government.

a Which is the better introduction and why?

b Write your own introduction in response to this exam question.

EXAMINER TIP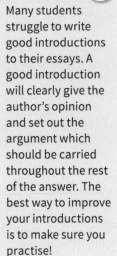

Many students struggle to write good introductions to their essays. A good introduction will clearly give the author's opinion and set out the argument which should be carried throughout the rest of the answer. The best way to improve your introductions is to make sure you practise!

REVISION SKILLS

Always check your answers. Good questions to ask yourself include: Does it clearly address all aspects of the question? Does it state a view (which will subsequently be upheld in the essay and repeated in the conclusion)? Does it use analysis rather than rely on description? You could also ask other students or a teacher for feedback on answers you write when revising.

3 Economic and social problems in Germany, 1919–24

Financial problems in the aftermath of the war

In 1919, the new Weimar Republic faced a serious debt in state finances. This was partly due to the legacy of the war as wartime governments had financed the war effort by borrowing and by printing more money. Government debt grew and the value of the German currency declined. This policy was based on the mistaken belief that Germany would win the war and recoup its losses by making its defeated enemies pay for the war. Governments in the years 1919–23 undoubtedly made this situation worse:

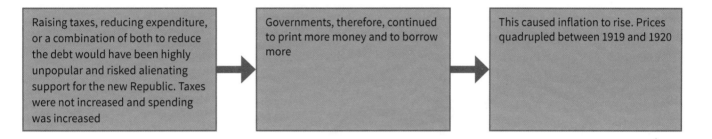

Raising taxes, reducing expenditure, or a combination of both to reduce the debt would have been highly unpopular and risked alienating support for the new Republic. Taxes were not increased and spending was increased	→	Governments, therefore, continued to print more money and to borrow more	→	This caused inflation to rise. Prices quadrupled between 1919 and 1920

There were some positive outcomes to this policy. Many politicians and businessmen thought inflation was beneficial as it stimulated investment and economic growth and government debt became less of a burden. The devaluation of the mark meant that Germany's exports became cheaper and foreign trade boomed. Unemployment was kept low.

The impact of reparations

In 1921 the Allied Reparations Commission set the level of reparations at £6.6 billion, to be paid in annual instalments.

- **Politically**, the demand in 1921 that Germany accept the terms of the Allied Reparations Commission's report provoked another political crisis in Germany and led to the resignation of the Fehrenbach government. Once again, Germany was bitterly divided.
- **Economically**, payment of reparations exacerbated Germany's debt and inflation. German governments in 1922 tried to negotiate a suspension of reparations payments for three years but the French would not agree.

The hyperinflation crisis of 1923

Inflation was already high at the beginning of 1923, as a result of the long-term causes mentioned above. The impact of the Franco-Belgian occupation of the Ruhr caused inflation in Germany to spiral out of control and reach the level of hyperinflation in October and November 1923.

1. In January 1923 French and Belgian forces occupied Germany's main industrial area in the **Ruhr** valley to extract reparations payments in the form of goods.
2. The Cuno government declared a policy of passive resistance to the occupation so workers in the area went on strike. The wages of the striking workers were paid by the government.
3. Tax revenue for the government was reduced.
4. Many goods in Germany were in short supply, further increasing prices.
5. The government printed more money to cover its debt.

Social welfare

Germany had had a system of unemployment benefits and Old Age Pensions since the 1880s but, under the Weimar Constitution, every German citizen had the right to work or welfare. The government extended the welfare system but the huge costs placed an additional burden on government finances. A large proportion of the additional money printed – which led to hyperinflation – was to pay for welfare benefits.

KEY CHRONOLOGY OF SOCIAL WELFARE MEASURES	
1919	The working day was limited to a maximum of eight hours
1919	Health insurance was extended to include wives, daughters and the disabled
1919	Aid for injured war veterans became the responsibility of national government; aid for war widows and orphans was increased
1922	All local authorities had to set up offices with responsibility for child protection

The social impact of hyperinflation

Money became worthless and commerce was severely disrupted, but the impact of hyperinflation varied across classes, age groups and regions.

Winners:
- Black-marketeers
- Those with debts, mortgages and loans
- Enterprising business people who borrowed, then repaid when the currency devalued further
- Long-term fixed renters
- People who had foreign currency
- Farmers

Losers:
- Pensioners, including war widows
- Those who had bought war bonds
- Landlords of fixed-rent properties
- Unskilled workers
- Small-business owners
- The long-term sick, as medical care rose
- Many experienced malnutrition

Hyperinflation also had significant political impact (see pages 23–24).

SUMMARY

- The legacy of the war left Germany with a serious debt, and post-war governments were unwilling to take the necessary corrective measures of reducing expenditure and increasing taxes.
- Governments printed more money to close the gap between revenue and expenditure, but this caused prices to rise.
- By late 1923, Germany was suffering from hyperinflation which brought chaos and suffering to millions of its citizens, though there were also beneficiaries.

APPLY

SOURCE ANALYSIS

SOURCE A

From the recollections of Erna von Pustau, the daughter of a Hamburg fish merchant. She is describing her experiences of hyperinflation in 1923 to an American writer in 1947.

We used to say, 'All of Germany is suffering from inflation.' I can say it was not true. There is no game in which everyone loses. Someone has to win. The winners in our inflation were big businessmen in the cities and the peasants and landowners in the country. The great losers were the working class and above all the middle class, who had most to lose. How did big business win? Well, from the very beginning they sold their goods at gold value prices and paid their workers in inflated marks. How did prices rise? Nobody really knew. Perhaps we thought somehow it had to do with the stock exchange, and somehow, maybe to do with the Jews.

SOURCE B

From Otto Strasser's book, 'Hitler and I', written in 1940. Strasser was a leading member of the radical wing of the NSDAP in the 1920s and was particularly anti-big business.

Inflation set in. Every week, every day, and every hour, the value of the mark declined; the consequence of a catastrophic defeat, which had ruined the country's economic life. A thing you wanted in the morning you bought at once, because by the afternoon the price might have doubled or trebled. Foreigners arrived in numbers, and with dollars, pounds, or francs bought objects of art or food and goods that ordinary Germans could not afford. In the face of this immoral spectacle hatred of foreigners grew. Anger mounted against ineffective government and business profiteers. The streets echoed with noisy demonstrations. Desperation was reflected on every face, desperation of the kind that can lead to outbursts of political violence. The future seemed hopeless.

SOURCE C

From a speech made to the Reichstag in February 1923 by Franz Bumm, the President of the Weimar government's Department of Health.

Unfortunately, this picture of accelerating and shocking decline in health conditions applies to the whole Reich. In rural areas where many farmers are able to feed themselves, conditions seem to be better. But in the towns and heavily populated industrial areas there has been a decided deterioration. Especially hard hit are the middle class, the widows and the pensioners who, with their modest incomes, can no longer afford the most basic necessities at present day prices. It is going just as badly for students. The expense of the most basic foodstuffs and the want of coal, linen, clothing and soap prevent any improvement in living conditions. A million and a half German families are inadequately provided with fuel. Thousands upon thousands spend their lives jammed together in the most primitive dwellings. More and more often one finds old age and weakness listed as the causes of death in the official records; these are equivalent to death through hunger.

 With reference to Sources A, B and C and your understanding of the historical context, assess the value of these three sources to an historian studying the impact of hyperinflation in 1923 on the German people.

a To help you assess the provenance of these sources, create an information card, one for each source, based on the card to the right. Include why this information may be of value to an historian studying the impact of hyperinflation on the German people from your own knowledge.

	Source A
Author:	
Date written:	
Who the source is for:	
Why it was produced:	
Tone:	
Emphasis:	

EXAMINER TIP

All sources in the exam will have a line or two of provenance information. Make sure you spend time studying this as well as the source itself as this is vital in assessing the value of any source.

EXAMINER TIP

Use examples of language and quotations from the sources to illustrate the points you make with regard to the tone of the source and what the author has chosen to emphasise.

b On the back of each card, list the key parts of the content of the source that would be of value to this historian.

c Using your answers to parts **a** and **b**, write a full answer to the exam question.

APPLY YOUR KNOWLEDGE

Draw a flow chart of the events and policies that led to the hyperinflation crisis of 1923. The first event has been completed for you.

> **1914–1918** The Kaiser's government financed the war by borrowing and printing more money, which led to increasing debt and inflation

ASSESS THE VALIDITY OF THIS VIEW

A LEVEL 'The Weimar government was the biggest loser in the hyperinflation of 1923–24.' Assess the validity of this view.

a Copy and complete this chart on the winners and losers of hyperinflation. Add more rows if you need to.

Group	Winner/loser/both?	Explanation
The Weimar government		
Students		
Mortgage holders		
Farmers		
Entrepreneurs		
Workers		
Black marketeers		
Big businesses		
Pensioners/widows		

b For each 'loser' from the table, give it a rating from 1 to 10 depending on how much people lost.

4 Political instability and extremism, 1919–24

 **RECAP**

The growth of political extremism

Parties of the extreme left and the extreme right fought elections but also used their armed paramilitary squads to attack their opponents. Political violence became the norm.

The challenge from the left

The Spartacists aimed for a communist revolution in Germany. They believed that the November 1918 revolution had been betrayed by Ebert and the SPD. They, and their heirs the KPD, attempted a number of armed revolts.

- The Spartacists staged an armed uprising in Berlin in January 1919 which was brutally put down by the army and Freikorps.
- In March 1919, the Spartacists attempted another armed rising in Berlin and a communist government was set up in Bavaria. Both were suppressed.
- In March 1920, a general strike in Berlin helped to defeat the Kapp Putsch (see below). Following this, the KPD formed a Red Army and seized control of the Ruhr, leading to armed clashes with the army and Freikorps.
- Other short-lived, left-wing revolts in 1920 occurred in Halle, Dresden, Saxony and Thuringia.
- In March 1921, the KPD tried to stage a revolution, beginning with a rising in Saxony. Disruption spread to the Ruhr and Hamburg but the risings were crushed.
- In 1923, during the hyperinflation crisis, a wave of strikes occurred in Saxony and Hamburg.

All of these revolts failed or were ruthlessly crushed but they engendered a fear of communism among the middle classes, driving many to support right-wing parties.

The challenge from the right

There were many right-wing, nationalist groups that were hostile to the republic, but did not all share the same objectives. Nationalist ideas had strong support among the old **conservatives** (landowners, industrialists, military officers, civil servants and judges) but also had some popular support, especially from ex-soldiers. Many of these ex-soldiers joined paramilitary groups, such as the Patriotic Leagues, which carried out assassinations of left wing opponents. There were also two attempts by right-wing nationalists to overthrow the republic.

Political assassinations

The Patriotic Leagues, formed from ex-Freikorps units, and having the support of officers in the German army, were dedicated to killing left-wing politicians and those associated with signing the Treaty of Versailles. Between 1919 and 1923 they carried out 354 political assassinations. In the same period, the left killed 22 of their opponents. Although the law was strengthened in 1922 to ban extremist organisations and severely punish political assassins, right-wing judges did not apply the law evenly. Only one right-wing assassin was executed in this period, compared to ten left-wing murderers.

The most high-profile victims of political assassinations were:

- Hugo Haase, leader of the USPD, gunned down in front of the Reichstag building in October 1919.
- Matthias Erzberger, who had led the German delegation to Versailles, shot in August 1921.
- Walther Rathenau, the foreign minister who had participated in the signing of the Armistice and the Versailles Treaty, shot in June 1922.

The Kapp Putsch

The **Kapp Putsch** in Berlin in March 1920, was an armed revolt against the government by Freikorps units.

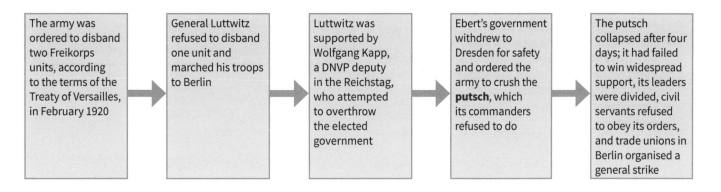

| The army was ordered to disband two Freikorps units, according to the terms of the Treaty of Versailles, in February 1920 | General Luttwitz refused to disband one unit and marched his troops to Berlin | Luttwitz was supported by Wolfgang Kapp, a DNVP deputy in the Reichstag, who attempted to overthrow the elected government | Ebert's government withdrew to Dresden for safety and ordered the army to crush the **putsch**, which its commanders refused to do | The putsch collapsed after four days; it had failed to win widespread support, its leaders were divided, civil servants refused to obey its orders, and trade unions in Berlin organised a general strike |

The Kapp Putsch revealed the depth of hostility towards the republic among army officers and among the judges who showed leniency towards those arrested in the aftermath of the putsch. The republic survived, but the putsch illustrated that its foundations were weak.

The Munich Putsch

The **Beer Hall Putsch**, in Munich in November 1923, was an attempt by the small NSDAP (Nazi party), led by Adolf Hitler, to seize power in Bavaria and lead a march on Berlin to overthrow the government. Several factors contributed to this attempted putsch:

- The occupation of the Ruhr by French and Belgian forces in 1923 resulted in a wave of anti-French feeling and an unusual degree of national unity. However, when the government abandoned the policy of passive resistance to the occupation in September, the nationalist right was outraged by what they saw as an act of betrayal.
- Many middle-class people, who had always believed in the virtues of hard work, careful spending and saving, had their values and confidence in the future shattered by the hyperinflation crisis. Hyperinflation therefore damaged middle-class confidence in the government and the republic as a whole.
- In Bavaria, a right-wing state government declared a state of emergency and nationalists agitated for a 'march on Berlin' to overthrow the federal government.
- One of the leading figures in this agitation was Adolf Hitler, the leader of the National Socialist German Workers' Party (Nazi Party).

On 8 November 1923, Hitler and his **Stormtroopers (SA)** took over a Munich Beer Hall, where a right-wing political meeting was taking place, and forced the State Commissioner (von Kahr) and the local army commander (von Lossow) to agree to join a march on Berlin. The Putsch failed because Hitler failed to secure the support of the police, and the army commander changed sides. A Nazi march through Munich on 9 November was fired on by the police and Hitler was arrested. The Nazis were banned and Hitler imprisoned (but only for nine months).

The Nazi Party

- Founded 1919; Hitler joined in 1920
- A 25-Point Programme set out its beliefs, which included **anti-Semitism**, anti-capitalism, anti-Weimar Republic, ultra-nationalism, pro-dictatorship
- Hitler became undisputed leader in 1921
- Limited support in Bavaria and unknown in rest of Germany

The problems of coalition government

There were ten coalition cabinets (cabinets made up of people from different political parties) between February 1919 and November 1923. Only one lasted more than a year. This instability was due to a number of factors:

- Under proportional representation, many small parties gained representation in the Reichstag.
- No one party ever gained enough seats to command a majority in the Reichstag.
- Many parties of the left and right were dedicated to the overthrow of the Weimar Republic.
- In a time of social and political upheaval, society became more polarised, and more extreme parties on the left and the right gained support.
- The onus was on moderate, pro-republic parties, to compromise and work together to ensure stable coalitions. They frequently failed to do this, especially in the face of unprecedented problems.

The state of the Weimar Republic by 1924

In the years 1919–24, the new Weimar Republic was beset by economic, social and political challenges. Stable government was difficult to achieve and there were a number of attempts, from left and right, to overthrow the republic. The army, police, judges and civil servants, whose responsibility it was to defend the state, could not be relied on to use their power in a fair and even-handed way, as they did not support the democratic values of the republic. Despite all of these challenges, however, the republic survived.

SUMMARY

- There were many coalition governments in the years 1919–23 but only one was able to survive for more than a year.
- The polarisation of German politics reflected the deep divisions in German society after defeat in the war.
- Political groups on both the extreme left and extreme right attempted to overthrow the republic but none succeeded.
- The invasion of the Ruhr and the hyperinflation crisis of 1923 put the political system under severe strain.

APPLY

APPLY YOUR KNOWLEDGE

Complete a mind-map of the problems of coalition government during the years 1919–24. Remember to draw connections between problems where there are links.

EXAMINER TIP

Knowledge of the problems of coalition government will be useful in answering questions on government policies and responses to economic, social and political problems as well as on political instability.

APPLY YOUR KNOWLEDGE

Define the terms in the table below. Then explain how each was connected to the instability of 1919–24.

	Definition	How it was linked to instability 1919–24
Coalition government		
General Strike		
Paramilitary forces		
Putsch		
Freikorps		
Patriotic Leagues		
Assassination		

EXAMINER TIP

Knowledge and understanding of specialist terms will enable you to write more effectively in your essays on the instability of 1919–24.

REVISION SKILLS

Compiling your own glossary of specialist terminology is a good way of making sure you understand and remember key words.

KEY CONCEPT

The political 'right' and 'left' is a key concept for the study of modern Germany.

a   On an A3 piece of paper, draw the political spectrum below.

Far left   Left wing   Centre left   Centre   Centre right   Right wing   Far right

b   Create information cards such as the example started for you on the right, for the active political groups/parties within Weimar Germany during 1918–24, stating their main beliefs and attitudes to the Republic. Cut them out and place them on your political spectrum for the correct time period.

Spartacist League

- Believed the November 1918 revolution to overthrow the Kaiser had been betrayed

- Wanted to incite a communist revolution in Germany

REVISION SKILLS

You may find political spectrum diagrams are a useful way of revising the different political groups and parties throughout the Weimar period.

HOW SIGNIFICANT?

 A LEVEL **How significant was the threat posed by political extremists to the Weimar Republic between 1919 and 1924?**

a To help you evaluate the threat of each challenge to the Weimar government posed by political extremists between 1919 and 1924 answer the following questions about each threat:

- What methods did they use and how threatening were these methods?
- How much support did they have? How widespread was that support in Germany?
- How quickly/well was the Weimar government able to suppress the threat?

b Give each individual threat a score out of 10 for how much it threatened the survival of the Weimar Republic. Then add up the scores to get an overall score for the threat of political extremists.

c Write an answer to the exam question using your answers to parts **a** and **b** to help you.

APPLY YOUR KNOWLEDGE

The Weimar government had to deal with a great many problems between 1919 and 1924. Copy and complete the chart below on the problems it faced and how well it dealt with them.

Problem	How well Weimar government dealt with the problem
Spartacist uprisings	

REVIEW

Look at pages 19–20 on the economic and social problems of the period if you need reminding of these.

EXAMINER TIP

This activity will help you answer any questions about how the government responded to problems in this period or why the Weimar Republic survived its first five years.

TO WHAT EXTENT?

 A LEVEL **To what extent was the Treaty of Versailles responsible for the growth of political extremism in Germany between 1919 and 1924?**

a List possible reasons for the growth of extremism, including the Treaty of Versailles. Draw lines and annotate them to show any links between reasons.

b Evaluate the degree to which each reason was responsible on the diagram below. You need to think carefully about the different factors and place them on the scale.

Slightly responsible   **Fairly responsible**   **Largely responsible**

c Write your answer to the exam question using your answers to parts **a** and **b** to evaluate how much responsibility you believe the Treaty of Versailles deserves compared to other reasons you identified.

EXAMINER TIP

Think about the aims and beliefs of the extremist groups that were prominent during this period.

REVIEW

To revise the Treaty of Versailles, see pages 15 and 16.

AS Level essay sample answer

REVISION PROGRESS

REVIEW

On these Exam Practice pages you will find a sample student answer for an AS Level essay question. What are the strengths and weaknesses of the answer? Read the answer and the corresponding Examiner Tips carefully. Think about how you could apply this advice in order to improve your own answers to questions like this one.

AS LEVEL 'The war guilt clause was the most hated aspect of the Treaty of Versailles in Germany.' Explain why you agree or disagree with this view.

25 marks

Sample student answer

The Treaty of Versailles was the peace treaty that ended the First World War. It was signed on 28 June 1919 in the Palace of Versailles, near Paris. The Treaty was almost universally hated in Germany and a major reason for this was that by signing the Treaty, Germany accepted responsibility for starting the war – the so-called war guilt clause. However, almost all aspects of the Treaty, including its other terms, the way those terms were decided, and the fact that Germany had very little choice but to sign it, were hated by Germans. Despite other reasons for hating the Treaty, the war guilt clause was probably the most hated aspect because Germans considered this to be extremely unfair and unjust but also because accepting responsibility for the war led to other hated aspects of the Treaty.

The German government sent a delegation to the peace conference, which led to the Treaty of Versailles, but to their surprise they were not allowed to take part in the discussions and negotiations with other countries about the terms of the treaty. Instead, once the Allied powers had decided the terms, Germany was only allowed to suggest small changes and was only given seven days to accept or reject it. The Allies warned Germany that if the Treaty was not signed then the war would restart so Germany had little choice but to sign. This was because the military advised the government that the German army would provide little resistance to the Allies and so Germany itself would be invaded. This is why Germans referred to the Treaty as the 'Diktat' or dictated peace.

The war guilt clause in the Treaty of Versailles was deeply resented in Germany. The vast majority of Germans believed that the First

REVISION SKILLS

AS essay questions will contain a quotation advancing a judgement followed by 'explain why you agree or disagree with this view'. Read the introductory pages of this Revision Guide on page 7 for details on how to master the essay question.

EXAMINER TIP

This introduction is extremely well-focused and does a good job of summarising the reasons why the Treaty of Versailles was hated. It also gives the clear judgment that the question requires.

EXAMINER TIP

Although this paragraph demonstrates good knowledge, it is overly descriptive and uses a storytelling approach. The student never clearly links the content back to the question by explaining that this 'Diktat' was a reason why the Treaty itself was hated in Germany. Starting each paragraph with a sentence which relates directly to the question will prevent the paragraph becoming overly descriptive.

World War had been a just war, that Germany had been forced to go to war because the Allies had tried to surround Germany. Therefore they felt that having to accept responsibility for starting the war was unfair, unjust and humiliating. However, it was also the consequences of accepting war guilt that meant this aspect of the treaty was much hated by Germans. Accepting responsibility for the war meant that paying compensation for damage caused to the Allies was justified. The reparations themselves were a major cause of German anger because most felt they would cause huge economic problems.

Accepting war guilt meant that Germany admitted being the aggressor and therefore justified other measures of the treaty which were designed to prevent Germany starting further conflict. The severe restrictions placed by the Treaty on the German armed forces was another clause that was resented and seen as humiliating for what Germans considered to be their powerful and proud nation. Germany had to surrender all heavy weapons and was forbidden from having an air force. The navy was limited to 6 battleships and no submarines and the army was limited to 100,000 men. Another clause stipulated that the Rhineland area of Germany had to be permanently de-militarised to prevent Germany threatening France and Belgium again. This meant that those Germans living in the Rhineland would be forced to endure an Allied army of occupation which was felt to be another humiliation.

Most Germans had believed that the peace terms would be based on US President Wilson's Fourteen Points, which were felt to be just. They included the right to national self-determination and Germans had believed they would be allowed to govern themselves and be included in peace discussions. However, the terms of the Treaty of Versailles brought about the loss of German territory to other countries so some people who considered themselves German no longer had a home in Germany. Another term was that Germany and Austria were forbidden from becoming one country, so again many people who considered themselves to be German in Austria were not allowed to be part of Germany.

Another humiliating aspect of the Treaty was that Germany was not allowed to join the League of Nations. The League was an international organisation that was established after the First World War to try to resolve disputes without resorting to armed conflict. Most countries except the USA joined the League but Germany was forbidden from joining. Most Germans still believed their country was an important one and would have resented not being part of international organisations in this way. Other terms

EXAMINER TIP

This paragraph is much better! It begins with clear links to the question, which continue throughout the paragraph to explain why the war guilt clause was hated in Germany.

EXAMINER TIP

This paragraph continues from the previous one by showing other terms of the Treaty that were a consequence of accepting that Germany was the guilty party in starting the war. It is well-written and shows good historical knowledge and understanding.

EXAMINER TIP

This paragraph is much less well linked to the question and some of the detail, although potentially very relevant is quite vague. Which countries were given former German territory, for example, and what impact would this have in terms of loss of people and resources? It tries to discuss too many separate factors without explaining how and why they caused resentment. The answer needed to clarify that the expectation that peace terms would be based on the Fourteen Points meant that Germans were shocked that this was not the case, besides being horrified at the terms of the Treaty itself. Greater awareness that different Germans hated different aspects of the Treaty would also have helped. For example, those Germans who were forced to live in France, Belgium, Denmark or Poland would have been most hostile to this aspect of the Treaty.

of the Treaty of Versailles which were resented were the loss of all overseas colonies and that Germany had to give to the Allies most of its merchant ships, trains, patents and overseas investments, which, as well as being humiliating, would also have economic consequences.

In conclusion, although the way in which the Treaty had been imposed on Germany was hated, as were clauses such as territorial losses and being excluded from the League of Nations, the war guilt clause was certainly the most hated aspect of the Treaty of Versailles. This was because Germans thought the clause was particularly unfair but also because admitting guilt for starting the war paved the way for some of the other clauses in the treaty such as demanding reparations in the form of money and resources to the Allies. It also justified severely reducing the capacity of Germany's armed forces and forcing Germans in the Rhineland to live under Allied occupation.

EXAMINER TIP

This paragraph becomes something of a list and perhaps an afterthought. It seems to mop up several ideas that should have been included earlier since they link to territorial losses and reparations.

EXAMINER TIP

The essay is well concluded with a summary of the reasons for the student's point of view, maintaining the argument set out in the introduction.

OVERALL COMMENT

The student presents well the view that the war guilt clause was the most hated aspect of the Treaty of Versailles, and the answer contains good knowledge and analysis in places. However, some parts of the essay are more descriptive and the 'balancing factors' are not well-developed. There is adequate analysis and precision for the essay to receive a mid-Level 4, but to reach the top of that level or higher it would need a stronger sense of balance.

OVER TO YOU

Give yourself 45 minutes to try to answer this question on your own. Consider this checklist when reviewing your answer:

❏ Did you provide details on the war guilt clause and why it was hated?

❏ Did you provide details and analysis on other aspects of the Treaty of Versailles?

❏ Did you write a conclusion showing a judgement on whether you agree or disagree with the statement?

Go back and look at pages 15–16 to help refresh your knowledge on the Treaty of Versailles.

2 The 'Golden Age' of the Weimar Republic, 1924–28

REVISION PROGRESS

5 Economic developments 1924–28

 **RECAP**

The stabilisation of the currency

After the trauma of the hyperinflation crisis, the German economy was stabilised and some sections of the economy began to grow and prosper. This turnaround was due to the actions of Gustav Stresemann's 'great coalition' government, which held office between August and November 1923. One of the key architects of this stabilisation was Hjalmar Schacht, the Currency Commissioner under Stresemann and subsequent governments.

Actions taken by Stresemann's government included:

- The ending, in September 1923, of passive resistance to the occupation of the Ruhr. This reduced government spending on payments to workers on strike.
- The introduction, in November 1923, of a new currency – the Rentenmark. The new currency was exchanged for the old at a rate one rentenmark for one trillion old marks. The currency was backed by a mortgage on all industrial and agricultural land.
- The government kept tight control over the amount of money in circulation to stop inflation getting out of control again.
- Stresemann's government cut spending and raised taxes in order to reduce government debt.

As a result of these changes, government debt was reduced, confidence in the currency was restored and business confidence began to grow. Not all companies thrived: those that were well-managed and avoided excessive debt were able to prosper; those that relied heavily on credit went out of business. The number of bankruptcies showed a sharp increase in 1924. People who had lost their savings in the hyperinflation crisis gained nothing from the introduction of the new currency.

The reparations issue and the Dawes Plan

Long-term stabilisation of the German economy depended on a settlement of the reparations issue. There were two attempts to reach a settlement. Firstly, in November 1923, Stresemann asked the Allies' Reparations Committee to investigate how the reparations issue could be resolved. Under the chairmanship of the American banker Charles Dawes, a committee of financial experts drew up an interim plan to reduce the burden of reparations payments. The result was the Dawes Plan of 1924.

- The total reparations bill remained unchanged but annual payments were reduced for the period 1924–29.
- A loan of 800 million marks from the USA would fund investment in the German economy and therefore help to stimulate economic growth. This would enable Germany to meet its reparations payments.
- The Allies took control over Germany's banks and railways.

The American loans that were a key part of the Dawes Plan helped the German economy to recover. The Plan also led to the withdrawal of French and Belgian troops from the Ruhr in 1924–25. Nevertheless, there was a heated debate in Germany about whether to accept the Plan. The 'national opposition' of DNVP, the Nazi Party and other right-wing groups attacked the government for agreeing to the Plan, arguing that Germany should defy the unjust Treaty of Versailles and refuse to pay any reparations. Stresemann believed that Germany had no alternative to accepting the Plan, but privately he called it 'no more than an economic armistice'.

The extent of economic recovery

Economic recovery	Economic weakness
• There was extensive foreign investment in industry • Industrial output grew • Inflation was low and the currency was stable • Exports increased • Advances in new industries e.g. cars, aircraft, chemicals, electrical • Companies rationalised and became more efficient • Fewer strikes as government introduced compulsory arbitration • More mechanisation in agriculture • Wages for industrial workers increased	• Unemployment was a perennial problem and, by 1926, 3 million people were out of work • Imports increased more than exports • Wage settlements increased costs • Farmers suffered from low prices and high debts – many farmers were forced to give up their farms, and rural incomes did not increase • Reliance on foreign loans made Germany vulnerable to shifts in the world economic climate • The professional middle class saw very little benefit from economic growth as they did not have trade unions to negotiate for higher salaries

The reparations issue and the Young Plan 1929

In 1929 a committee led by an American businessman, Owen Young, drew up a plan for a final settlement of the reparations issue.

- The total bill was reduced (from £6.6 billion to £1.8 billion).
- Annual payments were increased and the repayment period was set at 59 years.
- Allied control over banks and railways was relinquished.
- Allied occupation forces were to withdraw from the Rhineland by June 1930.

The Young Plan was accepted by the German government but not without fierce opposition from nationalist parties on the right. The DNVP's new leader, Hugenberg, organised a national campaign against the Plan and gave Adolf Hitler a leading role. This succeeded in forcing the government to put their 'freedom law' – which would require the government to repudiate the war guilt clauses of the Treaty of Versailles – to a referendum. Although the 'freedom law' was rejected by a majority in the referendum, nearly 6 million people voted in favour; the referendum campaign also gave Hitler the chance to make an impact on national politics for the first time.

> **SUMMARY**
> - The German economy was stabilised and became more prosperous, but only in some sectors.
> - The increase in incomes was not shared equally across all sections of society.
> - German reliance on foreign loans made its economic position rather precarious.

APPLY

APPLY YOUR KNOWLEDGE

Complete a spider diagram on methods the government took to resolve the economic crisis of 1923, describing how each method helped resolve the crisis.

Introduced the Rentenmark to replace the Reichsmark and stabilise the currency

Methods the government took to resolve the economic crisis

EXAMINER TIP

This activity will be useful for essays asking how successfully the government dealt with hyperinflation, or wider questions on how the Weimar government dealt with the problems it faced.

APPLY YOUR KNOWLEDGE

a   Complete a Venn diagram to show which people mostly benefited, which mostly lost out, and which had mixed fortunes during the German economy recovery of 1924–28.

EXAMINER TIP

Knowing who benefited and who lost out economically between 1924 and 1928 will be essential for answering questions on political developments and voting patterns.

b   Write a paragraph explaining your diagram.

PLAN YOUR ESSAY

AS LEVEL **'Gustav Stresemann was responsible for the economic recovery in Germany between 1924 and 1928.' Explain why you agree or disagree with this view.**

a To assess the different reasons for economic recovery, complete the table below.

Factor	How this contributed to economic recovery
Work of Stresemann	

b Write a list of ways to challenge the assumption in the question that the economy did recover.

c Use your answers to parts **a** and **b** to plan your answer to the exam question above.

ASSESS THE VALIDITY OF THIS VIEW

A LEVEL **'The apparent growth of the German economy in the years 1924 to 1928 was an illusion masking genuine economic problems.' Assess the validity of this view.**

a Complete the following table to assess economic growth and problems in these years.

Ways in which the economy grew 1924–28	Economic problems 1924–28

b Use your completed table from part **a** to help answer the exam question above.

SOURCE ANALYSIS

SOURCE A

An extract from the report of the Commissioner of the Reichsbank, 1928. This report was written to inform government ministers and business leaders about the state of the economy.

If we compare the present position with that of four years ago, we see a very great advance in regard to the economic development of the country as a whole.

There has been a far-reaching reorganisation and rationalisation of the industrial system of Germany; the standard of living of the masses of the people has appreciably risen, and in the case of a great part of the working-class has again reached or surpassed the pre-war level.

At the same time there are still considerable branches of the national economy that have had an inadequate share in the general recovery. The position of agriculture, though here and there improvement is apparent, remains on the whole less favourable than that of the rest of the national economy.

Whatever turn the future may take, it is certain that there is a serious temporary shortage of capital. The difficulties encountered in securing long-term loans have led to a growing reliance on short-term borrowing.

All source questions will need you to analyse the view of sources against your understanding of the historical context to help you assess their value.

a Using three different coloured pens, highlight the sections of the source above that contain:
  • information on aspects of economic recovery
  • areas that have seen less economic recovery
  • problems in the economy which the report is concerned about.

b Using your answer to part **a**, write a summary of this source. Leave space after each sentence you write for another sentence to be written.

c How does what this source says about economic recovery compare with your own knowledge? Add information to your summary of the source from your own knowledge in the gaps you left in part **b**.

EXAMINER TIP

There are two aspects to this question. Firstly, how much was Stresemann responsible for economic recovery compared with other factors? Secondly, how much the economy did actually recover?

REVIEW

To see more on Stresemann's work, see pages 42–43.

EXAMINER TIP

For all A Level source questions you will always have to analyse three sources rather than just one.

EXAMINER TIP

For A Level source questions, before analysing the content of the source, you will need to analyse the provenance of the source, including its tone and emphasis, also with reference to your own knowledge.

6 Social and cultural developments in Germany, 1924–28

RECAP

German society in the aftermath of the war experienced many far-reaching changes, especially affecting women, young people and the inhabitants of the larger cities. On the other hand, many Germans still lived a more traditional way of life and held onto traditional values. These years were marked by a continuing clash between those who embraced the freer atmosphere of the Weimar Republic and those who resisted change.

Social welfare reform

Before 1914 Germany had one of the most extensive systems of welfare benefits in the industrialised world. During the Weimar years, this system was extended and modified:

- In 1924, the Public Assistance system was modernised. This gave basic assistance to the poor.
- In 1925, the state accident insurance system was extended.
- In 1927, a national unemployment insurance system was introduced, financed by contributions from employers and workers.

The welfare system was expensive to administer and sustain, involving a large bureaucracy. Taxes on the better-off to pay for benefits often aroused resentment, while the introduction of **means tests** to hold expenditure down was often unpopular with welfare claimants.

Living standards and lifestyles

The economic changes of the years 1924–28 (see pages 30–31) resulted in social changes. Many Germans experienced rising living standards in these years but the gains were not evenly spread across society.

Those with rising living standards

- Owners of businesses that prospered during the trade boom
- Workers in trade unions that were able to negotiate wage increases
- Welfare recipients had some help to prevent them falling into poverty
- Some women who were able to take advantage of new employment opportunities

Those with stagnant or declining living standards

- People living on fixed incomes, especially pensioners and widows
- Those who had lost their savings in the 1923 hyperinflation
- Farmers and farm labourers

Position of women

There was much talk in Weimar Germany about the 'new woman' – free, independent, sexually liberated and having greater opportunities in employment and public life than earlier generations; for example, new opportunities arose in service industries, as clerks, typists, and shop assistants. There was some truth in this, but for many women in Germany, similar to the rest of industrialised Europe, very little had changed and there was fierce resistance to the changes from conservative forces in society.

Changes

1) The Weimar Constitution gave women equal voting rights in elections and the right to be Reichstag deputies, which was progressive for its time. Many more women became actively involved in politics at central and local levels

2) Women were given equal opportunities and the right to equal pay in civil service employment

3) There were increased employment opportunities for women

4) Birth control became more widely available, which empowered some women to exert control over the size of their families

Resistance to change

1) No women became cabinet ministers nor leaders of political parties

2) There was no regulatory requirement for equal pay in most occupations

3) In many occupations, women were required to give up employment when they married

4) The decline in the birth rate due to birth control was attacked by conservatives as a 'birth strike', and both Catholic and Protestant churches opposed birth control and divorce

Young people

In the Weimar period there was a perception that young people were becoming more rebellious and a concern that crime and anti-social behaviour was growing among young people. Worries were expressed over the activities of youth 'cliques' in large industrial cities. For young people themselves, a major concern was the rise in youth unemployment.

Germany had a well-developed system of state education but this divided young people along class lines and by religion. The education system had traditionally emphasised the virtues of obedience and respect for authority among the young. This continued but there were attempts to reform the school system in the Weimar years, to break down the religious and class barriers by introducing comprehensive, non-sectarian schools. This succeeded at elementary-school level but the educational divide persisted in secondary schools.

Youth groups had been a feature of German life since the 1890s and continued to flourish in the Weimar period. Many churches had their own youth groups to encourage young people to attend church and respect their teachings, but there were also more independent youth groups, such as the Wandervogel, which gave middle-class young people from the cities the opportunity to experience life in the countryside. A new development of the 1920s was the rise of youth groups for political parties. The SPD, KPD, DNVP and the Nazi Party all had groups for inculcating their ideologies in young people.

Jews

There were more than half a million Jews living in Germany in the 1920s, with 80% of them living in large cities. Most Jewish people were fully assimilated members of German society. During the Weimar period, many Jews were successful and achieved influence in the fields of politics, the press, business, the professions (16% of lawyers and 11% of doctors were Jewish) and the arts.

Anti-Semitism was strong among nationalist groups throughout the 1920s. However, hostility to Jews was greatest at times of national crisis, such as the period of 1918–24, as Jews were blamed for communist uprisings and Jewish financiers were blamed for the hyperinflation crisis. Between 1924 and 1930, Anti-Semitism was far less apparent, although Jewish bankers and businessmen were often accused of corruption.

The development of arts and culture in the Weimar Republic

The Weimar years were characterised by an atmosphere of cultural and personal freedom and experimentation in arts and culture.

This was epitomised by the flourishing night club scene in Berlin in which nudity, erotic dancing and American jazz music featured strongly in the cabarets.

The expressionist movement, which emphasised the importance of emotion, was very influential among German artists such as George Grosz and Otto Dix. Hannah Höch, a pioneer of photomontage, used her work to challenge gender stereotypes and link female liberation to left-wing political ideology.

Composers such as Hindemith and Schoenberg moved away from traditional musical forms. Schoenberg was associated with 'atonal' music.

Novelists such as Thomas Mann were also influenced by expressionism and focused on a character's internal mental state rather than on an external social reality.

Berlin was a leading centre in world cinema in the 1920s. Film-makers such as Fritz Lang, Billy Wilder and Joseph von Sternberg experimented with new cinematic techniques which influenced film-makers in Hollywood and elsewhere.

German playwrights such as Bertolt Brecht and Kurt Weill were part of a new wave of experimental theatre, particularly musical theatre, which was explicitly political and left wing, being anti-capitalist, anti-nationalist and anti-war.

In architecture, the Bauhaus school of art and design, founded by William Gropius, was highly influential in cultivating a 'modernist' approach to building design. Bauhaus students were encouraged to use materials such as steel, concrete and glass in their building designs, and to focus on the function of a building rather than superfluous ornamentation.

Not everyone in Weimar Germany was happy with the new trends in arts and culture. Away from the cities, traditional values and tastes still held sway and radical, experimental, modernist ideas were viewed with suspicion and hostility. There was a strong backlash from more nationalistic Germans who wished to preserve authority, traditional family values, conservative behaviour by women, respect for the teachings of the churches, and a Germanic culture. In the eyes of these people, the cultural experimentation of the Weimar years was leading to moral degeneracy and the influx of unwelcome foreign influences.

SUMMARY

- Weimar Germany gave its citizens more freedom than they had had before 1914.
- Germany in the mid-1920s had a vibrant intellectual climate in which experimentation, challenges to convention, and demands for reform were bringing social and cultural changes.
- The Weimar Constitution gave women more equality in politics and more widespread access to education. There were greater opportunities than before for women to pursue careers in the Weimar period and to make a mark in public life, but women were still far from achieving full equality in employment rights.
- There were attempts to reform Germany's education system to break down religious and class barriers in schools, but they were only partially successful.

APPLY

APPLY YOUR KNOWLEDGE

a How far did the lives of Germans change during the years 1924–28? Create information cards on each of the following groups:

- Women
- Young people
- Farmers
- Business owners
- Pensioners and widows
- Industrial workers
- The unemployed

For each group, give information on:

1 How their lives changed (for better or worse)
2 How they stayed the same
3 How much change there was within that group.

You should include both economic and social changes.

b When you have completed your cards, place them on the continuum line below, giving reasons for the position you give each group.

No change at all ←——————————————————→ **Substantial change**

EXAMINER TIP

This activity will be helpful for essays on the popularity of the Weimar Republic, as well as questions specifically about the economy or living standards and lifestyles.

REVIEW

Look back to page 31 for information on the economy during 1924–28.

KEY CONCEPT

- **The political 'right' and 'left' is a key concept for the study of modern Germany.**

How would people on the 'right' and 'left' of the political spectrum have responded to the social developments of the Weimar period? Complete the following table.

	'Left'	'Right'
Social welfare reforms		
Increasing power of trade unions		
'New' women		
Changes in education		
Cultural changes, e.g. night clubs, jazz music		
Expressionist and modern art and design		

TO WHAT EXTENT?

 A LEVEL **To what extent was there a 'social revolution' in Weimar Germany?**

a What is meant by 'social revolution'? Write a definition, then create a list or spider diagram of factors that might contribute to a social revolution.

b To consider different aspects of this question, copy and complete this grid.

Aspect of social change	Examples of social change	Examples of little or no change

EXAMINER TIP

Before beginning to plan any essay, you should take a moment to digest fully the wording of the question.

c Using your answers to parts **a** and **b**, write your answer to the exam question above.

APPLY YOUR KNOWLEDGE

Complete the circle diagram on changes to the arts and examples of artists during the Weimar years.

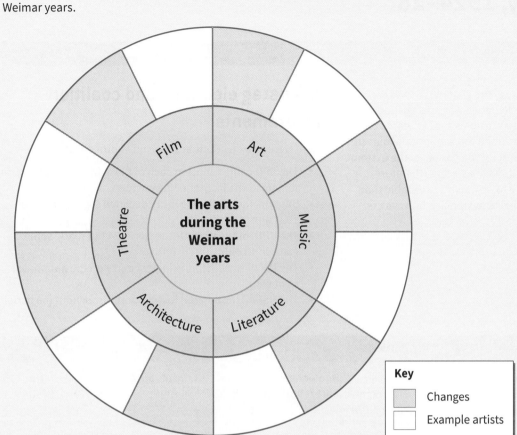

Key

■ Changes

□ Example artists

PLAN YOUR ESSAY

AS LEVEL 'Very few Germans experienced any social change in the years 1924 to 1928.' Explain why you agree or disagree with this view.

All essays require a balanced answer, whether or not you agree with the view given in the question.

a Write the points which agree with the view given in the question on one side of the scales and the points which disagree on the other. Which way your scales tip will determine your judgement.

b Now use your completed diagram to write an essay plan for the question above.

EXAMINER TIP

It's essential for you to give your opinion in AS essays. Using a diagram such as this one, or a simple chart, will help you decide whether to agree or disagree with the view given in the question before you start writing.

KEY CONCEPT

- **Anti-Semitism is a key concept for the study of modern Germany.**

  Write a paragraph explaining reasons for anti-Semitism among right-wing groups in Weimar Germany. Include the following ideas:

  - Jewish success
  - Jews as scapegoats for problems
  - Links to Bolshevism
  - Jewish influence on Weimar art and culture.

7 Political developments and the working of democracy, 1924–28

 **RECAP**

After the turmoil and instability of the years 1919 to 1923, the political life of the Weimar Republic was much calmer in the following five years. There were no further attempts to overthrow the government by armed force, political violence in general subsided, and support for the parties of the extreme left and extreme right declined. On the surface, therefore, the Weimar Republic appeared to be much more stable than previously. The extent of this political stability, however, is open to question.

Reichstag elections and coalition governments

There were two elections in 1924 and another in 1928.

- The SPD gained seats in each of these three elections and remained the largest single party.
- Support for the Centre Party declined slightly between 1924 and 1928.
- The KPD lost seats in December 1924 but made some gains in 1928.
- The DNVP remained the largest party on the nationalist right wing.
- The NSDAP (Nazi Party) lost support throughout the period.

Year	Left wing			Centre		Right wing		
	Communist (KPD)	Independent Social Democratic Party (USPD)	Social Democrat Party (SPD)	Democratic Party (DDP)	Centre (Catholic Zentrum)	Conservative (DVP)	Nationalist (DNVP)	Nazi (NSDAP)
1919	0	22	165	75	91	19	44	0
1920	4	84	102	39	85	65	71	0
May 1924	65	–	100	28	81	45	95	32
December 1924	45	–	131	32	88	51	103	14
1928	54	–	153	25	78	45	73	12

Coalition governments

- There were seven coalition cabinets between November 1923 and June 1928.
- Despite being the largest, and a pro-republican party, the SPD was not part of most of these coalitions.
- Few of the cabinets had majority support in the Reichstag and there were frequent disputes over policy.
- The DNVP, an anti-republican party of the right, joined a cabinet for the first time in January 1925.
- The formation in June 1928 of the 'grand coalition', led by Müller of the SPD, seemed to offer the prospect of a more broadly based, stable coalition government. It lasted nearly two years.

The development of political parties

Political parties were at the heart of the democratic process in Weimar Germany and vital to its success. If parliamentary democracy were to gain the support of the majority of German citizens, it was up to the pro-republican parties to engage with and represent the concerns of ordinary voters. They largely failed to do this because:

- Under the proportional representation system, deputies were chosen from party lists. There was no direct connection between deputies and constituents.
- The party list system gave party committees control over deputies who were therefore unable to show any independence or flexibility.
- There were factional rivalries within parties.
- Parties represented narrow sectional interests and none, therefore, was able to speak for the wider national interest.
- Forming coalitions inevitably involved the parties in making compromises on their principles.

Communist Party (KPD)

- Believed in revolutionary overthrow of political system.
- Large working-class following in industrial areas but never a mass party.
- Policy and tactics dictated by Soviet Union.
- Concentrated on attacking SPD, thus dividing the working-class vote.

Social Democrat Party (SPD)

- Largest party in Reichstag throughout period.
- A reformist, socialist party but still used old revolutionary rhetoric.
- Close links to trade unions which provided main base of support.
- Involved in only six cabinets, 1919–30.

Centre Party

- Represented interests of Catholic church in Germany.
- Appealed to Catholics of all classes.
- Involved in all coalition cabinets throughout the period.
- Supported Weimar democracy but shifted to the right after 1928.

German Democratic Party (DDP)

- A liberal, pro-republican party.
- Main support base among academics and professional groups.
- Serious splits and confused programme.
- In decline but participated in all coalition governments of this period.

German People's Party (DVP)

- Pro-republican.
- Participated in all coalition governments.
- Main support came from industrialists.
- Shifted to the right after the death of Stresemann in 1929.

German National People's Party (DNVP)

- Anti-democratic, monarchist and nationalist.
- Traditionally represented conservative landowners.
- Began to attract support from industrialists and professionals.
- Shifted to the right after 1928.

German National Socialist Workers' Party (NSDAP)

- Led by Adolf Hitler.
- Ultra-nationalist, openly anti-Semitic and anti-democratic.
- After failure of Beer Hall Putsch, changed tactics to fighting elections.
- Started as a fringe party in Bavaria and failed to make an impact in the rest of Germany after 1924, with small membership and few deputies in the Reichstag.
- After 1928, switched to campaigning in rural, Protestant areas in the north.
- 1929 campaign against Young Plan, opportunity to become a national party.

The election of Hindenburg as President in 1925

After the death of Ebert, Paul von Hindenburg was elected as President of the German Republic in 1925. This had both positive and negative effects for the Republic.

Positives	Negatives
As a former military commander who was revered by the right, Hindenburg's election reassured conservatives that the government of the Republic was in safe hands.	Hindenburg was fundamentally a monarchist and anti-democratic.
After his election, he respected the Weimar Constitution and did not abuse his powers.	He became increasingly impatient with party political rivalries and was prepared to use article 48 to bypass the Reichstag.
He appealed to political parties to work with him to restore national unity.	

Attitudes to the Republic from the elites and other social groups

- The old elites had been hostile to the republic from the beginning. The election of Hindenburg gave some reassurance to aristocratic landowners, army officers, civil servants and judges, but they remained anti-democracy.
- The middle class was diverse and not universally hostile to the republic. Those who had lost savings and did not share in the prosperity of the 'golden years' remained hostile, while business owners who prospered were broadly supportive.
- Most working-class voters, especially members of trade unions, supported the SPD and valued the democratic freedoms and social benefits of the period. A minority who supported the KPD were bitter at the brutal crushing of revolts by the army and police.

SUMMARY

- This period was more stable than the years that had preceded it. Political violence and extremism declined.
- On the other hand, the fundamental weaknesses of the Weimar Republic remained and it was as difficult in these years to establish stable coalition governments as it had been in the early years of the Republic.

APPLY

APPLY YOUR KNOWLEDGE

Match the acronyms for each party with their names and political leanings.

KPD	German National Socialist Worker's Party	Right wing	Anti-Weimar Democracy
SPD	German Communist Party	Right wing	Anti-Weimar Democracy
DDP	German National People's Party	Far right	Anti-Weimar Democracy
Centre	German People's Party	Far left	Pro-Weimar Democracy
DVP	German Democratic Party	Centre/ centre right	Pro-Weimar Democracy
DNVP	Catholic Zentrum	Centre left	Pro-Weimar Democracy
NSDAP	Social Democrat Party	Centre right	Pro-Weimar Democracy

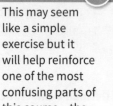

EXAMINER TIP

This will help give you a basic understanding of political parties during this period, which will be useful for essays on political stability and attitudes to the Weimar Republic.

REVISION SKILLS

This may seem like a simple exercise but it will help reinforce one of the most confusing parts of this course – the numerous political parties and the similarities of some of their names! Returning and completing simple exercises like this one from time to time will help reinforce knowledge and prevent you making silly mistakes in exams.

KEY CONCEPT

- **The political 'right' and 'left' is a key concept for the study of modern Germany.**

  In Chapter 4 you may have created a political spectrum for political groups and parties during 1918–24. Now try a similar exercise for 1924–28:

  a On an A3 piece of paper, draw the political spectrum below.

  Far left   Left wing   Centre left   Centre   Centre right   Right wing   Far right

  ⟵————————————————————⟶

  b Create information cards for each of the main parties within Weimar Germany during 1924–28, stating which groups supported them, their attitudes to Weimar democracy, and whether they were part of coalition governments in this period. Place them in the correct place on your political spectrum.

EXAMINER TIP

You could compare this political spectrum to the one you may have created for 1918–24 to give you an idea of how parties developed. Have any moved on the political spectrum?

ASSESS THE VALIDITY OF THIS VIEW

A LEVEL 'Germany was politically stable in the years 1924 to 1928.' Assess the validity of this view.

Take the different parts of this question in turn.

a Complete the following chart:

Evidence that Germany was politically stable	Evidence for political instability

b Was there a lack of support for extremist parties? What evidence could you use to support or challenge this view?

c Using your answers to parts **a** and **b**, write an answer to the exam question above.

APPLY YOUR KNOWLEDGE

Create a mind-map of reasons why the years 1924–28 saw little or declining support for extremist parties.

SOURCE ANALYSIS

SOURCE A

From 'An apolitical observer goes to the Reichstag', an article written for the Frankfurter Zeitung, a newspaper with a liberal/middle-class audience, in 1924 by the journalist Joseph Roth.

Here, in the German Reichstag, each party has not only its own political convictions but also its own ritual. There is no sense of overall decorum. Foreign ambassadors are sitting in the box. The eyes of America, France and Italy are directed at the representatives of the German people. And what do they see? The goose-stepping of the nationalists. Wrangling among the communists. Ludendorff in dark glasses. The apolitical observer cannot understand why, more than any other professional grouping in the world, German politicians are driven to make asses of themselves, before they've even embarked on their policies, which are a further reservoir of foolishness.

In the dome room there is a chandelier that weighs eight tons – as heavy as the fate of the people who own the chandelier. They've shelled out twenty six and a half million marks for their Reichstag. It looks imposing, no doubt about it. It would be nice if the delegates made it impressive as well.

Read Source A.

a Write a list of the kinds of enquiry for which an historian would find this a valuable source.

b Consider the provenance, tone and emphasis of this source. How might this affect the value of this source for a historian studying the problems of Weimar democracy?

c Write a short summary of the opinion given in this source.

8 Germany's international position, 1924–28

After the tensions between Germany and the Allied countries in the years 1919–23, culminating in the Franco-Belgian occupation of the Ruhr, there was an improvement in relations after 1924. During the years 1924 to 1928, Gustav Stresemann was the German Foreign Minister and he pursued the policy of **fulfilment** in relation to the Treaty of Versailles.

Gustav Stresemann and the policy of fulfilment

Aims

Throughout these years the consistent aim of German foreign policy was to revise the Treaty of Versailles, although not all Germans agreed on the extent of this revision, nor on the means to achieve it. For Stresemann the priorities were:

- A settlement of the reparations issue to reduce the burden on Germany.
- An end to Allied military occupation of the Rhineland.
- The protection of Germans living under the rule of foreign countries.
- The recovery of lands in the east, particularly Danzig and the Polish Corridor.
- The restoration of Germany as a great power.

Methods

Stresemann understood that Germany was too weak economically and militarily to risk another war. He therefore saw no alternative to peaceful cooperation between Germany and the Allies. This was designed to reassure Britain and France as to Germany's good faith and thereby win concessions from them. This was known as the policy of fulfilment.

Achievements

The Locarno Pact, 1925

Stresemann suggested a meeting of the Western European powers to resolve some of the tensions over borders and to prevent a hostile alliance against Germany between France and Britain. The outcome of this meeting, at Locarno in Switzerland in 1925, was the **Locarno Pact**:

- Germany, France and Belgium agreed to accept their existing frontiers.
- Britain and Italy agreed to act as the guarantors of the Pact.
- Germany, France, Belgium, Czechoslovakia and Poland agreed to settle any disputes peacefully.
- Germany agreed to keep its troops out of the Rhineland but the French agreed to start withdrawing their forces from the Rhineland.

Stresemann had therefore made concessions on Germany's western frontiers and on the Rhineland, but he did not agree to recognise Germany's eastern frontiers in the same way. This left open the possibility that, at some future date, Germany might try to regain lost territory in the east.

Relations with the USSR

Despite the enormous political differences between them, Germany and the USSR shared some important common ground:

- Both were treated as 'outcast' nations, excluded from the League of Nations.
- Both had a desire to regain lost territory in Poland.

The **Treaty of Rapallo** in 1922 was the start of a period of cooperation between the two countries. Trade and diplomatic relations were restored and Germany was allowed to secretly develop new weapons and train pilots in the Soviet Union, thus getting round the disarmament clauses of the Treaty of Versailles.

In 1926, the **Treaty of Berlin** renewed the earlier treaty.

The extent of disarmament

- Germany was subject to the disarmament clauses in the Treaty of Versailles and an InterAllied Control Commission was established to ensure compliance.
- The Treaties of Rapallo (1922) and Berlin (1926) with the USSR allowed Germany to get round the disarmament clauses by building aircraft in the USSR. Similar agreements with other countries allowed Germany to build submarines in Spain and tanks in Sweden.
- The Reichswehr also got around the limits on the size of the army by enlisting new recruits for short periods of intensive training, thereby creating a large reserve of trained soldiers.
- The Reichswehr also sponsored paramilitary groups, even after the Freikorps had been disbanded.

The end of allied occupation

Stresemann's policy of fulfilment succeeded in persuading the Allies to remove their occupation forces from Germany in a step-by-step approach.

- In 1926, Allied forces were withdrawn from Zone 1 of the Rhineland.
- In 1927 the Allies reduced their occupation forces in the Rhineland by 10,000 men.
- The remaining Allied forces were withdrawn from Zone 2 in 1929 and from Zone 3 in 1930.

Other diplomatic achievements

- In 1926, Germany was allowed to join the League of Nations.
- In 1928, Germany signed the Kellogg-Briand Pact, under which states voluntarily agreed to renounce war as a way of settling disputes.

Although these acts were largely symbolic, they nevertheless showed that Germany's diplomatic isolation was over and that the country was once again being treated as a great power.

Stresemann's achievements

An overall assessment of Stresemann's achievements must take account of a range of factors and opinions. As a staunch German nationalist, he wanted to revise the Treaty of Versailles in Germany's favour and re-establish Germany as a great power, and his policies were designed to promote German interests. On the other hand, he was a pragmatist and a realist who understood the need for compromise and for fostering good relations with the western Allies.

SUMMARY

- Stresemann was skilful diplomat and achieved much as Foreign minister, although he was undoubtedly helped by the willingness of Britain and France to find diplomatic solutions.
- His aims were substantially achieved:
  - Germany no longer had to fear a French invasion.
  - The reparations issue was resolved in the Young Plan of 1929.
  - Allied forces were withdrawn from the Rhineland by 1930.
  - Germany was admitted to the League of Nations.
  - The Treaty of Berlin enabled Germany to rearm in secret.
  - He made no concessions on Germany's eastern frontiers.
- On the other hand, he did not achieve all of his aims. He did not regain control over the Rhineland or the Saar region, and nor did he achieve a thorough revision of the Versailles Treaty.

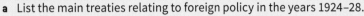

 **APPLY**

APPLY YOUR KNOWLEDGE

a List the main treaties relating to foreign policy in the years 1924–28.

b For each one, complete a card similar to the one below.

> Treaty: _____
>
> Date: _____
>
> Between: _____
>
> Main points: _____
>
> _____
>
> _____

 EXAMINER TIP

Knowledge of the main treaties negotiated by Stresemann will be useful for exam questions on foreign policy during these years or on the Treaty of Versailles.

IMPROVE AN ANSWER

 A LEVEL To what extent, by 1928, had the terms of the Treaty of Versailles been accepted in Germany?

Read the following paragraph from an answer to this exam question.

Answer

Stresemann negotiated the Locarno Pact with other Western European powers at Locarno in Switzerland in 1925. He managed to get France to agree that it would start withdrawing their troops from the Rhineland which revised some of the Versailles Treaty but agreed Germany would keep its own troops out too. He also accepted the existing western frontiers of Germany with France and Belgium which had been agreed at the Treaty of Versailles. This shows that he had mostly accepted the Treaty of Versailles by this time.

a List the strengths and weaknesses of this paragraph.

b Rewrite the paragraph removing the weaknesses or turning them into strengths.

c Write another paragraph on ways in which Stresemann had accepted the Treaty of Versailles. Make sure you begin with an analytical sentence.

 EXAMINER TIP

This question would need you to examine the debate over Stresemann's (and therefore the Weimar government's) acceptance of the Treaty, as well as the attitude of the wider German public.

 EXAMINER TIP

A good answer will directly address the question throughout and follow an analytical, rather than a descriptive approach.

 REVIEW

Look back to page 15 if you need to remind yourself of the terms of the Treaty of Versailles.

APPLY YOUR KNOWLEDGE

a   Place the following into the correct chronological order, adding the correct date for each.

- Young Plan
- Dawes Plan
- Locarno Pact
- Kellogg-Briand Pact
- Treaty of Berlin
- Treaty of Rapallo
- Germany joined the League of Nations

b   Create a flow diagram including each of the above. For each one, give a brief assessment of Gerrmany's international position before and after.

EXAMINER TIP

Detailed knowledge of the result of foreign policy will enable you to answer questions on how and why Germany's international position changed in the years 1924–28.

ASSESS THE VALIDITY OF THIS VIEW

 'The improvement of Germany's international position in the years 1924–29 was the work of Gustav Stresemann.' Assess the validity of this view.

a   Create a mind-map entitled 'Reasons for the improvement of Germany's international position 1924–29'. Then, using one colour, include all the ways you can think of in which Stresemann contributed to improving Germany's international position.

b   Then, using a different colour, add other reasons for the improvement of Germany's international position, and then, in a different colour again, add ways in which Germany's international position had not been improved.

c   Using your completed mind-map, write an answer to the exam question above.

REVIEW

You should also consider Stresemann's work in the Dawes Plan and the Young Plan in this answer. See page 30 if you need to remind yourself about these.

SOURCE ANALYSIS

SOURCE A

From a private letter of September 1925, from Gustav Stresemann to Kaiser Wilhelm II's son, the ex-Crown Prince, where he sets out his thoughts on German foreign policy.

In my opinion there are three great tasks that confront German foreign policy in the immediate future:

In the first place, the solution of the Reparations question in a way tolerable for Germany.

Secondly, the protection of Germans abroad, those 10 to 12 million of our kindred who now live under a foreign yoke in foreign lands.

The third great task is the readjustment of our eastern frontiers; the recovery of Danzig, the Polish Corridor, and a correction of the frontier in Upper Silesia. I refused at Thoiry to discuss the question of our eastern frontier and that of our colonies. One can only advance step by step. When the day arrives when, in one way or another, the question of our eastern frontier will come up for discussion, the atmosphere between us and France must already be such that we can broach this new problem. In the background stands the union with German Austria, although I am quite clear that this not merely brings no advantages to Germany but seriously complicates the problem of the German Reich.

a   Complete the following table to help you analyse the provenance of this source in relation to its value for an enquiry into the aims of Germany's foreign policy in the 1920s.

Who is the author?		Does this add to the value or diminish its value?	
When was the source written?			
Who is the audience for this source?			
Why do you think the author wrote it? (What is its purpose?)			

b   Describe the tone of the source. Identify some words and phrases that exemplify this.

c   What is the main emphasis in the source? What is the central point that the author is trying to convey? Why do you think he would emphasise this?

EXAMINER TIP

These questions all ask you to assess the provenance of a source. In an actual exam question you will also need to analyse the content in terms of its value for the purpose given.

9 The Impact of the Depression

 **RECAP**

In October 1929 there was a catastrophic fall in the value of shares on the New York Stock Exchange – the so-called Wall Street Crash. The resulting panic and economic dislocation quickly spread around the world. Germany was one of the worst hit countries, largely because the German economy had become heavily dependent on American loans, which now had to be repaid. By 1931, the German economy was suffering from a serious depression, which had a devastating impact on German society and on the political system.

Economic impact

Finance
- Loans from the USA were stopped and outstanding loans had to be repaid quickly. This led to a large outflow of foreign currency from Germany, which was therefore unable to pay reparations
- By the summer of 1931 the German banking system was in crisis, following the collapse of an Austrian bank. Banks were temporarily closed and taken under government control but the underlying problems were not resolved

Trade
- Germany had developed a strong export trade in the years 1924–29 that had underpinned its economic recovery
- During the post-1929 depression, world trade shrank, which hit Germany badly. Between 1929 and 1932, Germany's export trade declined by 61%, which severely damaged German industry

The economic impact of the Great Depression on Germany 1929–32

Industry
- In the years 1929–32, industrial production fell by 58% of its 1928 level
- Prices fell and many companies made heavy losses, causing them to become bankrupt
- Germany's main industrial areas in the Ruhr and Silesia, and in port cities such as Hamburg, were badly hit by factory and mine closures and the collapse of foreign trade

Farming
- The prices of agricultural products fell and exports declined
- Farmers were heavily indebted to the banks, which demanded repayment of loans
- Many farmers lost their farms

Social impact

The Depression created mass unemployment, a steep rise in poverty and undermined the confidence and security of the middle class. In these circumstances, society became more polarised.

Unemployment and the working class
- Unemployment grew; by 1932, approximately one third of all German workers were registered as unemployed.
- The official figures did not record the true scale of unemployment as many redundant workers did not register. Estimates of the true scale of unemployment in early 1933 suggest a figure of c8 million.
- Those who kept their jobs suffered cuts to wages and reductions in working hours.

Poverty
- Unemployment benefits were subject to strict means tests and were only provided for fixed periods.
- Poverty increased and more people became homeless; shanty towns grew up on the edges of large cities.
- Diseases linked to poor living conditions and malnutrition increased, especially among children.

Young people

- The unemployment rate for those under 25 was particularly high.
- Benefits for young unemployed were lower than for adults (those over 25).
- Juvenile crime increased, particularly crimes of violence, and more young men joined criminal gangs.
- More young men joined extremist political parties and were involved in political violence.

Women

- The female proportion of the labour force increased, as women were typically cheaper to employ than men.
- There was heightened hostility to married women in employment (on the basis that they were 'double-earners').
- In May 1932, a new law allowed married female civil servants to be dismissed.

Middle class

- Owners of businesses that went bankrupt lost their livelihoods and, in many cases, their homes.
- Many civil servants lost their jobs; those who remained in employment suffered cuts to their salaries.
- Economic insecurity further undermined the confidence of the middle class and raised fears that they would lose status.

Landowners and tenant farmers

- The collapse in agricultural prices hit farmers badly. Many tenant farmers could no longer afford to pay rents and left the countryside.
- Landowners lost out, as rents went unpaid and they fell into debt, especially in the east.

Political impact

The Depression placed enormous strain on the political system. Faith in parliamentary democracy was eroded, the parties of the extreme left and extreme right gained at the expense of the moderate parties of the centre, and political violence increased.

March 1930	Grand Coalition government collapsed.	This was due to splits over reducing unemployment benefits.
	Heinrich Brüning of the Centre Party was appointed Chancellor by Hindenburg.	Without the support of the SPD, Brüning did not have a majority in the Reichstag so increasingly had to rely on using Article 48.The Reichstag became increasingly irrelevant and met less frequently from this time.
	Brüning imposed cuts in unemployment benefits and government worker's wages and raised taxes (The Hunger Chancellor). His budget could be passed into law only by presidential decree.	The role of Hindenburg and the army: • Hindenburg observed the letter of the constitution but preferred an authoritarian style of government. • He relied on close advisers, especially Generals Groener and von Schleicher, to guide his decisions. • The army, and in particular von Schleicher, increasingly played a key role in political decisions.
September 1930	Reichstag elections.	The Nazis made a breakthrough into national politics, becoming the second largest party in Reichstag. The KPD also gained a lot of votes, mostly from SPD. In the election as a whole, two out of every five voters supported anti-democratic parties.
	The level of political violence on the streets increased.	Violence frequently took the form of street battles between Nazi Stormtroopers and communist **Red-Front Fighters' League**.
April 1932	Brüning banned the SA to try to reduce street violence.	The ban was ineffective and the SA continued to grow, and this ban lost Brüning the support of Schleicher, who feared that the ban could provoke a Nazi uprising.

May 1932	Brüning's government collapsed and he was forced to resign.	This was because: • the Depression had deepened (by February 1932, unemployment exceeded 6 million) and Brüning's policy of reducing state spending made the situation worse. • Street violence had increased, causing alarm among middle and upper classes about the threat of revolution.
	Hindenburg appointed Franz von Papen as the new Chancellor.	The appointment was made on Scheicher's advice and he became Defence Minister in the new government.
	Papen constructed a 'government of national concentration' in which most cabinet posts were held by landowners, businessmen and army officers (the 'cabinet of barons').	The only political support for Papen's government came from the DNVP, so Papen also ruled by Presidential decree. His government failed to resolve the political crisis.
June 1932	Papen lifted the ban on the SA.	This provoked a renewed wave of street violence.
July 1932	Using street violence as a pretext, Papen declared a state of emergency in Prussia and dismissed its SPD-led state government, making himself the Reich Commissioner in charge of Prussia.	This destroyed democratic government in Prussia, Germany's largest state.
July 1932	Reichstag elections – Nazis became the largest party, with 37.3% of the vote.	Hitler had agreed not to oppose Papen's government in return for a promise of new Reichstag elections in July. The election result strengthened Hitler's hand but did not give the Nazis an outright majority in the Reichstag. Hitler refused to join a coalition government unless he was Chancellor. Hindenburg and Schleicher wanted Nazi participation in government but refused to give Hitler outright power.
November 1932	Reichstag elections.	The Nazis in the Reichstag joined with other parties to force new elections in November but NSDAP suffered losses in this election (they lost 34 seats, and their share of the vote was reduced, to 33.1 %).
December 1932	Papen was forced to resign as Chancellor.	This was because Schleicher had withdrawn his support for him.
	Schleicher was appointed Chancellor.	Despite election losses, the Nazis remained the largest party in the Reichstag, but Hindenburg would not trust Hitler to become Chancellor. The Nazis were now short of money, and divisions within the Nazi Party were beginning to appear. It looked as though Hitler may have lost his chance. However, Schleicher's position was weakened in the eyes of Hindenburg as he had conspired against Papen.

SUMMARY

- The Depression of 1929–33 had devastating consequences for the German economy, society and politics. The rise in unemployment and the cost of providing unemployment benefits brought about the collapse of the Grand Coalition in March 1930.
- Extremist parties, especially the Nazi Party but also the Communist Party, gained most from the turmoil of the Depression.
- With the appointment of Brüning as Chancellor, and his need to rule by Presidential decree, parliamentary democracy in Germany collapsed and the army, and especially von Schleicher, came to play an increasingly important role in German politics.
- By 1932, Germany was in the throes of a political and economic crisis, which neither Brüning, nor his successor Papen, were able to resolve.
- After the July 1932 election, in which the Nazis became the largest party in the Reichstag, Hitler had the power to undermine Papen's government, but he was still not trusted by Hindenburg and Schleicher to become Chancellor. After the November 1932 election, Hitler's position was weakened.

APPLY

APPLY YOUR KNOWLEDGE

Briefly explain why the following economic problems occurred during the Great Depression in Germany:

- Collapse of export trade
- Fall in industrial production
- Fall in prices of goods
- Businesses going bankrupt and closing
- Unemployment
- Reductions in wages and working hours
- Lack of foreign investment
- Reduction in German government income

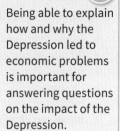

EXAMINER TIP

Being able to explain how and why the Depression led to economic problems is important for answering questions on the impact of the Depression.

IMPROVE AN ANSWER

AS LEVEL **'Unemployment was the worst consequence of the Great Depression in Germany.' Explain why you agree or disagree with this view.**

a Below is a paragraph from a student's answer to the exam question above. The student begins this paragraph by indicating that they are going to discuss the social effects of the Great Depression. However, the paragraph contains a mixture of social, economic and political problems. Using three different colours, highlight sections that deal with these three different types of problems.

b Rewrite the paragraph, removing the economic and political problems and including more on the social impact of mass unemployment.

c Use your answers to parts **a** and **b**, write a complete answer to the exam question above.

Answer

Unemployment was not the only devastating social effect of the Great Depression in Germany. Many businesses went bankrupt and industrial production and trade fell sharply. People's incomes rapidly diminished and they became dependent on savings or welfare benefits to survive. The rise in welfare dependents had a huge impact on reducing government income, as did the reduction in income tax receipts. Homelessness escalated as people could not afford to pay their mortgages or rents. Malnutrition and diseases caused by poor diets increased as people could not afford good food. People also had less money to spend on goods which further affected the economy and left many businesses struggling to survive. Many people blamed the Weimar government for unemployment and turned to extremist political parties which promised to provide more jobs if elected.

EXAMINER TIP

It's important that your essays follow a clear and coherent argument throughout. To help with this, each paragraph should usually focus on a particular consequence rather than trying to explain different ones as this can be confusing. However, you might need to mention several different consequences in a paragraph when showing how consequences link together.

REVIEW

The rise in extremism is another consequence of the Depression that should be explored in this essay. It is covered in more detail on pages 51 and 52.

APPLY

APPLY YOUR KNOWLEDGE

Create information cards for each of the following social effects of the Depression:

- Increased poverty
- Increased homelessness
- Increased disease and malnutrition
- Increased middle-class bitterness
- Increased street violence and violent crime
- Increased bitterness towards women workers

EXAMINER TIP

Knowing details such as dates and examples will impress the examiner. Knowledge of the social impact will be relevant for any essay on the impact of the Depression.

APPLY YOUR KNOWLEDGE

a Highlight the measures and policies taken by the Weimar government in response to the Depression in the Recap section on pages 46–48.

b For each measure write a sentence outlining the results and consequences of each policy.

EXAMINER TIP

Knowledge of government policies in response to the Depression will be vital in writing essays on reasons for the failure of Weimar democracy or the rise of extremism.

ASSESS THE VALIDITY OF THIS VIEW

A LEVEL **'The Weimar governments' failure to deal with the effects of the Depression was the reason for the growth of political extremism in Germany after 1929.' Assess the validity of this view.**

There are two aspects of this question which you will need to tackle in your essay.

a Do you agree with the view that the Weimar government failed to deal with the effects of the Depression? Make a list of measures the government took to try to deal with the impact of the Depression and whether or not these measures were successful? Was there anything the government could have done that it did not do?

b Create a mind-map of reasons for the rise of extremism after 1929, including the failure of the Weimar government to act effectively to deal with the Depression (if you believe that was the case).

c Use your answers to parts **a** and **b** to answer the exam question above.

REVIEW

You will need to include the appeal of **Nazism** and communism (covered on pages 51–52), and how these extremists used the Depression to gain support, as part of your answer.

EXAMINER TIP

Most A Level questions will include more than one area to analyse and you always need to address the question fully to gain a good mark.

10 The appeal of Nazism and communism

Electoral support for Nazism and communism up to July 1932

Both the NSDAP (Nazi Party) and the KPD (Communist Party) gained electoral support during the depression. However, the Nazis broadened the base of their support, both geographically and socially, while KPD gains were mainly at the expense of the SPD. The KPD did not succeed in broadening its support base beyond the working class.

	NSDAP	KPD
1928 Reichstag elections	Received only 2.6% of the votes.	Much more popular than the Nazis, with 10.6% of the votes.
1930 Reichstag elections	Became the second largest party in the Reichstag, with 18.25% of the vote.	Increased their share of the vote to 13.1%.
1932 Presidential elections	Hitler made a major impact, receiving nearly 37% of votes and coming second to Hindenburg.	Thälmann gained just 10% of votes.
July 1932 Reichstag elections	Became the largest party in the Reichstag, with 37.3% of the vote.	Won 14.3% of the votes and gained two million votes from 1928.

The appeal of Nazism

In 1928 the Nazis had a narrow base of support, attracting mainly the lower middle class (**Mittelstand**). These people – white-collar workers, small shopkeepers, independent craftsmen – continued to vote for the Nazis in the Depression years, but the NSDAP also broadened the base of its support, as shown in this diagram.

Protestants — Nazi support was strongest in the rural areas and small towns of the Protestant north, east and central areas of Germany

Catholics — The Nazis attracted limited support in the Catholic areas of the south and west. Most Catholics voted for the Catholic Centre Party and were less nationalistic than Protestants because of their allegiance to the Pope

Women — Women were also successfully targeted as Nazis played on common fears and emphasised traditional family values

Young people — The Nazis successfully targeted young people who had been disproportionately affected by unemployment. Many young men joined the SA

Farmers and rural communities — Farmers who were suffering from years of low prices and heavy indebtedness to the banks were targeted by the Nazis. Rural communities as a whole were particularly targeted by Nazi propaganda. Nazi support in rural areas grew strongly after 1928

Extended middle class — The extended middle class were increasingly worried by the growth in KPD support and the Nazis played on their fears of a communist revolution. Money from big business was crucial to Nazi success in election campaigns

Workers — Although working-class voters in the industrial areas had traditionally supported the SPD or KPD, the Nazis did attract some working-class support, especially among the unemployed

The importance of Hitler to Nazi success

Hitler had undisputed control over the Nazi Party by 1929. He was a powerful orator and displayed charisma. He also knew how to play on people's hopes and fears. As the most well-known and popular Nazi, Hitler was the focus of a huge amount of Nazi **propaganda**. He travelled extensively, giving speeches and attending rallies all over Germany. Total belief in Hitler was known as the *Führerprinzip*.

Racial theory

What distinguished Nazism from other types of right-wing Fascism was its racial theory. Nazis were strong believers in racialism – that the human species is divided into different races and each race has particular positive and negative characteristics. Derived from the Darwinist theory of evolution, the Nazis also believed in **Social Darwinism**, which advocated the improvement of 'racial hygiene' through selective breeding, birth control and sterilisation. The Nazis believed the Aryans were the master race and were, therefore, destined to lead. The Jews were at the bottom of the evolutionary hierarchy and, along with other groups, including the **Slavs** and black people, were deemed '**Untermenschen**' (sub-human).

The role of anti-Semitism in Nazi success

Most Nazi propaganda in 1932 had little to do with anti-Semitism; as the Party was trying to broaden the base of its support, it concentrated on economic issues. However, anti-Semitism still played a small role, as:

- The Nazis constantly described a link between Jews and communism.
- Jews were a convenient scapegoat to blame for all of Germany's problems.
- The Nazis were able to tap into a pre-existing tradition of anti-Semitism in Germany.
- The SA brought violent anti-Semitism to the streets of Germany.

The role of propaganda

- Hitler understood the importance of propaganda and concentrated Party resources on making it effective.
- The Nazi propaganda chief, Joseph Goebbels, was a skilled communicator and understood the importance of the 'propaganda of the deed'; rallies, marches and street battles against Communists conveyed a message of Nazi strength and discipline.
- Nazi propaganda was targeted at different audiences; the message was adapted to suit the specific target audience.
- Money provided by big business (Hugenberg and Thyssen) helped Nazis mount nationwide propaganda campaigns involving speeches, newspapers, rallies, posters and leaflets.
- The Nazis had their own newspapers.

The appeal of communism

The KPD had been a major force in Weimar politics since it was founded in 1920, As an avowedly working-class movement, it had built up a strong following among trade-union members in the industrial areas. Its appeal was based on an uncompromising commitment to supporting workers in class struggle, and it was involved in many strikes. During the Depression, however, many workers were unemployed and the KPD switched to setting up 'committees of the unemployed', organising hunger marches and campaigning against benefit cuts. It presented itself as the defender of working-class districts against the Nazis, and its Red Front Fighters' League fought many street battles against the SA. The KPD also focused on recruiting working-class youths – the so-called 'wild cliques' – and steering them into political campaigns. KPD membership grew from 117,000 in 1929 to 360,000 in 1932.

Policies and ideology

- The KPD emphasised revolutionary class struggle to overthrow capitalism as the only solution to the economic, social and political crisis of the time; KPD argued that the Depression was the 'final crisis of capitalism' which would inevitably lead to a Communist revolution.
- The party campaigned on immediate issues such as unemployment benefits and wage cuts. 'Bread and Freedom' was its rallying cry, aimed at the unemployed.
- The KPD attacked the SPD as 'social-fascists' who stood in the way of the overthrow of capitalism.
- It had links with the communist regime in the USSR and emphasised internationalism as opposed to nationalism.

Strengths	Weaknesses
<ul><li>Strong support in working-class districts of large cities.</li><li>Effective propaganda, using speeches, posters, marches and newspapers.</li><li>Strong organisation at street and neighbourhood level.</li><li>Red Front Fighters' League engaged in street battles with SA.</li></ul>	<ul><li>Membership turnover was high.</li><li>Failed to broaden base of support.</li><li>Short of money.</li><li>Limited appeal for women.</li><li>Fight against SPD 'social fascists' a tactical error when Nazis were the main threat.</li><li>Growth of KPD drove middle class to support Nazis.</li></ul>

Strengths and weaknesses of the KPD 1929–32

SUMMARY

- Both the Nazis and the KPD gained from the depression, but the Nazis more than the KPD.
- The KPD grew at the expense of the SPD but did not broaden the base of its support.
- Rise of the KPD benefited the Nazis, as they were able to play on middle- and upper-class fears of a communist revolution.

- The Nazis succeeded in becoming a broad-based movement. By the summer of 1932, NSDAP was the largest party in Reichstag and Hitler was able to make a bid for power.

APPLY

APPLY YOUR KNOWLEDGE

Complete the mind-map of Nazi ideology.

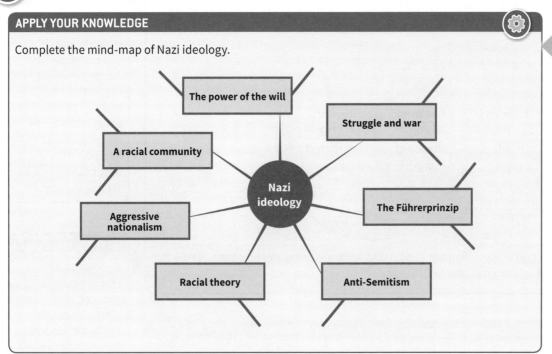

APPLY YOUR KNOWLEDGE

For each group in the table below, give an indication of the amount of support the Nazis managed to attract from this group in the July 1932 election. Then explain why they managed to gain that amount of support from each group.

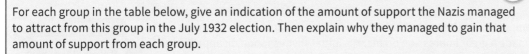

	How much support was there for the Nazis from this group?	Reasons for that amount of support
Lower-middle classes		
Farmers		
Workers		
Industrialists		
The young		
Housewives		
Catholics		
Protestants		

KEY CONCEPT

Anti-Semitism, Social Darwinism and racialism are key concepts for the study of modern Germany.

a   Write a definition of each of the key concepts above.

b   Explain how each was connected in Nazi ideology.

APPLY YOUR KNOWLEDGE

a Complete the following Venn diagram on reasons why the Nazi Party and the Communist Party attracted more supporters in Germany in the elections of 1930 and 1932.

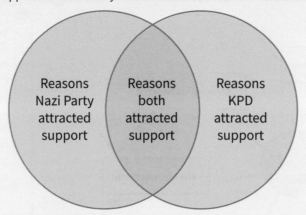

Reasons Nazi Party attracted support

Reasons both attracted support

Reasons KPD attracted support

b Using your completed chart or Venn diagram to help you, write a summary explanation of why the Nazi Party gained more support than the KPD.

SOURCE ANALYSIS

SOURCE A

From the autobiography of Albert Speer, written in prison after 1946 and published in 1970. Speer was appointed Armaments Minister in 1942. Here he recalls listening to Hitler speak in 1930.

Hitler entered and was tempestuously hailed by his numerous followers among the students. This enthusiasm in itself made a great impression on me. His initial shyness soon disappeared; his pitch rose, he spoke urgently, with hypnotic persuasiveness. I was carried on the wave of enthusiasm which bore the speaker along from sentence to sentence. It swept away my scepticism. Opponents were given no chance to speak. This furthered the illusion, at least momentarily, of unanimity. Finally, Hitler no longer seemed to be speaking to convince; rather, he seemed to feel that he was expressing what the audience, by now transformed into a single mass, expected of him. The peril of communism, which seemed unstoppable, could be checked, Hitler persuaded us, and instead of hopeless unemployment Germany could move towards economic recovery.

Read Source A and consider its value to an historian studying the appeal of Nazism.

a How would the author, date, audience and purpose of writing affect the value of this source for an historical study into the appeal of Nazism?

b What is the tone and emphasis of this source? Include examples of words or phrases that help convey this. Does this affect the value of the source for this study?

c How would the content of the source be valuable for this study? What are its limitations?

ASSESS THE VALIDITY OF THIS VIEW

A LEVEL 'It was Hitler's anti-communist stance that won support for the NSDAP in 1932.' Assess the validity of this view.

a Create a list of all the factors involved in the Nazi Party's electoral success.

b Give each factor a rating out of 10 for its importance in winning votes for the Nazis and explain why you have given this rating. Remember to consider the different groups that attracted most Nazi support in the 1932 elections.

c Use your answers to parts **a** and **b** to write an answer to the exam question above.

REVISION SKILLS
This activity involves a Venn diagram, but you could use another method to complete this activity. Experiment with your revision techniques and find which are the best ways for you to retain information.

REVIEW
If you need a reminder on the general reasons why extremist parties attracted support go back to page 46–48.

EXAMINER TIP
You should always consider the provenance of sources before analysing the content. Both are important, however, the provenance will help you assess and evaluate the value of the content. You also need to apply your own knowledge when analysing both provenance and content.

EXAMINER TIP
Always take time to read all exam questions carefully so that you fully understand what is being asked. In this case, the question is about both the appeal of Hitler and the fear of communism as the main factors that won the Nazi Party electoral support.

11 The appointment of Hitler as Chancellor

The appointment of Hitler

Hitler was appointed as Chancellor by President Hindenburg in January 1933. The process that brought him to power was long and complex and, although the Nazis became the largest party in the Reichstag in the July 1932 elections, there was no inevitability about Hitler becoming Chancellor.

November 1932: Fall of Papen's government but setback for Nazis in Reichstag election

July 1932: Reichstag election, Nazis became largest party in Reichstag with over 37% of the vote

May 1932: Collapse of Brüning's government and start of political crisis with Papen as Chancellor

April 1932: Presidential election, Hitler received nearly 37% of the second-round vote

1931: Depression deepened, and street violence between Nazi SA and KPD Red Front intensified

September 1930: Reichstag election, major gains for Nazi Party and KPD, losses for moderate parties

March 1930: Collapse of Müller's Grand Coalition and replacement by Brüning; rule by presidential decree signalled end of parliamentary democracy in Germany

December 1929: Campaign against Young Plan gave Hitler a chance to make a breakthrough as a national politician

October 1929: Wall Street Crash led to a severe depression in Germany and mass unemployment, placing Weimar democracy under strain

The rise of the Nazi Party

The situation in November 1932

The election did not resolve the political crisis, as Papen's government still did not have an overall majority in the Reichstag. Papen himself was weakened and he had lost the support of the army and of Schleicher, forcing him to resign. This left Schleicher, a man who preferred to manipulate politicians from behind the scenes, with no alternative but to become Chancellor himself. Schleicher wanted to restore an authoritarian form of government in Germany, dominated by the old elites, but he understood that realistically this could be achieved only through an alliance with the Nazi Party.

At the same time, the position of Hitler and the Nazi Party had been weakened by the election of November 1932:

- They lost two million votes and 34 seats, although they remained the largest party in the Reichstag.
- In state elections in December, their support continued to fall.
- Middle-class voters had been alienated by Hitler's attacks on Papen, his refusal to join a coalition, and Nazi support for a transport strike in Berlin.
- Three elections in eight months had exhausted the Nazis' funds.
- Hitler's previous refusals to join a coalition government unless he was the Chancellor had alienated Hindenburg, who was not prepared to trust him to lead a government.
- Divisions were beginning to appear in the Nazi Party over Hitler's tactics.

Being the largest party in the Reichstag, the Nazis had the ability to frustrate the governments of Papen and Schleicher. That was not enough, however, to give Hitler the chancellorship. Without a willingness on Hitler's part to compromise on joining a coalition government, or a change of mind by Hindenburg, Hitler could not gain power by legal means.

The role of 'backstairs intrigue'

Hindenburg was surrounded by a small group of advisers who guided his decisions. These included his son, Oskar, and Otto Meisner, a civil servant who controlled access to the President. Schleicher was part of this inner circle, but because of his plotting against Papen he had lost some of his previous influence with Hindenburg. These men were all involved in the 'backstairs intrigue' that finally brought Hitler to power in January 1933.

The failure of Schleicher's government

Schleicher needed broad support to construct a stable government, he tried two tactics to achieve this:

1 As the largest party, only the Nazis could provide this from within the Reichstag. Schleicher therefore tried to persuade Gregor Strasser, a radical Nazi, to join his government, thereby putting pressure on Hitler to do the same. Hitler purged Strasser and reasserted his control over the Nazi Party.

2 Schleicher tried to persuade the trade unions to support his government with the promise of a progressive social policy with measures to help the unemployed and restore wage levels. This also failed as it did not attract much trade union support and alienated industrialists and landowners.

Hitler becomes Chancellor

As Schleicher tried to construct a stable government, Papen conspired with Hitler, who now agreed to be part of a coalition, providing he was Chancellor; Hugenberg (leader of the DNVP) was prepared to be part of the coalition	Further talks took place between Hitler, Papen, Hindenburg and Meisner where it was agreed to bring down Schleicher and form a coalition government in which Hitler would be Chancellor	President Hindenburg had doubts about Hitler's suitability but Papen and Oskar Hindenburg convinced him that as Hitler was poorly educated and had no experience in government, they would be able to control him	Schleicher asked Hindenburg to suspend the constitution and give him dictatorial powers; Hindenburg refused and Schleicher resigned	Hitler was appointed Chancellor on 30 January 1933 at the head of a coalition government in which Nazi ministers were in a minority; the cabinet included Papen and Hugenberg

SUMMARY

- Success in elections was very important to the Nazis in their bid for power, but their support was waning before Hitler became Chancellor in January 1933.
- By the end of 1932, Hitler's refusal to join a coalition government unless he was the Chancellor appeared to have been a serious tactical error as Hindenburg was not prepared to concede this.
- With their position as the largest party in the Reichstag, and their willingness to use street violence, the Nazis could destabilise any government that excluded them.
- Papen and Hindenburg's close advisers came to the conclusion that it would be safer to have Hitler in government, and that they could manipulate and control him once he became Chancellor.

APPLY

APPLY YOUR KNOWLEDGE

Number the following events in order, then add the correct dates.

- Hindenburg appoints Hitler Chancellor.
- Hindenburg appoints Papen Chancellor.
- Hindenburg appoints Schleicher Chancellor.
- Hindenburg appoint Brüning Chancellor.
- The Nazis become the largest party in the Reichstag for the first time.
- The Nazis lose votes but remain the largest party in the Reichstag.

EXAMINER TIP

Knowledge of the complex events of 1932 and January 1933 will be important for questions on reasons why Hitler became Chancellor or how the Nazis came to power, as well as questions on why Weimar democracy collapsed.

SOURCE ANALYSIS

SOURCE A

From the Memoirs of Franz von Papen, which were written after the Second World War and were published in 1952.

We were to learn in the course of time into what hands Germany had fallen. There was little hint of either domination or genius in Hitler's manner or appearance, but he had immense powers of persuasion and an extraordinary and indefinable capacity for bending individuals and, above all, the masses, to his will. He was fully aware of this power and completely convinced of his infallibility. One thing, however, must be understood. The first Hitler government was formed in strict accordance with parliamentary procedure. He had been brought to power by normal democratic processes. It must be realised that neither he nor his movement had acquired the character or carried out the atrocities for which they were to be condemned fifteen years later. We believed Hitler when he said that, once he was in a position of power and responsibility, he would steer his movement into more ordered channels.

Read Source A and consider the following three historical studies:

1 How Hitler became Chancellor of Germany.

2 Papen's role in Hitler becoming Chancellor of Germany.

3 The establishment of the Nazi dictatorship.

a Complete the basic provenance details in the table below, then using your understanding of the historical context, assess the value of each of the provenance details for Source A.

REVIEW

The establishment of the Nazi dictatorship is covered on pages 59–60 if you need to remind yourself of events in order to consider the value of this source to an historical study of it.

	Historical study 1	Historical study 2	Historical study 3
Author:			
Date:			
Audience and reason for writing the source:			

b What is the tone of the source and what has the author chosen to emphasise?

c How, if at all, do the source's tone and emphasis affect its value for historical studies 1, 2 and 3?

TO WHAT EXTENT?

 To what extent was Hitler's appointment as Chancellor in January 1933 due to 'backstairs intrigue'?

Consider how useful each of the following information would be to include in an answer to the exam question above.

Individual	Very useful	Of some use	Not very useful
Reichstag election results of 1928.			
The collapse of the Grand Coalition government in March 1930.			
Reichstag election results of 1930.			
Brüning's government took temporary control of the banks to prevent more of them collapsing in 1931.			
The exclusion of the SPD from government meant that no government after 1930 had a majority in the Reichstag.			
The fall of Brüning's government in May 1932.			
The Presidential election of 1932.			
The banning of the SA in April 1932.			
Reichstag election results of July 1932.			
Papen imposed authoritarian rule in Prussia July 1932.			
Hitler refused to join Papen's government after July 1932 election.			
Reichstag passed a vote of no confidence in Papen's government.			
Reichstag election results of November 1932.			
Schleicher persuaded Hindenburg to appoint him Chancellor in December 1932.			
Schleicher negotiated with Gregor Strasser about the Nazis joining his government.			
Schleicher's resignation as Chancellor.			
Papen's negotiations with Hitler in December and January 1933.			
The Wall Street Crash of October 1929 saw share prices on the New York Stock Exchange drop rapidly and many American companies were badly hit.			
Papen and Hindenburg believed they would be able to control Hitler once he became Chancellor.			
Papen and Oskar von Hindenberg persuaded President Hindenberg to appoint Hitler Chancellor.			

b Add any other highly relevant or partly relevant information you think you should include.

c Use your answers to parts **a** and **b** to help answer the exam question above.

EXAMINER TIP

This question will require an analysis of the factors responsible for Hitler becoming Chancellor. You should consider all the factors before reaching a judgement on the extent of the importance of 'backstairs intrigue'.

REVIEW

You will need to consider other factors that led to Hitler becoming Chancellor, such as the impact of the Depression and the appeal of Nazism, which led to the Nazis becoming the largest party in the Reichstag (see pages 46–48).

12 The establishment of the Nazi dictatorship, January–March 1933

 **RECAP**

When Hitler was appointed as Chancellor at the end of January 1933 he was not yet the dictator he aspired to be, as his power was still limited:

- Hindenburg, as President, had the ultimate authority under the constitution.
- The Nazis were in a minority within the coalition cabinet.
- The constitution, which was still in force, guaranteed the rights of German citizens under the law.

By the end of March 1933, a Nazi legal dictatorship had been established. This involved both the use of terror and the use of legal powers.

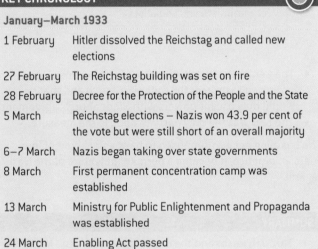

KEY CHRONOLOGY	
January–March 1933	
1 February	Hitler dissolved the Reichstag and called new elections
27 February	The Reichstag building was set on fire
28 February	Decree for the Protection of the People and the State
5 March	Reichstag elections – Nazis won 43.9 per cent of the vote but were still short of an overall majority
6–7 March	Nazis began taking over state governments
8 March	First permanent concentration camp was established
13 March	Ministry for Public Enlightenment and Propaganda was established
24 March	Enabling Act passed

The coalition cabinet

Chancellor – Adolf Hitler

Vice Chancellor – Franz von Papen (non-party)

Defence Minister – General Blomberg (non-party)

Foreign Minister – Freiherr von Neurath (non-party)

Minister of the Interior – Wilhelm Frick (NSDAP)

Minister without Portfolio – Hermann Goering (NSDAP)

Minister for Economics – Alfred Hugenberg (DNVP)

Minister of Labour – Franz Seldte (non-party)

The use of terror

- With control over the police, and with sympathetic judges, the Nazis were able to use terror with impunity.
- The SA was expanded (from 500,000 to c3 million in a year), merged with the **Stahlhelm**, and was given the position of 'auxiliary police'. The regular police were ordered not to interfere in SA activities.
- The Nazis unleashed a wave of violence against trade unions, SPD and KPD offices and members, and against newspaper offices.
- Thousands of political opponents were put into makeshift concentration camps. Dachau was the first permanent camp, established on 8 March 1933.

The use of terror intimidated opponents. It also heightened the feeling that Germany was on the brink of civil war and that only extraordinary measures would prevent the country descending into chaos.

The 'Pact of 1933'

Hitler also moved quickly to gain the support of powerful institutions and groups within German society, especially the army and big business.

- On 3 February 1933 he met with the army's senior officers to reassure them that the Nazi regime did not pose a threat to the army's position as the most important institution in the state.
- On 20 February he met leading industrialists to reassure them that there would be no Nazi attacks on large capitalist enterprises and to get their financial backing.

This so-called 'Pact of 1933' was a compromise with the old elites but it gave Hitler vital backing in his bid to establish a legal dictatorship.

The March 1933 Reichstag election and the Reichstag fire

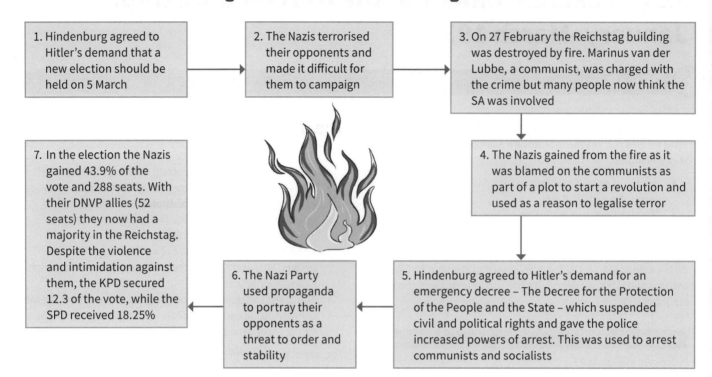

1. Hindenburg agreed to Hitler's demand that a new election should be held on 5 March

2. The Nazis terrorised their opponents and made it difficult for them to campaign

3. On 27 February the Reichstag building was destroyed by fire. Marinus van der Lubbe, a communist, was charged with the crime but many people now think the SA was involved

4. The Nazis gained from the fire as it was blamed on the communists as part of a plot to start a revolution and used as a reason to legalise terror

5. Hindenburg agreed to Hitler's demand for an emergency decree – The Decree for the Protection of the People and the State – which suspended civil and political rights and gave the police increased powers of arrest. This was used to arrest communists and socialists

6. The Nazi Party used propaganda to portray their opponents as a threat to order and stability

7. In the election the Nazis gained 43.9% of the vote and 288 seats. With their DNVP allies (52 seats) they now had a majority in the Reichstag. Despite the violence and intimidation against them, the KPD secured 12.3 of the vote, while the SPD received 18.25%

The use of legal power and the end of democracy

The Nazi victory in the March election and the Decree for the Protection of the People and the State severely weakened the opposition to the Nazis and laid the groundwork for the establishment of a legal dictatorship. For this dictatorship to be fully established, however, Hitler needed more wide-ranging powers.

At the first meeting of the new Reichstag on 23 March, the deputies were presented with a Nazi demand to pass 'The Law for Removing the Distress of the People and the Reich' – the so-called **Enabling Act**. This provided the legal basis for the Nazi dictatorship as it gave Hitler the power to issue decrees without the support of the Reichstag and without needing Hindenburg's agreement. This law, which required a two-thirds majority of the deputies, was passed because:

- The SA created an atmosphere of intimidation at the Opera House (where the Reichstag now sat).
- KPD deputies were not allowed to attend, as the party was now banned.
- The DNVP deputies were willing allies of the Nazis.

- The Centre Party deputies voted for it because Hitler promised to protect the Catholic Church and that he would only use his powers with Hindenburg's agreement.
- The SPD was the only party to oppose the measure.

The Enabling Act was supposed to have a time limit of four years. In practice, it became a permanent feature of the Nazi regime.

SUMMARY

- Through terror and the use of legal power, the Nazi regime established the legal foundations of their dictatorship within two months of Hitler becoming Chancellor.
- There were still limits to Hitler's power; Hindenburg retained the ultimate authority in the republic, the army was still loyal to Hindenburg, and political parties were still legal.
- Hitler met the army leaders and big-business leaders in February 1933 and gained their support. This 'Pact of 1933' was vital to Hitler's success in the next stage of consolidating his dictatorship and reshaping Germany.

APPLY

APPLY YOUR KNOWLEDGE

Create a mind-map of ways in which the Nazis created a legal dictatorship between Hitler's appointment as Chancellor and the end of March 1933. Use the branches of the map below to get started. Colour code your mind-map, with examples of the use of terror in one colour and the use of legal powers in another colour.

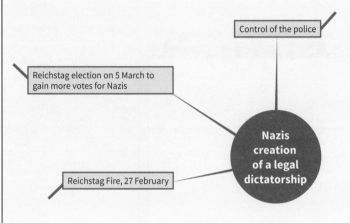

EXAMINER TIP

This activity will be useful for any exam questions on how Hitler consolidated his power or established a dictatorship.

HOW SIGNIFICANT?

A LEVEL **How significant was Hindenburg's underestimation of Hitler in the establishment of Nazi rule in Germany by March 1933?**

a Complete the table below to help you evaluate the significance of the different factors that enabled the establishment of Nazi rule in Germany by March 1933.

Factors that enabled Nazi rule by March 1933	How significant were these factors?
Hindenburg's underestimation of Hitler	

b Use your completed table from part **a** to help you write an answer to the exam question above.

REVIEW

You will need to include factors that led to Hitler being appointed Chancellor. See pages 55–56 if you need a reminder.

EXAMINER TIP

It is vital to take note of any dates in the exam question. In this case, for example, anything you include after March 1933 will be irrelevant and will therefore not gain any marks but instead lose you valuable time.

PLAN YOUR ESSAY

 'The activities of the SA were the main contributor to Hitler's consolidation of power between January and March 1933.' Explain why you agree or disagree with this view.

All AS essay questions will require you to balance points of agreement against points of disagreement. It is a good idea to use a two-column chart to prepare for this. See if you can create a plan for this question for your revision.

Before you begin to write you will need to decide whether you will agree or disagree with the statement. This two-column chart should help you to decide.

Agree	Disagree

EXAMINER TIP

Planning your exam essay is essential, so you should practise writing essay plans as much as you practise writing full answers.

SOURCE ANALYSIS

SOURCE A

From account by the SPD deputy, Wilhelm Hoegner, describing a Reichstag session on 23 March 1933 when the Enabling Act was discussed.

The wide square in front of the Kroll Opera House was crowded with dark masses of people. We were received with wild choruses, 'We want the Enabling Act!' Youths with swastikas on their chests eyed us insolently, blocked our way, in fact made us run the gauntlet, calling us names like 'Centre pig', 'Marxist sow'. The Kroll Opera House was crawling with armed SA and SS men. In the cloakroom we learned that Severing (the SPD member who had previously been Prime Minister of Prussia) had been arrested on entering the building. The assembly hall was decorated with swastikas and similar ornaments. When we Social Democrats had taken our seats on the extreme left, SA and SS men lined up at the exits and along the walls behind us in a semi-circle. Their expressions boded no good.

a What is the tone of this source? Highlight all the parts of the source where the author uses language to create this tone.

b How might the provenance of the source explain the tone?

c How valuable would this source be to an enquiry on how the Nazis established a dictatorship in Germany? Write a paragraph giving your view, including a comment on how the provenance of this source may affect the value of it for this enquiry.

EXAMINER TIP

You would need to consider all aspects of the provenance of a source in an exam question, including the author, date, audience, the reason the source was written, and the tone and emphasis of the source.

AS Level sources sample answer

REVISION PROGRESS

 REVIEW

On these Exam Practice pages you will find a sample student answer for an AS Level sources question. What are the strengths and weaknesses of the answer? Read the answer and the corresponding Examiner Tips carefully. Think about how you could apply this advice in order to improve your own answers to questions like this one.

AS LEVEL With reference to these sources and your understanding of the historical context, which of these sources is more valuable in explaining the effect of the Great Depression on German society?

25 marks

REVISION SKILLS

The AS source question will focus on two primary sources or sources contemporary to the period. Read page 6 of this Revision Guide for details on how to master the sources question.

SOURCE A

From the autobiography of Lea Grundig, published in 1964. Grundig was a German painter and member of the KPD from 1926. Here she describes living through the Depression.

The unemployed had to do a lot to get their benefits. They stood in endless lines in every kind of weather at the unemployment offices. There they stood and waited until it was their turn. Unemployment became a tragedy for many. Not only because of the poverty that mutely sat at their table at all times. Not working, doing nothing, producing nothing – work that not only provided food, but also, despite all the harassment and drudgery, was satisfying, developed skills, and stimulated thinking; work, a human need – was not available; and wherever it was lacking, decay, malaise, and despair set in.

SOURCE B

From 'Twilight for Women', an article written by Hilde Walter in July 1931. Walter was a former social worker who worked as a journalist for *Die Weltbühne*, a left-wing magazine.

Women have become unpopular. An uncomfortable atmosphere is gathering around all working women. Along the entire spectrum from left to right, the meaning of women's employment and their right to it are suddenly being questioned. At the moment it is not even the old discussion over so-called 'equal rights' or 'equal pay for equal work' that occupies the foreground. Suddenly we are obliged to counter the most primitive arguments against the gainful employment of women.

Sample student answer

The author of Source A, Lea Grundig, lived through the Great Depression and so she provides an eyewitness account of the effects of unemployment, which was a major effect of the Depression on German society. This makes this source valuable. However, she was a Communist which might mean that she wanted to exaggerate the experiences of the unemployed. Nevertheless, her comments can be supported by other evidence. For example, the Weimar government placed tight restrictions on unemployment benefits during the Depression to try to reduce government spending so this matches the evidence of Source A. The tone of

EXAMINER TIP

The student provides some analysis of the content and provenance of Source A, mentioning author, date and tone, although purpose and audience have not been considered. There is also only limited use of contextual own knowledge. There is a little to support the source content but no attempt to challenge it.

Source A is quite depressed and gloomy, using words and phrases such as 'endless', 'tragedy', 'doing nothing, producing nothing', 'decay', 'malaise' and 'despair set in,' which is valuable as this gives us a good idea of the impact of the Depression for society.

Source B is also a valuable source for explaining the impact of the Great Depression on society because it describes the feelings of resentment towards women workers. This can be confirmed by other evidence that there was rising hostility towards women workers, who were seen as taking jobs away from men. The numbers of women in work actually rose throughout the Depression because women were cheaper to employ. Most hostility was reserved for married women who were called 'double-earners' as it was assumed their husbands had jobs too. Source B comments on how the 'old discussion' about equal rights and equal pay, which were topics of debate in the 1920s, was replaced by the question of whether women should be employed at all. This gives us a very good insight into a key social issue during the Depression. Source B has limitations, however, because it is only focused on one effect of the Depression and does not give any information on how working women felt about this increased resentment.

Although both sources have value, I think Source A is more valuable because the source describes several ways in which unemployment, caused by the Great Depression, affected people, whereas Source B focuses on one effect – the hostility towards women workers. Source A looks at the broad issue of poverty which affected all and the sense of despair that was strong in German society. Although Source B is of value in explaining a specific effect of the Depression, this is a more limited source overall.

EXAMINER TIP

There is a very good analysis of the value of the content of Source B in which the student applies some good contextual own knowledge. However, the student focuses entirely on the content of Source B and does not analyse the provenance at all. This would severely limit the level awarded.

EXAMINER TIP

This conclusion clearly explains why the student believes Source A is more valuable than Source B, with an explanation of why. This provides substantiation for the judgement.

OVERALL COMMENT

This student's answer analyses the content of both sources well and demonstrates a sound contextual understanding. It also provides a substantiated judgement as to which is the more valuable. However, it is limited in its analysis of the provenance of the sources, and its failure to address the provenance of Source B would hold it to a maximum of low Level 4, despite its other promising qualities.

OVER TO YOU

Give yourself 45 minutes to answer this question on your own. Consider this checklist when reviewing your answer:

❏ Did you analyse both the provenance and content of both sources?

❏ Did you support your analysis with your own knowledge?

❏ Did you come to a clear judgement on which source is more valulable and explain why?

Go back and look at pages 46–48 to refresh your knowledge of the impact of the Great Depression.

4 The Nazi dictatorship, 1933–39

REVISION PROGRESS

13 Hitler's consolidation of power, March 1933 to August 1934

RECAP

By the end of March 1933, Hitler had established the legal foundations for his dictatorship but he still did not have total control over Germany. The existence of other political parties, the independence of the civil service and democratic control over local government were all obstacles to the establishment of a complete dictatorship. These obstacles were removed during the period from March 1933 to August 1934 in a process the Nazis referred to as *Gleichschaltung*, meaning coordination or 'bringing into line'.

Government and administrative changes

Creating a one-party state

The KPD had already been suppressed under the Reichstag Fire Decree in February and communists were persecuted. Some were imprisoned while others fled into exile

Socialists were persecuted and imprisoned or fled into exile

From July 1933, the NSDAP was the only legal political party in Germany

On 14 July 1933 the Nazis issued a 'Law against the Formation of New Parties' which made forming a non-Nazi political party illegal

The SPD had voted against the Enabling Act and continued to oppose the Nazi government but were banned as a 'party hostile to the nation and state' in June 1933

The DNVP voluntarily disbanded on 27 June and the Centre Party followed on 5 July. The Centre Party had been appeased by the signing of the Concordat between the Nazi regime and the Roman Catholic Church

Control over local government

31 March 1933	7 April 1933	30 January 1934	14 February 1934
The 'First Law for the Coordination of the Federal States' dissolved elected assemblies in the federal states and replaced them with Nazi-dominated assemblies	The Second Coordination Law created the post of Reich Governor to rule over the federal states	The 'Law for the Reconstruction of the Reich' abolished state assemblies	The Reichsrat was abolished

Control over the Civil Service

Many civil servants were conservative and supportive of Hitler's appointment. Where their loyalties were in doubt, local officials were forced to resign and were replaced by Nazi Party members, many of whom had no experience of government. The Nazis also placed Party officials in government offices to watch over civil servants.

The Night of the Long Knives

The SA had made a major contribution to the rise of the Nazi Party and to the reign of terror which was unleashed against the Nazis' opponents thereafter. After July 1933, when Hitler declared that the Nazi revolution was over, the violence of the SA increasingly became an embarrassment to Hitler.

- The SA, led by Rohm, pressed for a 'Second Revolution', including using the SA as a basis for a national militia to replace the regular army.
- Many SA members became disillusioned and restless as they lost their auxiliary police status and lacked any clear role.
- SA violence and political pressure threatened to undermine Hitler's relationship with Hindenburg and the army.

The army was the only institution with the power to remove Hitler from power, and the primary loyalty of its commanders was to Hindenburg, not Hitler. The situation came to a head in the summer of 1934 when:

- SA units began to attack army convoys and stole weapons.
- Papen, with Hindenburg's approval, made a speech attacking Nazi excesses and SA violence.
- The Defence Minister, von Blomberg, threatened to give the army the power to crush the SA.

Hitler had been warned about the risks posed by the SA but had done nothing. These developments convinced him that he could not delay action against the SA any longer. Therefore, in the 'Night of the Long Knives', on 30 June 1934, Hitler purged Rohm and the SA. Eighty-four were executed, and c1000 arrested. The SA was neutralised as a threat, but Hitler also took the opportunity to eliminate many other political opponents, including Schleicher, while Papen was put under arrest. By presenting the massacre as necessary to prevent an SA coup, Hitler won public support for his actions.

The impact of President Hindenburg's death

After Hindenburg died in August 1934, Hitler moved quickly to merge the offices of Chancellor and President, thereby making himself the undisputed leader of Germany - the **Führer**. After the Night of the Long Knives, the army had no objections to this and Hitler was able to achieve his aim. Soldiers had to swear an oath of allegiance to Hitler as their Commander in Chief, giving Hitler more control over the army.

SUMMARY

- The Nazis moved quickly to assert control over the political and administrative systems of Germany.
- By the summer of 1934 the Nazi dictatorship had been firmly established.
- With the allegiance of the army and no independent President, there appeared to be no forces capable of removing Hitler from power after August 1934.

APPLY

KEY CONCEPT

- **Problems of democratic states is a key concept for the study of modern Germany.**

Reflecting on Part One of this book, create a mind-map of reasons why the Weimar Republic collapsed. Include factors such as the problems of the constitution, actions taken by the government, events outside the government's control and actions of opponents of the Republic.

REVIEW

Look back through Chapters 1–12 if you need to remind yourself of reasons why Weimar collapsed.

APPLY YOUR KNOWLEDGE

a Write a definition of what is meant by 'dictatorship'.

b Complete the table below with a brief explanation of why each action was necessary for Hitler's establishment of a dictatorship and then give some brief detail of how he managed to achieve this.

	Why?	How was this achieved?
Creating a one-party state		
Controlling local government		
Controlling the civil service		
Controlling the armed forces		

EXAMINER TIP

Knowledge and understanding of what is meant by dictatorship, and how the Nazis established one, will be useful for any questions asking about how the Nazis established total control.

REVIEW

Look back to pages 59–60 if you need to remind yourself of events from 30 January 1933 until the end of March 1933.

APPLY YOUR KNOWLEDGE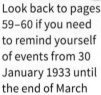

a On an A3 sheet of paper, create your own timeline of events that led from Hitler becoming Chancellor in January 1933 to Hitler becoming Führer in August 1934. This will provide an overview of how the Nazis consolidated power.

30 January 1933　　　　　　　**19 August 1934**

Hitler appointed Chancellor by President Hindenburg

Hitler declares himself Führer

b Colour code the events in your timeline using a highlighter pen. Choose one colour to show when violence, or the threat of violence, was the main method being used, and another colour to show when legislation was the main method being used.

EXAMINER TIP

Knowledge of the events and legislation of the period between when Hitler became Chancellor and when he became Führer will be important for questions on how Hitler established a dictatorship or consolidated power.

PLAN YOUR ESSAY

A LEVEL **How significant was the Night of the Long Knives in Hitler's consolidation of power?**

a Draw a mind-map to show the different ways in which the Night of the Long Knives could be considered significant. Include reasons why Hitler ordered it as well as the consequences of this event.

Ways in which the Night of the Long Knives was significant

Removing the SA secured the army's support for Hitler's government

b Write a list of events, policies or legislation that helped Hitler consolidate power. Include the Night of the Long Knives in the list. Then number each of the items on your list in order of significance for consolidation of Hitler's power.

c Use your completed list to help you write an essay plan for the above question.

TO WHAT EXTENT?

A LEVEL **To what extent was the elimination of opposition from within the Nazi Party more important than the elimination of opposition from outside it in Hitler's consolidation of power in the years 1933 to 1934?**

a Explain how the Nazis eliminated opposition from within the Party. Then create a list of ways in which the Nazis eliminated opposition from outside the Party.

b One of the main ways of evaluating importance in this case would be to decide how much of a threat was posed by opposition from inside and outside the Party to Hitler's consolidation of power. Write one paragraph of explanation of why eliminating opposition from inside the Party was important, and another on why eliminating opposition from outside the Party was important.

c Use your answers to parts **a** and **b** to help you write an answer to the exam question above.

14 The 'Terror State'

A Terror State is one in which citizens are ruled by fear and violence and have no legal protection. Under the leadership principle (Führerprinzip), Hitler was a 'man of destiny' whose role was to interpret and implement the will of the people. Therefore, Hitler's word was law. German citizens were no longer considered equal under the law and they lost the legal rights and freedoms which had been enshrined in the Weimar Constitution. Moreover, the Nazis introduced new laws, new courts and new police forces alongside the existing systems, which were expected to adapt and bend to Hitler's will.

The police system in the Third Reich

The Nazis created new political police forces alongside the existing criminal police. This created overlap and confusion as each competed for their place in the system. Gradually, the SS, under Heinrich Himmler, took control over the various police agencies.

The SS (Schutzstaffel)	The Gestapo	The SD (Sicherheitsdienst)
Originally Hitler's bodyguard, it became the main organisation that arrested political opponents and ran concentration camps.	A secret police force whose role was the elimination of political opposition.	The internal security service of the Nazi Party; an offshoot of the SS.
Membership was based on perceptions of racial purity, discipline and absolute obedience to the Führer.	A relatively small number of professional agents, mostly office-based.	Led by Reinhard Heydrich, like the Gestapo, a relatively small organisation.
Neutralised the SA as a political police force in the Night of the Long Knives, June 1934.	Relied on a network of informers and Nazi Party activists who reported on their neighbours.	Similar role to Gestapo but staffed by amateurs.
In 1936 Himmler and the **SS** took overall control of the SD and **Gestapo**. In 1939, the Reich Security Department Headquarters was established, placing all Party and state police forces under Himmler's command.	Created an atmosphere of fear and suspicion because people believed, wrongly, that there were Gestapo agents everywhere.	Also had responsibility for monitoring public opinion.

Concentration camps

Concentration camps were a major tool used by the different police agencies for imprisonment. They were greatly feared by many Germans.

- The first permanent camp was set up at Dachau in 1933; many other camps across Germany followed, some of which were temporary.
- Originally used to imprison political opponents for 're-education' through torture, beatings and hard labour; after 1936, the emphasis changed to imprisoning those who were deemed 'undesirables' according to Nazi racial ideology.
- From 1934, the SS took control of and ran all camps.

The courts and the justice system

In 1933, judges and lawyers were mostly conservative but remained independent of Nazis control. The Nazis brought the justice system under control through:

- The Front of German Law, established in April 1933, which made clear that the careers of those in the legal profession depended on doing what the Nazis wanted.
- Nazi Special Courts, which were established alongside existing courts in 1933, followed by People's Courts in 1934. These functioned alongside the existing courts but dealt with political crimes, had Nazi judges as well as professionals, and there were no juries.

The extent and effectiveness of opposition and non-conformity

In a one-party state, with repressive laws and an extensive police and prison apparatus, opposition to the regime was illegal and dangerous. It must also be remembered that there was a strong base of support for the regime and that Nazi propaganda and censorship was effective in controlling access to information. There was, therefore, limited active opposition to the regime once the Nazi dictatorship had been established in 1933. Nevertheless, there were individuals and organisations who resisted the pressure to conform and to be 'brought into line'.

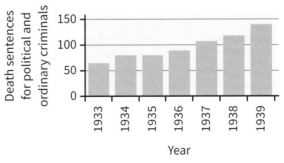
The death penalty was used increasingly in the Third Reich

Political opposition

- The SPD was banned in 1933, members were arrested and the leadership fled into exile. The Party established small cells of supporters in factories and cities to continue its propaganda work in secret.
- The KPD was more prepared than the SPD for secret, underground organisation and established a network of cells in industrial areas.
- Both SPD and KPD cells were broken up by the Gestapo but others appeared to take their places.

Trade union and worker resistance

- Official union resistance to the Nazis crumbled very quickly in 1933.
- Trade unions were absorbed into the Labour Front (DAF).
- Nazi propaganda promoted the idea of class solidarity.
- Many workers were unhappy with their wages and working conditions and strikes did occur, although strikers were imprisoned.
- Absenteeism and sabotage of machinery were used by workers to express dissatisfaction.

Resistance by the churches

- Christian churches retained some independence from the Nazi state but were under severe pressure to conform. Church leaders had to try to protect their organisations, often by avoiding conflict.
- Resistance by some Protestants to the Reich Church (which was under Nazi control) resulted in the formation of the Confessional Church, led by Pastor Niemoller.
- The Roman Catholic Church in Germany was traditionally more independent of the state than the Protestant church.
- Catholic desire for self-preservation led to the Concordat with the Nazi regime in 1933.
- The 1937 Papal Encyclical 'With Burning Grief' protested against Nazi pressure on Catholics to conform but led to increased repression.

Resistance from young people

- Membership of the Hitler Youth, including the League of German Girls, became compulsory in 1936.
- By the mid-1930s there were signs of disillusionment with the Hitler Youth and of young people opting out.
- There was no organised resistance among young people but non-conformist behaviour such as through dress and musical tastes provided ways to express individuality.

Resistance by the elites

- Aristocratic civil servants and military officers shared many of the Nazis' nationalist ideals but were disdainful of their methods.
- The Pact of 1933 between Hitler, the army and big-business leaders was vital to the Nazi consolidation of power.
- In 1937, Hitler purged General Fritsch, the army Commander in Chief, and General Blomberg, the Defence Minister, after they expressed doubts about his foreign policy. Nazi control of the army was strengthened by this.
- Despite the purge, there was resistance in September 1938 to Hitler's plan to annex the Sudetenland area of Czechoslovakia, which would risk war with Britain and France. General Beck (Head of General Staff) and other senior officers, planned to overthrow Hitler if war was declared, believing Germany was not prepared for war. When war was averted, the plot evaporated.

All open opposition to the Nazis was crushed and the death penalty was used increasingly against those convicted of political crimes. The atmosphere of fear and suspicion worked insofar as it, at least, created an appearance of conformity.

The use of propaganda

Hitler regarded propaganda as a vital tool in the creation of the Third Reich. His propaganda chief, Joseph Goebbels, established a new Ministry of Public Enlightenment and Propaganda in March 1933.

The aims of propaganda

Hitler and Goebbels wanted to 'unite the nation behind the ideals of the national revolution'. Propaganda was an essential tool for achieving this through:

- controlling the access and flow of information to ensure that resistance was silenced
- promulgating only positive images of the regime and its leader
- mobilising people to actively support the aims and policies of the regime.

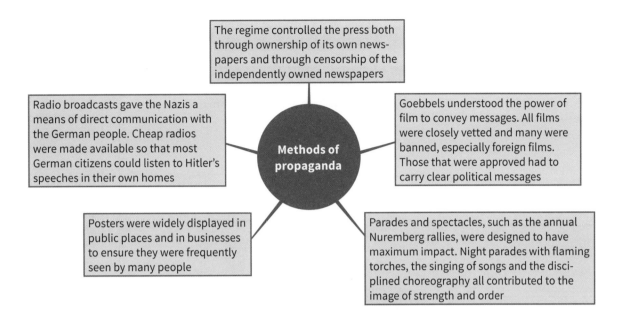

The regime controlled the press both through ownership of its own newspapers and through censorship of the independently owned newspapers

Radio broadcasts gave the Nazis a means of direct communication with the German people. Cheap radios were made available so that most German citizens could listen to Hitler's speeches in their own homes

Methods of propaganda

Goebbels understood the power of film to convey messages. All films were closely vetted and many were banned, especially foreign films. Those that were approved had to carry clear political messages

Posters were widely displayed in public places and in businesses to ensure they were frequently seen by many people

Parades and spectacles, such as the annual Nuremberg rallies, were designed to have maximum impact. Night parades with flaming torches, the singing of songs and the disciplined choreography all contributed to the image of strength and order

The effectiveness of propaganda

The Nazis were skilled at using various forms of propaganda, especially new media such as radio and film. Moreover, Nazi propaganda was all-pervasive in German society. However, it's difficult to gauge the effectiveness of propaganda and how fully the German people were indoctrinated. From the sources of private individuals and the monitoring of public opinion by the SD, as well as the absence of organised opposition and the degree of support at rallies, there are some conclusions that can be reached:

- Most Germans believed in the Hitler Myth and in Nazi economic success. Foreign policy successes were also popular.
- Evidence from Gestapo reports suggests that Nazi rule was generally popular but that there was some scepticism.
- Nazi propaganda was most successful in winning support from young people and when it built upon existing beliefs and values.
- Nazi propaganda was less successful with older Germans and when it challenged deeply held beliefs, especially religious beliefs.

The extent of totalitarianism

The Nazis aspired to having total control over every aspect of people's lives. The totalitarian regime they wished to create was to be a political dictatorship, in which all power at central and local levels was concentrated into their hands, no opposition was to be tolerated, the flow of information was to be strictly controlled and the German people would give their full and unqualified support to the aims of the regime. In the Nazi *Volksgemeinschaft*, all aspects of the economic social, cultural and religious activities of German citizens were to be controlled by the state.

The Nazis achieved some success in creating a totalitarian state:

- A one-party state was created.
- The Nazi regime controlled the flow of information and used education to indoctrinate the young.
- Nazi propaganda pervaded every aspect of society.
- The 'terror state' machinery of police, courts and concentration camps was effective in crushing overt opposition.
- Party activists insinuated themselves into every aspect of people's daily lives – neighbourhoods, workplaces, leisure, schools and universities – to deny people the space to think and act for themselves.
- The Nazis crushed independent trade unions and replaced them with the Labour Front.
- The Hitler Youth movement became, by 1939, the only legally permitted youth movement.

On the other hand:

- The SPD leaders in exile maintained contact with supporters in Germany.
- The KPD maintained an underground organisation based on factory cells.
- Despite repression and terror, pockets of resistance to the Nazis remained among young people, workers, and within the Churches.
- Most businesses remained under private ownership and managers resented the increase in state controls over the economy, although the opportunities for companies to profit from rearmament ensured their cooperation.
- Some aristocratic generals and civil servants continued to regard the Nazis with disdain and retained the capacity for independent thought.
- The structure of the Nazi dictatorship was chaotic, with many competing and overlapping party and state agencies and leading Nazis competing for Hitler's attention.

SUMMARY

- The Nazis created an extensive political police system which instilled fear and suspicion into the minds of German citizens and silenced all open criticism.
- Resistance to the Nazis was fragmented and highly risky but there were pockets of resistance among young people, workers, the Churches and the elites.
- The Nazis saw propaganda as vital to their aim of consolidating power and establishing a totalitarian regime. Goebbels was a skilled propagandist and the evidence suggests his methods were effective.

⚙ APPLY

APPLY YOUR KNOWLEDGE

Complete the mind-map of reasons why there was little opposition and resistance to the Nazi regime between 1933 and 1939.

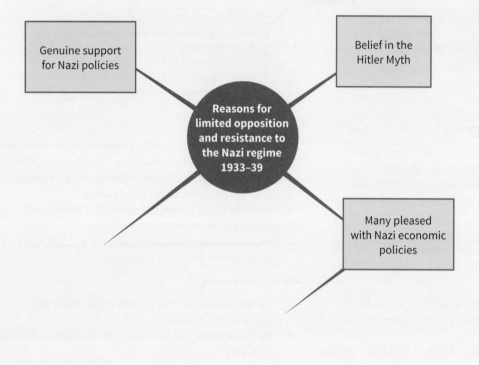

Genuine support for Nazi policies

Belief in the Hitler Myth

Reasons for limited opposition and resistance to the Nazi regime 1933–39

Many pleased with Nazi economic policies

EXAMINER TIP

Reasons for limited resistance to the Nazi regime will be important for questions relating to the extent of totalitarianism, as well as those directly about opposition to the Nazis.

REVIEW ↻

Other sections of the book, such as economic policies (page 74), social policies (page 78) and the establishment of the one-party state (page 65) are all relevant for this question.

ASSESS THE VALIDITY OF THIS VIEW

> **A** **LEVEL** 'Propaganda was more important than terror in maintaining Nazi control over the German population in the years 1933 to 1939.' Assess the validity of this view.

a Copy and complete the following table, adding comments on strategies and success. Then assign a value from 1 to 10 (with 10 being the most important) to each point of each column, to help assess the relative importance of the points you make.

Ways in which 'terror' was used to maintain control	Ways in which propaganda was used to maintain control

b Use your completed table to help you write an answer to the exam question above.

EXAMINER TIP

This is an example of an exam question which does not require you to examine factors others than those named in the question – terror and propaganda.

APPLY YOUR KNOWLEDGE

Create information cards on each of the following:

- Political resistance
- Worker resistance
- Resistance by the Churches
- Resistance by young people
- Resistance by the elites

On each card give details of the ways in which members of these groups opposed the Nazis, how the Nazis tried to deal with resistance from these groups, and how effective the resistance was.

EXAMINER TIP

Knowledge of different opposition groups will be useful for any questions on resistance to the Nazis.

IMPROVE AN ANSWER

A LEVEL   **How significant was the Gestapo in the implementation of Nazi terror in the years 1933 to 1939?**

a Read the following two student paragraphs from different answers to the exam question above. Which is the better answer? Why?

Answer 1

The Gestapo played a highly significant role in the implementation of Nazi terror. As a secret police force whose main role was to monitor and root out opponents, or potential opponents, of the Nazi regime, it played a vital role in both preventing opposition and dealing with it. Contrary to the widespread belief that there were Gestapo agents everywhere, listening and watching for signs of dissent, there were actually only a small number of agents and most were office-based. The Gestapo therefore depended on informers, but this made them no less significant. Whether their information was obtained from 'block leaders' who were Nazi Party members reporting on their block of flats or street, or given voluntarily by ordinary Germans, the Gestapo's reputation for being 'all-knowing' ensured that most Germans feared its presence and conformed. Furthermore, from a desire to appear loyal, they were quick to incriminate others, at the least rumour, and opposition stood little chance of growing.

Answer 2

The Gestapo was an important secret police force which was responsible for dealing with opposition to the Nazi regime. The Gestapo had a terrible reputation and the name is still feared to this day. During Nazi times, everyone was scared of the Gestapo because it was said that they were everywhere. People really believed the Gestapo was listening and watching them all the time and they became scared to say or do anything which might be held against them and lead to their arrest. We now know that the Gestapo rumours were exaggerated and that there were not actually as many of them as people thought at the time. Even so, there were plenty of informants around and some people tried to settle old scores with people they didn't like by reporting them to the Gestapo. All this shows how the Gestapo inflicted terror on the German population and shows that they were really significant.

b Write a second paragraph on another significant factor in the implementation of Nazi terror.

15 Economic policies

Nazi economic policy

The Nazis had no clear plan for the economy in January 1933 but they did have priorities:

- In the short term, the aim was to revive the economy and reduce unemployment.
- In the long term, they aimed for 'economic **autarky**' (or self-sufficiency) as part of their desire to create an economy geared to the needs of a future war.

The role of Schacht

Dr Schacht was the President of the Reichsbank and, from 1934, the Economics Minister. He was an experienced banker and a financial expert with a good reputation among business leaders. He introduced a range of policies to stimulate the economy:

- Public spending on public works schemes such as building autobahns, homes and hospitals helped to reduce unemployment.
- Tax concessions gave some people, e.g. farmers, more money to spend on consumer goods.
- Subsidies to private firms encouraged them to employ more workers.
- Wages and prices were controlled.
- Trade deals were signed with other countries, e.g. in Southern and South-Eastern Europe, to increase German exports of manufactured goods and to secure supplies of food and raw materials, while placing strict controls on imports of goods into Germany (The New Plan of 1934).
- The Reich Labour Service was introduced in 1935, obliging unemployed young men to do six months labour in farming or construction.
- Schacht used **Mefo Bills** to finance rearmament. These were a form of credit note which guaranteed that the state would pay businesses for their work, but encouraged them to defer asking for their money for five years by offering a high interest rate (4% p.a.) on what was, in reality, a loan. Rearmament thus began before the government had the money to pay for it, and the expenditure could also be kept secret.

Schacht was undoubtedly successful in reviving the German economy but he was fortunate in that economic recovery in Germany and elsewhere had begun before January 1933. He did not succeed, however, in resolving the imbalance between Germany's imports and exports, which led to a serious shortage of foreign exchange by 1935–36. Moreover, he opposed the Nazis' policy of autarky, believing it to be uneconomic, and for this reason he lost his influence in 1936 after Goering was given responsibility for the Four Year Plan.

Goering, rearmament and the creation of a war economy

By 1935–36 the German economy was showing signs of strain, with shortages of various foods and rising prices. The Nazi regime wanted to step up rearmament but this would be expensive and require more imports of raw materials. This raised the question of priorities, which has been described as a choice between 'guns or butter'. In order to satisfy consumer demand and avoid rationing, Germany needed to import essential foods, but in order to achieve rearmament the country needed to import essential raw materials. Germany, however, did not have the reserves of foreign currency to pay for both. Hitler was unable to make a clear choice between the two but believed Goering when he claimed that the economy could be reoriented towards achieving maximum self-sufficiency in food and raw materials – otherwise known as a policy of economic autarky. This was the basis of the **Four Year Plan** introduced by Hermann Goering in 1936 to make Germany ready for war within four years:

- Controls were imposed on labour supply, wages, prices and access to supplies of raw materials and foreign currency.
- Production targets were set for private companies.
- New state-owned plants were established to increase capacity of vital commodities, e.g. the Hermann Goering Steelworks.
- Production of key commodities such as chemicals, iron and steel increased.
- Research was launched into substitute products, such as oil from coal.

Propaganda was vital to the success of the Four Year Plan:

- The quest for self-sufficiency was presented as a battle for the whole 'people's community'.
- Germans were encouraged to buy German products.
- Savings campaigns encouraged Germans to consume less and save more, releasing funds for investment.
- People were encouraged to collect scrap metal for melting down.

Nazi policy towards management and the industrial elites

Most (but not all) business leaders were supportive of the Nazis and welcomed their policies of suppressing trade unions and creating political stability, though many private businesses did not welcome increased state controls. Some firms took advantage of the opportunities for increased profits which the Four Year Plan offered, and, where firms were less enthusiastic, the Nazis by-passed them by creating new enterprises.

The degree of economic recovery by 1939

Positive developments	Limitations
• Unemployment was reduced dramatically after 1933 due to job-creation schemes, companies taking advantage of subsidies to employ more workers, Reich Labour Service and rearmament. • Businesses were able to increase their profits. • Incomes for many workers increased during 1933–36; despite official attempts to restrict wages, pay for some workers increased because of longer hours worked. • Farmers were helped by increased tariffs on imports and higher prices.	• Much of the reduction in unemployment was achieved by taking people out of the labour market (e.g. conscription of young men into the armed forces from 1935; persuading married women to give up work; the active removal of a number of women from their jobs e.g. in 1936 women were banned from working as judges, prosecutors and doctors). • Employment figures were inflated through counting unpaid and occasional contract workers as employed. • By 1939 there were labour shortages in some parts of the economy. • Living standards were under pressure from wage controls and rising prices. People could afford to buy enough food but consumption of higher value foods decreased. • There were serious shortages of key commodities by 1936. • Many targets of the Four Year Plan were not met and Germany still needed to import one third of its raw materials in 1939.

SUMMARY

- Schacht had some success in reviving the German economy and reducing unemployment but the revival created a new set of problems, with Germany importing more than it was exporting and reserves of foreign exchange getting seriously low.
- Unemployment was reduced but there were still high levels of 'hidden unemployment'.
- The Four Year Plan placed the economy under strain and its targets were not fully achieved.
- There was pressure on living standards.

APPLY

APPLY YOUR KNOWLEDGE

Define the following terms, then explain how each relates to Nazi economic policies between 1933 and 1939.

	Definition	Relationship to Nazi economic policies
Autarky		
Rearmament		
Autobahns		
Subsidies		
Tariffs		
Mefo Bills		

EXAMINER TIP

Correct knowledge and use of specialist terms will demonstrate to the examiner that you have a good understanding of the topic. These terms will be useful for any questions on Nazi economic policies.

APPLY YOUR KNOWLEDGE

a Copy and complete the spider diagram below with ways in which the Nazis reduced unemployment.

> After 1936 rearmament created many jobs

> From 1935 conscription meant most young men were counted as employed

How the Nazis reduced unemployment

b Use two different colours to highlight your spider diagram. With one colour, show ways in which new jobs were created, and, with a different colour, show other methods that were used to reduce unemployment.

EXAMINER TIP

Knowledge of the methods used to reduce unemployment will be useful when answering questions on Nazi economic policies or the degree of economic recovery.

ASSESS THE VALIDITY

A LEVEL 'Despite the official claims, Nazi economic policies between 1933 and 1939 mostly failed in what they set out to achieve.' Assess the validity of this view.

a Copy and complete the table below to help assess what the aims of economic policies were, what the Nazis claimed had been achieved, and how far these aims were actually achieved.

Aim of economic policies	Nazi claim	Was the aim achieved? Was the Nazis' claim true?

b Use your completed table to help you write an answer to the exam question above.

EXAMINER TIP

As well as tackling the direct points in the question, your essay might consider whether the German people's belief that the economy was improving and that targets were being met was in itself a success (and was just as important as whether their economic policies actually succeeded).

APPLY YOUR KNOWLEDGE

Did businesses benefit from the Nazi regime?

Think of ways in which the industrial elites benefited and ways in which they failed to gain from Nazi policies 1933–39. Place your ideas on the weighing scales and tilt the scales according to the number of points you have made for each side.

TO WHAT EXTENT?

A LEVEL To what extent did the Nazis achieve an economic miracle in the years 1933 to 1939?

There are really two parts to this question. Firstly, to what extent was there an economic miracle and secondly, to what extent were the Nazis responsible for economic growth.

a Copy and complete the table below to help you see the results of Nazi economic policies. Then, using two different colours, highlight those results that show economic growth and those that indicate stagnation or economic problems.

Nazi economic policies	Result of these policies

b Write a list of any other factors besides Nazi policies which played a role in economic growth.
c Write a paragraph considering how far there was an economic 'miracle'.

EXAMINER TIP

You would need to consider what is meant by 'economic miracle' before you begin planning an answer to this question.

REVIEW

Look back to pages 46–48 to find out what the policies of the previous governments were, as this may have led to success as well.

16 Social policies

📖 RECAP

Nazi social policy was based on the concept of a 'people's community' or *Volksgemeinschaft*:

- The nation would be unified by blood, race and ideology.
- There would be no opposition.
- All 'national comrades' would be fit and healthy, loyal to the Führer, show self-discipline and be ready to make personal sacrifices.
- The Nazis aimed to create a new German man and new German woman.

Nazi policies towards young people

The starting point for creating the *Volksgemeinschaft* was Germany's young people, who were to be indoctrinated through the education system and through Nazi youth organisations.

- In schools, the Nazis removed teachers who were deemed to be politically unreliable or who were Jewish.
- A strong emphasis on PE and military drill in schools reflected the Nazis' obsession with racial 'health' and war.
- Control over the curriculum and the issuing of new textbooks ensured that schools became a channel for the Nazi indoctrination of youth.
- In universities, entry to courses was restricted and lecturers who were deemed politically unreliable or who were Jewish were dismissed.
- Women were limited to 10% of available university places, and Jewish students to 1.5%.
- University students were expected to join the German Students' League and to do four months' labour service.
- After 1933, the Nazi youth groups were the only legal youth organisations, apart from Catholic youth groups. Catholic groups were banned in 1936.
- The emphases of activity in the Hitler Youth (HJ) were on political indoctrination, physical activity and military drill. Membership became compulsory in 1936.
- The League of German Girls (BDM) prepared girls for their future role as housewives and mothers. Membership became compulsory in 1936.

Degree of success

There was considerable success in this area. For example, the regime succeeded in bringing schools and universities under their control, and by 1939 the HJ and BDM were the only legal youth movements and membership was compulsory. However, attendance at HJ meetings began to slip after 1936 and the re-emergence of 'youth cliques' indicated that youthful desire for independent activity had not been extinguished.

Nazi policies towards women

The Nazis wanted to raise the birth rate and to discourage married women from working:

- Marriage loans were available for women who left work and married an **Aryan** man.

- Medals were given for having larger families – 'donating a baby to the Führer'.
- Birth control was discouraged and abortion restricted.
- Women were encourged to adopt a healthy lifestyle.
- The Reich Mothers' Service was introduced, to train 'physically and mentally able mothers'.
- In 1933, the German Women's League (DFW) was established, giving advice to women on cooking and healthy eating

Degree of success

The campaign to raise the birth rate had some success, although this may have been due to other factors (e.g. an improved economic situation encouraged couples to have more children). However, contrary to Nazi ideology, the number of women in employment increased, especially after 1936, when labour shortages created pressure to employ them.

Nazi policies towards workers

In the Nazi *Volksgemeinschaft*, there would be no class differences or conflicts. The trade unions were seen as an obstacle to this ideal and were banned in May 1933. They were replaced by the Nazi-run **German Labour Front (DAF)**.

- Led by Robert Ley, the DAF was the largest organisation in Nazi Germany.
- Membership was not compulsory but the DAF was the only legal organisation representing workers.
- Membership included employers as well as workers.
- Its main role was to spread Nazi propaganda among the workers.
- DAF built up its own business empire, including banks, housing associations, construction companies, the Volkswagen car plant and a travel company.
- Workers in the Third Reich had to work harder for longer hours, and wages were controlled.
- The Strength through Joy (**KdF**) branch of the DAF offered subsidised holidays and leisure activities for workers, making it one of the regime's most popular organisations.

Degree of success

Strength through Joy was generally popular, and membership increased. However, despite the lack of independent trade unions, strikes still occurred because of pressure to hold down wages and for people to work harder.

Nazi policies towards the Churches

Religious loyalties were too deeply rooted for the Nazis to sweep them aside. On the other hand, religious faith was an obstacle to the Nazi aim of making the Führer the sole focus of loyalty for all Germans. The Nazis, therefore, proceeded cautiously in dealing with the churches, especially with the Roman Catholic Church.

Protestant Churches

- Nazis had their own pressure group, the German Christians, operating within the German Church, with large membership (c600,000) and strict adherence to Nazi ideology.
- In 1933 the Nazis 'coordinated' the Protestant Church into a centralised Reich Church under their control. Ludwig Müller, a Nazi, was appointed Reich Bishop.
- The Reich Church was reorganised on the leadership principle (fuhrerprinzip).
- The Reich Church adopted the 'Aryan paragraph', under which pastors who had converted from Judaism were dismissed from the church.
- The adoption of the Aryan paragraph prompted a breakaway, in September 1933, by a group of dissident pastors, led by Martin Niemoller and Dietrich Bonhoffer, who established the Confessional Church.
- Support for Confessional Church was patchy but attracted some rural congregations who wanted to retain traditional forms of worship.
- The Nazi regime tried to weaken the Confessional Church by repression.
- Church schools were abolished in 1938–39 to give the Nazis complete control over the education system.
- The regime also launched a Church Secession campaign to persuade party members to renounce their Church membership.

The Roman Catholic Church

- Roman Catholics were more difficult to 'coordinate' because of their long tradition of independence from the state and their loyalty to the Pope.
- The Roman Catholic Church wished to avoid conflict with the regime and the Pope signed a Concordat with the Nazi regime in 1933 under which each side agreed not to interfere in the other's affairs.
- The Nazis did not honour the agreement but there were only sporadic protests from Catholics.
- When Cardinal Galen spoke out against the regime, in 1935–36, the Nazis responded with increased repression, including restrictions on Catholic newspapers and on public meetings.
- Goebbels launched a propaganda campaign against financial corruption in Catholic charities, leading to the seizing of their funds and closing of their offices.
- After the Pope issued an encyclical 'With burning grief', in 1937, which was critical of the regime, Nazi repression was again increased. Church schools were closed and Catholic youth groups banned. Monasteries were closed and their assets seized. Many priests (c200) were arrested and tried on sex charges, some of which were founded and some of which were not.

Degree of success

The regime's policy towards the churches was inconsistent and confused. The Church Secession campaign succeeded in persuading c5% of the population to renounce formal membership of the Churches, and repression ensured that resistance to Nazi policy towards the Churches was confined to a small minority of individuals. By 1939, although the Concordat between the regime and the Roman Catholic Church was dead, the Church as an institution did not directly challenge Nazi policies. However, the Nazis failed to establish a single, united Protestant church under their control, and religion remained a powerful force in German society.

Benefits and drawbacks of Nazi rule

A post-war survey showed that nearly half of Germans viewed the years 1933–39 as a positive experience due to:

- Full employment by 1936.
- Regular employment, even though wages were held down.
- Political stability and an ordered society.
- The benefits through leisure activities and holidays the KdF brought.
- Healthy profits made by large corporations.

On the other hand, not all groups benefited, and political stability came at the cost of individual freedom:

- Living standards for the majority did not improve.
- Farmers and the Mittelstand saw few benefits from Nazi rule.
- Nazi repression created an atmosphere of fear and suspicion.
- German Jews experienced increased discrimination and repression from 1933.
- Nazis did not succeed in creating a classless national community as inequalities remained.

SUMMARY

- The Nazi *Volksgemeinschaft* was an attempt to create a national community based on race and ideology, united behind the Führer.
- Control over schools, universities and youth movements was vital to the Nazis' long-term aim of creating a new German man and a new German woman.
- The Nazis opposed feminism and sought to indoctrinate women to accept their traditional roles as homebuilders and child-rearers.
- Independent trade unions, seen as divisive, were abolished and replaced by the Labour Front. Strength through Joy offered benefits to workers who joined the Labour Front in order to raise productivity and develop a classless society.
- The Nazis were cautious in their approach to the Roman Catholic Church in the early years of the regime but became increasingly repressive as some Catholics began to resist.
- The regime had more success in bringing the Protestant Reich Church into line, but the breakaway Confessional Church was a sign that Nazis failed to fully coordinate the Churches.

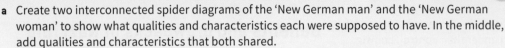

APPLY

APPLY YOUR KNOWLEDGE

a   Create two interconnected spider diagrams of the 'New German man' and the 'New German woman' to show what qualities and characteristics each were supposed to have. In the middle, add qualities and characteristics that both shared.

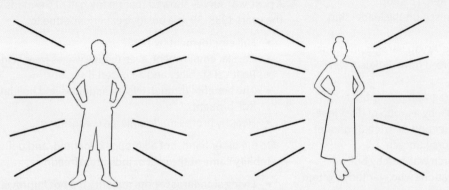

b   Take each characteristic and give at least one example of a Nazi policy to encourage this.

EXAMINER TIP

Knowledge of Nazi social policies and what the Nazis were trying to achieve will help with questions on *Volksgemeinschaft* and how far society was changed under Nazi rule.

TO WHAT EXTENT?

 A LEVEL   **To what extent did the Nazis change the lives of women in the years 1933 to 1939?**

a   Copy and complete the following table with ideas on how women's lives changed due to Nazi policies.

Ways in which women's lives changed	Ways in which women's lives stayed the same

b   List the 'types' of women whose lives would have been changed the most. Whose would have changed the least?

c   Use your ideas from parts **a** and **b** to answer the exam question above.

REVIEW

You could also consider how the lives of 'non-desirable' women such as Jews, were changed by Nazis policies during this period (see pages 94–106).

SOURCE ANALYSIS

SOURCE A

From a 1934 Sopade report into the attitudes of young people towards the Hitler Youth. These reports were compiled in secret by SPD members in Germany for the leadership in exile.

Youth is still in favour of the system: the novelty, the drill, the uniform, the camp life, the fact that the school and the parental home take a back seat compared to the community of young people – all that is marvellous. A great time without any danger. Many believe that they will find job opportunities through the persecution of Jews and Communists. The more enthusiastic they get the easier are the exams and the sooner they will get a position, a job. For the first time the peasant youth is associated with the state. Young workers also join in. They see the national community as better than being the lowest class. The new generation has never had much use for education and reading. Now nothing is demanded of them; on the contrary, knowledge is publicly condemned.

Young people follow the instructions of the HJ and demand that their parents become good Nazis. It seems that the secret of National Socialism is the secret of its youth. They believe in nothing but their Hitler.

SOURCE B

From *Youth in the Third Reich*, the memoirs of Arno Klonne, published in 1982. Klonne had been a leader in the Hitler Youth.

If other people rave about their time in the Hitler Youth, I cannot share their enthusiasm. I have oppressive memories. In our troop, the Jungvolk activities consisted almost entirely of boring military drill. Even if sport or shooting practice or a sing song were scheduled, we always had to do drill first. The slightest signs of recalcitrance, the slightest faults with our uniforms, the slightest lateness on parade were punished with extra drill. But there was method in the madness: from childhood onwards we were drilled in toughness and blind obedience. How did we put up with that for four years? The only explanation I can find is that we were in the grip of ambition, we wanted to impress our sub-leaders with exemplary discipline, with our powers of endurance, with our military bearing. For, those who did well were promoted, could put on stripes and braid, could give orders, even if only for the five minutes when the leader disappeared behind the bushes.

SOURCE C

From a speech given by Hitler to a Hitler Youth rally in Berlin in October 1932.

You youngsters should ignore social barriers, ignore everything that threatens to divide you, and seek and find the German community. You must hold on to it and preserve it and let no one rob you of it. It is never too soon to bring up the youth of Germany to feel themselves to be, above all else, German. The National Socialist education of youth shall not be for the benefit of one party but of the German people. The unanimous willingness of the youth of Germany to dedicate itself to the National Socialist ideal gives clear proof of this. Let others mock and laugh; you will one day be Germany's future.

 With reference to Sources A, B and C, and your understanding of the historical context, assess the value of these three sources to an historian studying the Hitler Youth.

a   Copy and complete the following table by adding the information for each source.

Source	What do you know about the authorship?	How might the authorship affect the value of the source?	When was the source written? How might this affect its value?	Audience and purpose; how might this affect the value of the source?	Tone; what does the source emphasise about the Hitler Youth?
A					
B					
C					

b   Write an overview of the opinion given in each source. Then annotate your overview, citing your knowledge to support or challenge the view in each source.

c   Use your answers to parts **a** and **b** to write a full answer to the exam question above.

 EXAMINER TIP

Remember that to answer source analysis questions effectively, you need to consider the provenance and content of each source and apply your own knowledge to your evaluation of both.

A Level essay sample answer

REVISION PROGRESS

REVIEW

On these Exam Practice pages you will find a sample student answer for an A Level essay question. What are the strengths and weaknesses of the answer? Read the answer and the corresponding Examiner Tips carefully. Think about how you could apply this advice in order to improve your own answers to questions like this one.

A LEVEL 'The lack of organised resistance to the Nazis in the years 1933 to 1939 was due to terror.' Assess the validity of this view.

25 marks

REVISION SKILLS

A Level essay questions may contain a quotation advancing a judgement, in which case the quotation will be followed by 'assess the validity of this view'. Read page 7 of this Revision Guide for details on how to master the essay question.

Sample student answer

There was a lack of organised resistance to the Nazis in the years 1933 to 1939 and terror was indeed a reason for this. The Nazis exerted terror through the police system, the law and violence and used harsh punishments to deal with opponents as well as frighten others into behaving how they wanted them to. However, there was a variety of reasons for the lack of organised resistance, including propaganda, censorship and indoctrination, as well as a genuine support for Nazi policies. It was a combination of these factors that led to the lack of organised resistance rather than one particular factor that predominated.

A major reason for the lack of organised resistance to the Nazi regime in the years 1933–39 was that the Nazis removed rival political parties using both terror and legal means. Large numbers of communists and socialists, who opposed Nazi policies, were arrested and many were placed in concentration camps while others fled into exile shortly after Hitler became Chancellor on 30 January 1933. Persecution of opponents intensified after the Reichstag Fire in February 1933 which was blamed on a Communist (although it is likely that the SA were involved) and used as an excuse to ban the KPD (German Communist Party). The offices of trade unions, left-wing newspapers and the SPD were damaged and people attacked in an attempt to frighten them into silence. The SPD was also banned in June 1933 and the DNVP and Centre Party dissolved themselves before the Nazis passed the Law Against the Formation of New Parties on 14 July 1933 which ensured that the Nazi Party was the only political party left in Germany. This effectively reduced the chance of resistance through political means.

EXAMINER TIP

This introduction clearly sets out the argument the student should now follow through the rest of the essay. However, it would have been good to include something on what is meant by 'lack of organised resistance' here. The introduction is also quite mechanical – providing a list of factors without further comment to provide 'depth'.

EXAMINER TIP

This first paragraph explains how the Nazis effectively removed political opposition and reduced the potential for organised resistance but, although implied, it never explicitly states that the methods employed were a form of 'terror'. A closer link to the question is needed.

Terror was achieved through a variety of methods which helped to remove those people most likely to resist and to frighten others into conforming with what the Nazis wanted. A police system was developed alongside the traditional police which had different but also overlapping roles. The SS, led by Heinrich Himmler, was the main organisation that arrested political opponents, ran concentration camps and after 1936, took control over the SD and Gestapo. The Gestapo was a secret police force whose role was to track down opposition by monitoring people. The SD also gathered intelligence and had responsibility for monitoring public opinion.

The Gestapo and SD therefore played a central role in the implementation of Nazi terror. They used agents and 'block wardens' who were Nazi Party members and monitored housing for signs of opposition activities. Despite the belief that the Gestapo were everywhere, the Gestapo and SD were both relatively small forces. This made them no less effective however, at making Germans greatly fear them and therefore conform, which kept resistance to a minimum. The Gestapo were reliant on information being given to them by ordinary Germans and since many cooperated, opposition groups stood little chance of developing.

Concentration camps were also a very effective part of the Nazis machinery of terror. Makeshift concentration camps were used from the very start of Hitler's rule. By July 1933 there were around 70 temporary camps. The first permanent camp was Dachau, near Munich which opened on 8 March 1933. In 1933 and 1934 the concentration camps were used for the 're-education' of opponents. Hard labour, poor living conditions, lack of food and torture and brutality were used to 're-educate' mostly communists, socialists and trade unionists into conforming with the regime. Many were released in 1934 and most were too frightened to resist again. After 1936 concentration camps were mostly used to imprison asocials, Jews or gypsies, probably because most political opposition had effectively been dealt with by this time.

There were other reasons for a lack of organised resistance. The Nazis used propaganda and censorship effectively to make sure that people were only informed of what they wanted them to know and to promote Nazi ideology and policies. A variety of propaganda methods were used, such as posters or newspaper articles, films giving a clear Nazi message, radio broadcasts of Hitler's speeches and parades such as the Nuremberg rallies which showed military strength and helped to make Germans proud of

EXAMINER TIP

These paragraphs on the police system describe how the different agents used terror to control the population and keep resistance to a minimum. However, it is more descriptive and analytical with no linking sentence at the beginning of the paragraph and no actual analysis of the 'terror'.

EXAMINER TIP

This paragraph continues with more description and contains unnecessary information such as the final sentence. It mentions that concentration camps 're-educated' political prisoners so they would not oppose the regime, but the point is not well-explained. It also fails to explain the fear generated by concentration camps which helped ensure people conformed.

EXAMINER TIP

While the student is correct to include propaganda and censorship, this paragraph does not effectively link these back to the question by explaining how they were an important part of ensuring people conformed to the regime and kept resistance to a minimum. Censorship is mentioned but not explained at all and it is not necessary to list all the methods of propaganda in this way.

their nation. Propaganda was everywhere in German society to ensure that everyone received the Nazi message.

There was also genuine support for Nazi policies. This was partly due to indoctrination as schools, youth groups, women's groups and the German Labour Front all taught Nazi ideology. However, some Nazi policies were genuinely popular, which ensured people conformed to what the regime wanted. The Nazis created jobs and helped Germany recover from the Depression. Traditional, conservative values leading to policies such as rewarding women for marrying and having many children were also popular with many Germans. Genuine support and Nazi successes therefore meant that Hitler had widespread support. Many believed in the Hitler Myth – of Hitler as a father figure. This popularity was a major reason for the lack of organised resistance to the regime.

Therefore there were many reasons which all worked together to ensure there was a lack of resistance to the Nazis in the years 1933 to 1939. Terror was a major reason but lack of resistance was equally due to propaganda and censorship and genuine support for Nazi policies. Although some individuals spoke out against the regime and there were minor acts of defiance, people mostly conformed. By cracking down on political opponents from the very start using a combination of terror and the law, the Nazis ensured that those most likely to resist were prevented from doing so, although there were underground cells of SPD and KPD supporters that continued their opposition throughout Nazi rule.

EXAMINER TIP

This paragraph again tends to description, although it makes the valid point that many people genuinely supported the Nazis which meant they had no desire to resist.

EXAMINER TIP

This conclusion starts well by explaining the student's view that there were several factors that were responsible for the lack of organised resistance. However, the overall judgement is quite superficial and the conclusion inappropriately introduces new content that has not been previously used in the argument in the final two sentences.

OVERALL COMMENT

This answer examines some reasons for the lack of organised resistance to the Nazis. However, in places, it is overly descriptive and it lacks depth of analysis, particularly in its failure to examine what 'terror' or 'organised opposition' actually meant. Any continuing resistance is ignored until the conclusion and other potentially relevant material is also omitted – for example, detail on the Churches, legislation such as that banning the trade unions, the practice of *Volksgemeinschaft*, and Nazi youth policy. Overall this answer might reach a low Level 4, but to obtain a higher mark it would need greater range and depth.

OVER TO YOU

Give yourself 45 minutes to try to answer this question on your own. Consider this checklist when reviewing your answer:

☐ Did you provide details on what is meant by organised resistance?

☐ Did you provide details and analysis on the role of terror as a reason for lack of organised resistance?

☐ Did you provide details and analysis on the role of other factors as reasons for lack of organised resistance?

Go back and look at page 69–71 to help refresh your knowledge of Nazi terror and resistance.

A Level sources sample answer

REVISION PROGRESS

 ## REVIEW

On these Exam Practice pages you will find a sample student answer for an A Level sources question. What are the strengths and weaknesses of the answer? Read the answer and the corresponding Examiner Tips carefully. Think about how you could apply this advice in order to improve your own answers to questions like this one.

 With reference to these sources and your understanding of the historical context, assess the value of these sources to an historian studying women in Nazi Germany.

30 marks

REVISION SKILLS

The A Level exam paper will have one source question that is compulsory; the question will be focused on three primary sources or sources contemporary to the period. Read page 6 of the Revision Guide for details on how to master your source analysis skills.

SOURCE A

From 'Mothers who give us the future', an article written by Emilie Müller-Zadow, published in Germany in 1936. Müller-Zadow was a prominent member of the Nazi organisation, the German Women's League.

The place that Adolf Hitler assigns to woman in the Third Reich corresponds to her natural and divine destiny. Limits are being set for her, which earlier she had frequently violated in a barren desire to adopt masculine traits. The value and sanctity of goals now being set for her have been unrecognised and forgotten for a long time; and due respect is now being offered to her vocation as mother of the people, in which she can and should develop her rich emotions and spiritual strengths according to eternal laws.

It is therefore not at all surprising that the state and party claim the education of mothers as exclusively their task. For the way a mother sees her child, how she cares for, teaches, and forms him, the principles that she instils in him, the attitude that she demands of him, all of this is crucial for the national health, for a German morality, and for the unified overall mind-set of the future nation

SOURCE B

From Martha Dodd, *My Years in Germany*, published in 1939. Martha was the daughter of the American ambassador to Germany and lived there from 1933 to 1937.

Young girls from the age of ten onward were taken into organisations where they were taught only two things: to take care of their bodies so they could bear as many children as the state needed and to be loyal to National Socialism. Huge marriage loans are floated every year whereby the contracting parties can borrow substantial sums from the government to be repaid slowly or to be cancelled entirely upon the birth of enough children. Birth control information is frowned on and practically forbidden.

Despite the fact that Hitler and the other Nazis are always ranting about 'Volk ohne Raum' (a people without space) they command their men and women to have more children. Women have been deprived of all rights except that of childbirth and hard labour. They are not permitted to participate in political life – in fact Hitler's plans eventually include the deprivation of the vote; they are refused opportunities of education and self-expression; careers and professions are closed to them.

From an official Nazi publication, *Basic Principles and Organisation Guidelines of the German Women's League,* **written in 1933.**

1 We desire the awakening, the training, and the renewal of women's role as the preservers of the nation's springs, the nation's love life, marriage, motherhood and the family, blood and race, youth and nationhood. The whole education, training, careers and position of women within the nation and state must be organised in terms of their physical and mental tasks as well.

2 We recognise the great transformation which has taken place in women's lives over the past 50 years as a necessity produced by the machine age, and approve of the education and official integration of women for the good of the nation insofar as they are not performing their most immediate service for society in the form of marriage, the family and motherhood.

3 We regret, however, the false paths of the democratic-liberal-international women's movement because it has not found new paths for the female soul but has created a womanhood which has lost its deepest sources of female strength.

Sample student answer

Source A is written by a prominent member of the National Socialist Women's League. This is valuable because she is likely to have agreed with and understood Nazi policies towards women, although she is equally likely to give a one-sided opinion because of this. The source was written in 1936, which is valuable because it is in the middle of Nazi rule when policies had taken shape but before the start of the Second World War, which affected all policies. As all publications in Nazi Germany were heavily censored, this may also lessen its value as the source may have been adapted before publication, although this seems unlikely as the author was a prominent member of the Women's League.

The audience is likely to have been all Germans – particularly women – and the purpose of the source is to explain the role of women in the Nazi state. This adds value as the source demonstrates the Nazi attempt to win over minds and spread Volksgemeinschaft, although there are limitations to the explanation of the policies and how they affected women. The content of the source is therefore linked to its purpose. It gives a valuable summary of the aims of Nazi policies for women as being to fulfil women's natural role as mothers and as being crucial for Germany.

Source B is written by an American woman who lived in Germany from 1933 to 1937. This is valuable because she would have witnessed the lives of women in Nazi Germany. It was published in 1939 so shortly after she had lived in Germany.

EXAMINER TIP

The answer begins well by focusing on the question immediately and examining one source at a time, which is exactly what is required.

EXAMINER TIP

The student covers most aspect of provenance here but omits an examination of the tone and emphasis of the source, which it is important to include.

EXAMINER TIP

The analysis of the value of the content of the source is very vague. The student should have added more on how the content would be valuable and included far more of their own knowledge to support their analysis.

Therefore her memories are recent and she would be in a position to know. The audience would be an American or international one so this adds value insofar as she would be opening herself up to criticism should she deliberately attempt to mislead. The purpose, which is indicated in the title of the book, 'My Years in Germany', also increases the value, as she wanted to inform people of her experiences from living in Nazi Germany and clearly felt she had something worthwhile to say. However, the source emphasises the restrictions placed on women and the tone is scathing and critical, emphasising what the author views as the repressive nature of the regime by using language such as: 'frowned upon'; 'forbidden'; 'command'; 'deprived of all rights'; 'not permitted'; 'refused opportunities of'. This might detract somewhat from the value as it is clearly opinionated and may be an attempt for the author to convey her American view of Nazism.

The content of the source would be valuable because it gives an overview of what the Nazi Party wanted from women – loyalty and to bear many children. This is supported by other evidence from Nazi Party sources and speeches by Nazi leaders. The source refers to Nazi women's policies, which would include the loans given to women who got married whereby the amount owed was reduced when the woman had more children, and the lack of information allowed on contraception. The source also says that Hitler planned to deprive women of the vote but this would have meant little in the context of Nazi Germany and its one-party state. The content of the source is also limited as it does not give any information on how German women felt about Nazi policies. The author of the source is obviously very hostile but other evidence suggests that many German women welcomed Nazi policies which valued their roles as housewives and mothers.

Source C is written by the German Women's League organisation. Therefore it is valuable for a study on women in Nazi Germany because it gives the opinions on what the organisation wants. The source states that the organisation wants a return to women's primary role as mothers. This equates to what is known about this Nazi organisation which, among other things, ran classes for women on running the home and rearing children. Although welcoming some aspects of modern society for women, such as greater education and making women more central to society, the source says the organisation rejects the women's movement because it doesn't recognise women's greatest role and area of fulfilment as wives and mothers. This is also supported by

EXAMINER TIP

The provenance information for Source B is well covered (although there is no need to restate what is in the attribution at the beginning of the paragraph) with comment on authorship, date, purpose, audience, tone and emphasis. There is also a strong attempt to link all this to value, although in places the answer seems a little mechanical and list-like.

EXAMINER TIP

This paragraph provides some analysis of the value of the content of Source B, well-supported by own knowledge. However, the evaluation needs a summary at the end to provide an overall judgement.

EXAMINER TIP

The student has made a very common mistake when analysing Source C, which is focusing almost entirely on the content of the source and paying little attention to the provenance. Both are equally important.

other evidence from Nazi sources which was horrified with what it saw as many of the consequences of the women's movement in Weimar Germany which saw a reduction in the birth rate, greater promiscuity and more women in the work force. The source is limited, however, because it does not give any information on the policies of the Nazi government or on how women's lives would be affected under Nazi rule.

OVERALL COMMENT

This answer provides some useful evaluative comment on each of the three sources but fails to give an overall judgement on any of them. It also omits the provenance elements of Source C and there are other limitations, as indicated above. Overall this would obtain a low Level 4 mark.

OVER TO YOU

Give yourself 55 minutes to try to answer this question on your own. Consider this checklist when reviewing your answer:

☐ Did you analyse both the content and provenance of all three sources?

☐ Did you support your analysis with your own knowledge?

☐ Did you come to an overall judgement on the value of each source?

Go back and look at page 78 to help refresh your knowledge of Nazi policies towards women.

5 The racial State, 1933–41

17 The radicalisation of the State

Phases in the development of the Nazi State

There were three phases in the development of the Nazi regime:

1 **The legal revolution, 1933–34**
   - Hitler consolidated his power by legal means.
   - The SA was used to terrorise opponents and there were sporadic attacks on Jews.
   - Hitler was constrained by his need for the support of the army and Hindenburg.

2 **Creating the new Germany, 1934–37**
   - Hitler focused mainly on economic revival and social coordination.
   - With concerns about public opinion, Hitler did not have a free hand to act as he wished. Anti-Semitism was played down during the Berlin Olympics of 1936.
   - He avoided confronting powerful groups such as the army and the Catholic Church.

3 **The radicalisation of the State, 1938–39**
   The regime took bold steps, or extreme steps, that it would not have risked taking earlier, focusing on the persecution of 'racial enemies' and furthering measures to create the 'racially pure' state the Nazis desired.

As the years continued, Nazi racial policy became more and more extreme. This was partially because of the effect of cumulative **radicalism** as Nazi officials sought to outdo one another in fulfilling the Führer's ideology. It was from 1938 that racial policies became more radical. There were a number of reasons for this:

- The regime was secure.
- The economic recovery was firmly established, and the economy was preparing Germany for war.
- The SS had control over the police and security system.
- Control over the army was achieved with the purge of Blomberg and Fritsch.
- Those who had been urging caution in anti-Semitic policies had been removed from positions of power (see pages 78–79).

Nazi racial ideology

Nazi racial theory was rooted in Social Darwinist ideas of natural biological selection and on the quasi-science of **eugenics**, a popular theory among Western cultures in the late 19th and early 20th centuries, which advocated the improvement of 'racial hygiene' through selective breeding, birth control and sterilisation.

- Hitler viewed humanity as consisting of a hierarchy of races, in which the Aryan peoples, the 'master race', were inherently superior to all other racial groups. At the bottom of the hierarchy were the '*Untermenschen*' (those 'less than human') among whom he included Jews, Slavs and black people.
- Nazi racial ideology stressed the need to 'purify' the Aryan race by preventing intermarriage with people of inferior races.
- The Nazis also believed that 'racial hygiene' had to be protected through the sterilisation or elimination of 'biological outsiders' – i.e. the mentally and physically disabled – and the removal of people such as homosexuals, pacifists, Roma people and Jews.

The Nazi concept of the *Volksgemeinschaft* (people's community) was also based on racial ideology. It was not enough to be a loyal German; only 'racially pure' Germans could qualify as members of the *Volksgemeinschaft*. In the racially unified state that the Nazis wished to create, the interests of the individual were to be subordinate to those of the nation – or 'Volk'. National comradeship was not available to political enemies, '**asocials**' or 'racial enemies'.

Nazi racial ideology placed great emphasis on the German right to, and need for, **Lebensraum** ('living space').

- Many Germans believed that their country was over-populated and that they needed more land.
- Nazi racial ideology stated that land to the east of Germany – populated by the inferior Slav peoples of Poland and Russia – should be taken over by Germany to settle to provide 'living space' for German farmers, manufacturers, etc.
- Hitler's concept of *Lebensraum* was driven by a racial element. Conquest of lands to the east would enable Germany to wage a war of racial annihilation against the Jews and Slavs there.

Policies towards the mentally ill and physically disabled

- Nazis considered the mentally and physically disabled to be 'biological outsiders' who threatened the fitness and purity of the Aryan race.
- In July 1933, the Law for Prevention of Hereditarily Diseased Progeny introduced compulsory sterilisation for various 'inferior' groups, including schizophrenics, manic-depressives, epileptics, alcoholics, and those with inherited physical disabilities.
- In 1935, compulsory abortion was introduced for these same groups.
- In the years 1933–45, 400,000 people were sterilised.
- In 1939, euthanasia was introduced for mentally and physically disabled children. The T4 programme was responsible for the killing of over 5000 children in special hospitals where they were either starved to death or given lethal injections.
- After protests from a Protestant pastor (Braune), Roman Catholic Cardinal Galen, and intervention by the Pope, the euthanasia programme was halted in 1941.

Policies towards asocials and homosexuals

- The term 'asocial' covered criminals, tramps and beggars, alcoholics, prostitutes, homosexuals, juvenile delinquents and the 'work-shy' (long-term unemployed).
- In 1933, and again in 1936 and 1938, there were mass round-ups of 'tramps and beggars'. Some were forced into work, others were sent to concentration camps.
- In 1936, an 'asocial colony' was set up at Hashude in northern Germany to 're-educate' asocials.
- Many of the so-called 'work-shy' were forced to undergo compulsory sterilisation.
- The Nazis regarded gay men as 'degenerate', so, in 1933, the regime purged homosexual organisations and banned gay literature.
- The law was amended in 1935 to broaden the definition of homosexuality and to impose harsher penalties, e.g. imprisonment. Gay men were rearrested after release from prison and sent to concentration camps under so-called 'preventive custody'.
- Many gay men in concentration camps were castrated to 'cure' them of their 'perversion'; many were beaten to death in the camps and around 60% of gay prisoners died.

Policies towards religious sects

- The Nazis were suspicious of all religious sects, especially those with international links.
- Most sects were banned in November 1933, including the Mormons, Jehovah's Witnesses, Christian Scientists, Seventh Day Adventists and the New Apostolic Church.
- Bans were lifted if sects showed willingness to cooperate with the regime, e.g. The Seventh Day Adventists and the Mormons.
- The Jehovah's Witnesses refused to cooperate with the Nazi regime because they felt this would require too great a compromise of their beliefs. Many were arrested and sent to concentration camps.
- By 1945, c10,000 Jehovah's Witnesses had been imprisoned and many had died.

Policies towards the Roma and Sinti

- There was discrimination against Roma and Sinti people before 1933 but the Nazis made it more systematic.
- In 1935, the Nuremberg Laws were applied to Roma and Sinti as well as to Jews, so gypsies became German subjects, not citizens and were banned from marrying or having sexual relations with Aryans. In 1936, the SS set up a Reich Central Office for the Fight against the Gypsy Nuisance, which collected information to identify Roma and Sinti.
- In 1938, a Decree for the Struggle against the Gypsy Plague led to a more systematic classification process.
- In September 1939, the regime began deporting Roma and Sinti from Germany to settlements in Poland.

SUMMARY

- Nazi racial policy evolved in the years 1933–39, as the regime began to feel more secure and policies became more radical, especially after 1938.
- Nazi racial theorists adopted quasi-scientific theories, such as Social Darwinism and eugenics, to support their belief in a hierarchy of races and the need to protect the racial purity of the master race.
- The Nazi concept of the *Volksgemeinschaft* demonstrated that, in the Third Reich, individual rights and interests were overridden by the interests of the state.
- The mentally and physically disabled were deemed to be a threat to the 'racial hygiene'of the Aryan race; they were subjected to compulsory sterilisation and to a euthanasia programme.
- Groups that were excluded from the *Volksgemeinschaft* on racial grounds were subjected to increased persecution; those described as 'asocials, homosexuals, religious sects and the Roma and Sinti peoples were persecuted, imprisoned in concentration camps and subjected to brutal treatment. There is limited evidence to suggest that the policies were effective in changing the mindset of the German people.

⚙ APPLY

APPLY YOUR KNOWLEDGE

a Copy and complete the following table, and define each of the terms in the context of Nazi ideology.

Term	Definition
Degenerate	
Asocial	
Biological outsiders	
Untermenschen	
Master race	
Euthanasia	
Sterilisation	
Deportation	

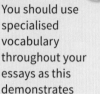

EXAMINER TIP

You should use specialised vocabulary throughout your essays as this demonstrates detailed knowledge of topics.

b At least one of the terms from part **a** describes the Nazi attitude or policy towards each of the different groups of people in the table below. Copy and complete the following table, and, for each group of people, explain the Nazi attitude or belief towards that group and, if applicable, the Nazi policies towards the group in 1933–39. Make sure you use the terms from part **a** as much as you can.

Group	Nazi attitudes towards this group	Nazi policies towards this group 1933–39
Roma and Sinti		
Tramps and beggars		
Slavs		
Homosexuals		
Mentally ill		
Aryans		
Mentally or physically disabled		

EXAMINER TIP

Knowledge of Nazi racial ideology and attitudes and policies towards different groups will be essential for any questions on racial policies or the impact of Nazi rule on people in Germany.

APPLY YOUR KNOWLEDGE

Stick together several pieces of paper and use this to create a combined timeline of all racial policies during this period. Use different colours for policies affecting the following groups:

- Asocials
- Homosexuals
- Gypsies
- Mentally ill and mentally and physically disabled.

REVISION SKILLS

Timelines are a great way of reinforcing chronology. You could use them for a variety of topics. You could even create one large timeline of all racial policies in the years 1933–1941.

KEY CONCEPT

Racialism and Social Darwinism are key concepts for the study of modern Germany.

Racialism and Social Darwinism were central to Nazi racial ideology. A major aim of Nazi racial policies was to breed a master race of Aryans. Give three examples of policies between 1933 and 1941 that were based on ideas of racialism and Social Darwinism and which aimed to increase 'racial purity'.

SOURCE ANALYSIS

SOURCE A

A directive from Himmler on the treatment of gypsies, issued in December 1938:

Experience gained in combating the Gypsy nuisance, and knowledge derived from race-biological research, have shown that the proper method of attacking the Gypsy problem seems to be to treat it as a matter of race. Experience shows that part-Gypsies play the greatest role in Gypsy criminality. On the other hand, it has been shown that efforts to make the Gypsies settle have been unsuccessful, especially in the case of pure Gypsies, on account of their strong compulsion to wander. It has therefore become necessary to distinguish between pure and part-Gypsies in the final solution to the Gypsy question.

The aim of the measures taken by the State to defend the homogeneity of the German nation must be the physical separation of Gypsydom from the German people and the regulation of the Gypsy way of life. The necessary legal foundation can only be created through a Gypsy Law which prevents further intermingling of blood.

Consider the following questions, then provide a bullet-point outline of the value of this source to an historian studying Nazi racial ideology:

- How does the provenance of this source affect its value?
- How does the information in the source compare with your own knowledge of Nazi racial ideology?
- Which would be of greater value to an historian using this source to study Nazi ideology – its provenance or its content?
- What are the limitations of this source for an historian studying Nazi racial ideology?

EXAMINER TIP

Remember that all exam questions on sources will require using your contextual knowledge. This means contextual knowledge of both the content and the provenance.

HOW SIGNIFICANT?

 How significant was the persecution of the non-Jewish minorities for the implementation of *Volksgemeinschaft* in the years 1933 to 1941?

a Define what was meant by '*Volksgemeinschaft*', then complete the table below.

Who was excluded from *Volksgemeinschaft*	Reason for exclusion	How they were persecuted

b List ways in which *Volksgemeinschaft* was implemented, besides persecution of non-Jewish minorities.

c Use your answers to parts **a** and **b** to write an answer to the exam question above.

REVIEW

For a reminder about the implementation of *Volksgemeinschaft*, see pages 78–79.

18 Nazi policies and actions towards the Jews, 1933–37

RECAP

Soon after Hitler became Chancellor in January 1933 the Nazis began to persecute the Jews. Because the regime was in the process of consolidating its power in the period before August 1934, Hitler had to steer a careful course. On the one hand, he needed to satisfy the demands of the Nazi Party rank-and-file for immediate persecution of the Jews while not allowing this to damage his fragile relationship with the army, big business and Hindenburg. The main emphases of Nazi anti-Semitic policy in this early period were on propaganda and on legislation, although the boycott of Jewish shops in 1933 was a gesture to the SA and Nazi rank-and-file. Nevertheless, all Jewish teachers were dismissed from schools and universities in 1933 and the school curriculum was changed to give an anti-Semitic bias in subjects such as Biology and History.

One of the first difficulties was in defining who was Jewish, as there was no scientific way of identification. After some discussion, people were considered 'Jewish' if either of their parents or a grandparent were practising Jews.

The boycott of Jewish shops, April 1933

- The boycott of Jewish shops was claimed to be a retaliation against Jews in Germany and elsewhere calling for a boycott of German goods.
- The boycott was enforced by the SA, which set up pickets outside Jewish-owned businesses.
- Other targets were Jewish professionals such as lawyers and doctors, many of whom were attacked in the street. Jewish school teachers and lecturers were also attacked by the SA.
- It was accompanied by a propaganda campaign launched by Goebbels.
- The boycott lasted only one day, as many Germans defied the SA and continued to use Jewish shops and there were difficulties in identifying Jewish-owned businesses.
- Hitler was not enthusiastic about allowing the SA to control events and threaten his relationship with his conservative allies. It is likely that he allowed the boycott to go ahead to placate the SA but that he never intended it to last very long.

The Civil Service Laws, 1933

- The Law for the Restoration of a Professional Civil Service (April 1933) required that Jews be dismissed from the Civil Service.
- Hindenburg insisted on exemptions for Jews who had served in the armed forces in the First World War and for those whose fathers had been killed in the war. This lessened the law's impact until after Hindenburg's death, in 1934, when no Jews were exempt.
- The new law alarmed Germany's Jewish population. Around 37,000 Jews emigrated in 1933.

Further anti-Semitic legislation in 1933

- Laws were passed to exclude Jews from professional jobs, but these laws were slow to take effect as there were large numbers of Jewish lawyers, doctors and teachers.
- A ban was introduced in April 1933 on Jewish doctors treating non-Jewish patients, though many continued to do so.
- A Law against Overcrowding of German Schools and Universities was introduced in April 1933 to restrict the number of Jewish children who could attend state schools and universities. The process of removing Jewish children from schools was not completed until 1938.
- The Reich Press Law of October 1933 introduced strict censorship and control of the press, and gave the regime the right to remove Jewish journalists from employment.

The Nuremberg Laws, 1935

The Nuremberg Laws were announced at the Nazi Party rally in Nuremberg in 1935 and introduced on 15 September.

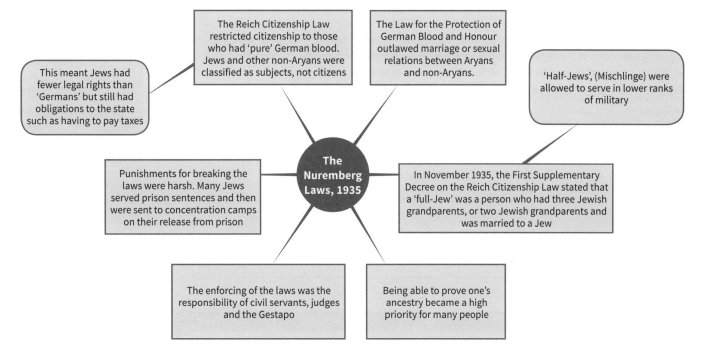

The Reich Citizenship Law restricted citizenship to those who had 'pure' German blood. Jews and other non-Aryans were classified as subjects, not citizens

The Law for the Protection of German Blood and Honour outlawed marriage or sexual relations between Aryans and non-Aryans.

This meant Jews had fewer legal rights than 'Germans' but still had obligations to the state such as having to pay taxes

'Half-Jews', (Mischlinge) were allowed to serve in lower ranks of military

Punishments for breaking the laws were harsh. Many Jews served prison sentences and then were sent to concentration camps on their release from prison

The Nuremberg Laws, 1935

In November 1935, the First Supplementary Decree on the Reich Citizenship Law stated that a 'full-Jew' was a person who had three Jewish grandparents, or two Jewish grandparents and was married to a Jew

The enforcing of the laws was the responsibility of civil servants, judges and the Gestapo

Being able to prove one's ancestry became a high priority for many people

Discrimination

Alongside national laws, there were widespread instances of discrimination.

- Local authorities introduced many restrictions on Jews using public facilities such as swimming pools.
- Some privately owned businesses, such as pubs and restaurants, advertised that Jews were not welcome.

However, Gestapo reports suggest that many Germans did not support this open discrimination but it was dangerous to express these opinions openly. The extent of discrimination varied from area to area; some signs were displayed to satisfy local Party officials and were not rigorously enforced.

Mindful of Germany's reputation in foreign countries, Hitler ordered that anti-Semitic signs and the enforcement of the laws should be downplayed during the Berlin Olympics of 1936.

SUMMARY

- There was a gradual increase in discrimination against Jews in the years after 1933.
- The boycott of Jewish shops in April 1933 was short-lived as Hitler was wary of offending his conservative allies.
- The Civil Service Laws of 1933 and the Nuremberg Laws of 1935 established a legal framework for discrimination against the Jews.
- Evidence suggests that many Germans did not fully support these measures.

APPLY

APPLY YOUR KNOWLEDGE

a Start a timeline of anti-Semitic policies and actions throughout the years of Nazi rule. Complete the sections for 1933–37.

b Use the timeline to help you create a line graph charting the extent of Jewish persecution throughout the years of Nazi rule. Complete the graph for the years 1933–37. Include labels at points of your choosing to describe levels of persecution at these points.

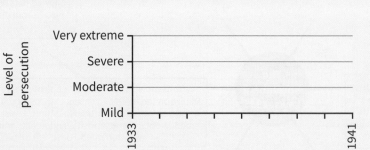

TO WHAT EXTENT?

 To what extent were Jews affected by Nazi anti-Semitic laws in the years 1933 to 1937?

a For each of the anti-Semitic laws of this period, decide who was directly affected and how far. Copy and complete the table below.

	Which Jews were directly affected and how much?
Law for the Restoration of a Professional Civil Service (April 1933)	
Laws to exclude Jews from the professions (1933)	
Banning Jewish doctors from treating Gentiles (April 1933)	
Law against overcrowding of German schools and universities (April 1933)	
Reich Press Law (October 1933)	
Reich Citizenship Law (1935)	
Law for the Protection of German Blood and Honour (1935)	

b Now consider the indirect effects of these laws for German Jews. Summarise the:

- social effect
- economic effect
- likely psychological effect.

APPLY YOUR KNOWLEDGE

Copy and complete the spider diagram below to show ways in which Jews were affected by Nazi policies and actions up to 1938.

| Some Jews who owned businesses would have lost money due to discrimination and the boycott of Jewish shops in April 1933 | **How Jews were affected by Nazi policies and actions up to 1938** | Some left Germany – around 37,000 emigrated in 1933 alone |

EXAMINER TIP

Knowledge of Nazi policies and how they affected Jews will be essential for any questions on anti-Semitic policies.

ASSESS THE VALIDITY OF THIS VIEW

A LEVEL 'Jews were the main target of Nazi persecution in the years 1933 to 1937.' Assess the validity of this view.

a Read the statements below and decide whether each statement supports or challenges the view given in the exam question above. Copy and complete the table by adding more statements of your own.

	Supports	Challenges
The Nuremberg Laws applied to all non-Aryans, not just Jews.		
Many communists were sent to concentration camps or fled into exile after the Reichstag Fire.		
Many local authorities and private businesses discriminated against both Jews and gypsies.		
Laws were passed to prevent Jews being employed in the civil service or the professions.		
The SPD party was banned in 1933. Many members were sent to concentration camps.		
Jehovah's Witnesses were banned as well as persecuted.		
Many gay men were sent to concentration camps, some were castrated.		
Some Jewish children were removed from state schools by the authorities.		
Remaining non-Nazi politicians were murdered during the Night of the Long Knives.		
Disabled people were forcibly sterilised from July 1933.		
Jews were attacked on the streets during the boycott of Jewish shops.		
Early anti-Semitic laws were slow to take effect and were sometimes ignored.		

b Use your answer to part **a** to decide on what argument you are going to take in your answer. Then write an answer to the exam question above.

EXAMINER TIP

Good essays follow a line of argument throughout. This does not mean that you don't have to consider other points of view, but you must explain why you have rejected these arguments in favour of another.

REVIEW

If you need a reminder of the treatment of other minorities see pages 89–91. Also see pages 59–60 and 65–66 and for information on persecution of political opponents.

19 The development of anti-Semitic policies and actions, 1938–40

The effect of the *Anschluss* with Austria, March 1938

After 1938, Nazi policies became more radical, none more so than in their policies towards the Jews. The **Anschluss** with Austria, in March 1938, was an important milestone in this radicalisation process:-

- The *Anschluss* was achieved without a shot being fired. The fact that the Allies did not intervene to uphold the Treaty of Versailles led Hitler to believe that nothing could stand in the way of his ambitions.
- The occupation of Austria by Germany gave the Nazis the opportunity to persecute the large numbers of Jews living there and to force Jews to emigrate. Jews in Austria were immediately stripped of their legal rights, property, employment, and the right to enter restaurants, public baths and parks. Many were physically assaulted and publicly humiliated by the Nazis, and Jewish shops were looted.

The radicalisation of Nazi policy had actually begun before the *Anschluss*. Schacht, who had argued strongly against radical anti-Semitism in business, for fear of alienating foreign investors, was marginalised. Blomberg and Fritsch, who had advised Hitler to be cautious in his foreign policy to avoid a war for which Germany was not yet prepared, were purged in January 1938. More radical Nazis, such as Goering, gained influence. Goering, in charge of the Four Year Plan, cared much less about foreign public opinion and wanted to remove Jews from businesses as soon as possible.

Anti-Semitic decrees in 1938–39

Date	Detail	Significance
April 1938	Decree of Registration of Jewish Property – Jews had to register all property they owned.	This allowed the state to confiscate all Jewish-owned property worth over 5000 marks. This marked another step in the Aryanisation of Jewish businesses.
June/July 1938	Jewish doctors, dentists and lawyers were forbidden from treating Aryans.	This effectively meant many could no longer practise.
July 1938	Jews were banned from working as travelling salesmen, security guards, travel agents and estate agents.	Employment opportunities for Jews were further diminished.
August 1938 – to begin from January 1939	Jews who were deemed to have non-Jewish first names had to change them. All Jewish women had to take the name of Sarah, and all Jewish males to take the name Israel.	Helped people identify (and therefore discriminate against) Jews.
September 1938	Jews were banned from visiting theatres, cinemas, concerts and circuses.	By this time, few places of entertainment admitted Jews, but this ensured all places were closed to Jews. Jews set up their own places of entertainment to compensate.
October 1938	All Jews had to have their passports marked with a letter 'J'.	This made identification of Jews easier.
November 1938	Jews lost their entitlement to state welfare benefits.	Poor Jews became heavily dependent on Jewish charities.

Reichkristallnacht, 9–10 November 1938

The Night of Broken Glass (also known as the 'November **pogrom**'), on 9–10 November 1938, was an organised pogrom against Germany's Jewish population in which homes and businesses were looted, synagogues were burned down, and thousands of Jews attacked. The event that triggered the pogrom was the killing of a German diplomat, von Rath, in Paris, by a young Jewish man. The Nazis presented the violence that followed as a spontaneous explosion of anger by the German people. In reality, the events were coordinated by Joseph Goebbels, who had issued instructions to Nazi officials across the country to organise the violence. Goebbels was anxious to regain Hitler's favour after incurring the Führer's disapproval over an extra-marital affair. The fact that Himmler and Goering disapproved of the pogrom underlines the chaotic nature of the Nazi regime.

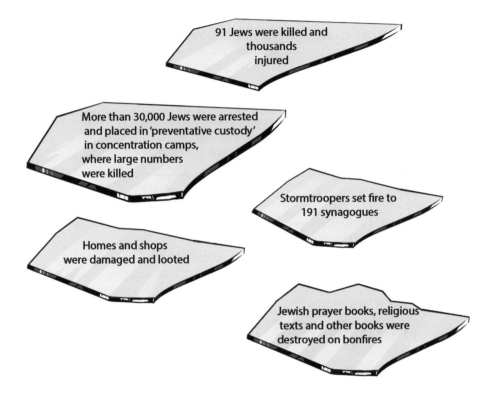

91 Jews were killed and thousands injured

More than 30,000 Jews were arrested and placed in 'preventative custody' in concentration camps, where large numbers were killed

Stormtroopers set fire to 191 synagogues

Homes and shops were damaged and looted

Jewish prayer books, religious texts and other books were destroyed on bonfires

The aftermath of Reichkristallnacht

- Goering prevented insurance companies from paying compensation to Jews for damage and loss.
- The Decree for Restoration of the Street Scene (12 November) ordered that Jews had to pay the cost of repairs, amounting to a fine of 1 billion Reichsmarks.
- The 12 November Decree Excluding Jews from German Economic Life completed the Aryanisation of Jewish businesses.
- From 13 November, Jewish pupils were only allowed to attend Jewish schools.

Emigration

The Nazis wanted Germany to be 'Jew free', and the first attempt to achieve this was through emigration.

- 150,000 Jews chose to leave Germany between March 1933 and November 1938. After *Reichkristallnacht*, Jewish interest in emigration grew. Many families were keen to send their children to a safe haven in other countries e.g. 9000 Jewish children were sent to Britain in 1938–39 on the **Kindertransport** scheme.
- Although Jews who supported Zionism were keen to emigrate to Palestine, the majority of German Jews had a strong attachment to Germany and did not want to leave.
- Younger Jews, and those with enough money to pay for resettlement, were more likely to leave than older or less affluent Jews.
- Before 1938, many German Jews did not believe that the Nazis would make their lives intolerable, or indeed threaten their lives.
- Few foreign countries were keen to accept large numbers of Jewish refugees, so emigration was difficult.
- Although the Nazis encouraged emigration they also placed obstacles in its way by confiscating the assets of those who did emigrate.

Controlled emigration

- After the *Anschluss* in March 1938, Reinhard Heydrich and Adolf Eichmann used Austria as a testing ground for SS policy on emigration.
- Under the aegis of the Central Office for Jewish Emigration, 45,000 Austrian Jews were forced to emigrate.
- The confiscation of Jewish property was used to finance the emigration of poorer Jews.
- In January 1939 this policy was extended to the whole of Germany.

The impact of the war against Poland

German forces invaded western Poland on 1 September 1939, which led Britain and France to declare war on Germany. The outbreak of war brought about a further radicalisation of Nazi policies towards Jews. The conquest of Poland provided the regime with new territory for settling Jewish people, and the emphasis of Nazi policy shifted from forced emigration to deportation and resettlement of Jews. However, the conquest also massively increased the number of Jews living under Nazi control and therefore posed significant problems for the regime.

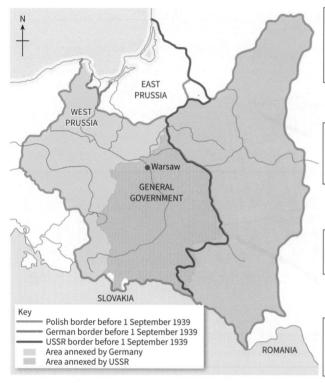

Key
- Polish border before 1 September 1939
- German border before 1 September 1939
- USSR border before 1 September 1939
- Area annexed by Germany
- Area annexed by USSR

- Poland was carved up into three zones – eastern Poland, occupied by the USSR; western Poland, incorporated into the German Reich; and central Poland, designated the 'General Government' and ruled by a Nazi governor

- The Nazi plan was to settle Germans in western Poland by driving out the Jews living there (*Lebensraum*), forcibly relocating them into the General Government region

- Between September 1939 and February 1940, the SS deported more than half a million Jews from western Poland to the General Government

- Hitler demanded the mass deportation of Jews from Germany and Austria but the authorities in the General Government could not cope with the sheer numbers involved

The Madagascar Plan

Madagascar, a large island off the east coast of Africa, was part of the French empire, so, after the conquest of France by Germany in June 1940, the Nazis looked at Madagascar as a possible area for resettling four million European Jews. The living conditions in Madagascar would be so harsh that, in time, most of the Jewish emigrants would die of disease and starvation.

After Germany failed to defeat Britain in the autumn of 1940, the Madagascar Plan was abandoned, as the British Royal Navy would be able to intercept the ships transporting Jews to the island. The Nazis' attention turned back to the east. After the forthcoming invasion of the Soviet Union, the Nazis planned to send Europe's Jews to Siberia.

SUMMARY

- The *Anschluss* with Austria led to a significant radicalisation of Nazi policy towards the Jews.
- During 1938, a series of decrees deprived Jews of their property, their employment, entitlement to welfare and their education.
- Reichkristallnacht, in November 1938, was an important turning point, leading to further violence and persecution of the Jews.
- The Nazis experimented with emigration as a way of removing Jews from Germany, but their policies were chaotic and contradictory.
- The outbreak of war in September 1939 brought many more Jews under Nazi control and led to a further radicalisation of policy.

APPLY

APPLY YOUR KNOWLEDGE

Fill in your timeline of Nazi anti-Semitic policies and actions and complete your graph on the extent of Jewish persecution for the years 1938–39.

REVIEW

You began this activity in Chapter 18.

TO WHAT EXTENT?

 A LEVEL **To what extent did Nazi anti-Semitic policies and actions change in the years 1933–39?**

a Write three bullet points of key ways in which policies and actions changed, and three bullet points on how they stayed the same.

b Use your answer to part **a** to help answer the exam question above.

REVIEW

See pages 94–95 for a reminder of anti-Semitic policies before 1938.

APPLY YOUR KNOWLEDGE

Many historians see 1938 as a turning point in Nazi anti-Semitic policies. In what ways did anti-Semitic policies and actions intensify between 1938 and 1940? Copy and complete the following mind-map.

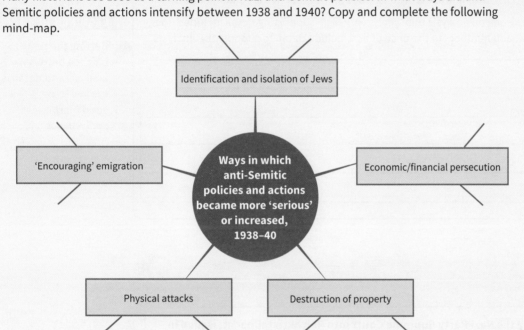

EXAMINER TIP

Knowledge of ways in which persecution increased will help you with any question on how and why policies changed or persecution escalated.

APPLY YOUR KNOWLEDGE

Copy and complete the table below on the factors that encouraged and discouraged Jewish emigration from Germany during the years 1933 to 1939. Include Nazi policies and actions as well as reasons why Jews did/did not emigrate.

Factors encouraging Jewish emigration	Factors discouraging Jewish emigration

EXAMINER TIP

Factors that encouraged and discouraged Jewish emigration will help answer questions on the results of Nazi anti-Semitic policies during this period.

IMPROVE AN ANSWER

A LEVEL 'The main aim of Nazi anti-Semitic policies and actions between 1938 and 1940 was to drive the Jews out of German territory.' Assess the validity of this view.

Below is a paragraph taken from the middle of a student's answer to the question above.

Answer

Although there were other motives, it can be convincingly argued that a major aim of all anti-Semitic laws and actions in this period were initially to encourage Jews to emigrate, and then to force them to do so. Measures that helped identify Jews and isolate them, damaged Jews economically and hurt them physically can all be seen as actions that were taken to frighten Jews so they would leave Germany. In addition, the range of ideas put forward as to where Jews could be deported to, such as Poland and Madagascar also supports emigration as a main aim of Nazi anti-Semitic policies and actions.

a Summarise the argument the student seems to be taking in this answer. List points you could make to counter the argument then decide whether you agree with the student's argument or not.

b This paragraph is quite strong on analysis but there's very little supporting detail included. In a table like the one below, add numbers to the answer and include detail to support the analysis.

1	
2	
3	
4	
5	

SOURCE ANALYSIS

SOURCE A

From a secret report by the Nazi Party Supreme Court into Reichkristallnacht, issued in February 1939.

The first known case of the killing of a Jew, a Polish citizen, was reported to Dr Goebbels on 10 November at about 2 o'clock and in this connection the opinion was expressed that something would have to be done in order to prevent the whole thing from taking a dangerous turn. Dr Goebbels replied that the informant should not get excited about one dead Jew, and that in the next few days thousands of Jews would see the point. At that time most of the killings could still have been prevented by an official order. Since this did not happen, it must be deduced from that fact as well as from the remark itself that the final result was intended or at least considered possible and desirable. In which case, the individual agent carried out not simply the assumed, but the correctly understood, wishes of the leaders, however vaguely expressed. For that he could not be punished.

a Summarise the content of the source.

b In what ways would the content of this source be valuable to a historian studying Reichskristallnact? Evaluate the content against your own knowledge.

c In what ways would the content of this source be limited for this study? Again, use your own knowledge to do this.

20 Policies towards the Jews, 1940–41

 **RECAP**

KEY CHRONOLOGY		
1940	February	First Jewish ghetto set up in Lodz
	April–June	German invasion of Western Europe
	October	Warsaw ghetto established
		German Jews excluded from wartime rationing
1941	June	German invasion of Soviet Union
	July	*Einsatzgruppen* ordered to kill Jews and communists in Soviet Union
	December	Jews in Germany ordered to wear Star of David badge

The spreading war and the development of anti-Semitic policy

By the summer of 1940, Germany had defeated and occupied part of Poland, Norway, Holland, Belgium and part of France. Italy joined the war on Germany's side. In June 1941, Hitler launched the invasion of the Soviet Union (Operation Barbarossa) in pursuit of *Lebensraum*, to eliminate communism and to facilitate the extermination of Germany's racial enemies. The German attack took the Soviet Union by surprise and by the end of the year German forces were in control of the rest of Poland, the Ukraine, the Baltic states and much of western Russia. The invasion of the Soviet Union brought over three million Soviet Jews under German control.

The war brought a further tightening of restrictions on Jews living in Germany:

- Radio sets were confiscated from Jews and they were banned from buying them.
- In 1940, Jews were excluded from wartime rationing allowances of clothing and shoes and they were allowed only restricted access to shops.
- In 1941, Jews were required to have a police permit to travel.
- In December 1941, all Jews in Germany were compelled to wear a yellow Star of David badge.

Deportations and ghettoization

The conquest of Poland brought millions more Jews under Nazi control but also gave the Nazis the opportunity to develop new policies for dealing with them. As the Germanisation of western Poland proceeded during 1939–40, the Nazis began to establish ghettos (districts restricted to particular groups of people) in selected cities in Eastern occupied countries, to which Jews from other areas were forcibly deported. In February 1940, the first Jewish ghetto was set up in Lodz, Poland. Other ghettos were established across the occupied territories in the following months and years, including the Warsaw ghetto and others in Cracow, Lvov and Lodz (in modern Poland), Bialystok (in modern Ukraine) and Vilnius (in modern Lithuania).

- Life in the ghettos was overcrowded, insanitary and harsh. Food, clean water and fuel were limited.
- Jewish inhabitants had to do forced labour.
- Jewish authorities were responsible for running the ghettos under German supervision; Jewish Councils of Elders organised food distribution, allocation of rooms, registration of new arrivals, and the policing of the ghettos.
- Huge restrictions were put on anything entering the ghettos, including food and medical supplies.
- Terrible conditions ensured that Jews died of hunger, diseases such as typhoid, typhus and tuberculosis, or exhaustion. Around half a million Jews died in ghettos.
- Ghettos were sealed by brick walls or barbed wire. Any Jews trying to escape would be shot by police patrols.

The *Einsatzgruppen*

The *Einsatzgruppen* (Special Groups) were temporary units comprising troops and police commanded by men from the Gestapo, the SD or the Criminal Police but under the overall direction of the SS

After the invasion of the Soviet Union, four Special Groups of 600–1000 men were sent in to eliminate communist officials, Red Army Commissars, partisans and the 'Jewish–Bolshevist intelligentsia'

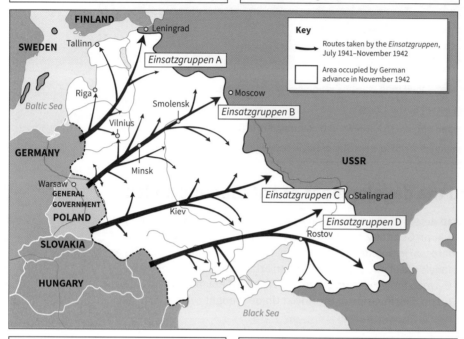

Einsatzgruppppen were supported by police reserve units and by auxiliary units recruited from local populations in the occupied territories

Up to half a million Soviet Jews were killed in June–July 1941 alone, while overall the *Einsatzgruppen* and auxiliary troops were responsible for the killing of an estimated 1.3 million Jews. Most were shot and buried in mass graves

SUMMARY

- The war in the east brought millions more Jews under Nazi control and also led to a tightening of restrictions on Jews in Germany.
- Beginning in Poland in 1940, the Nazis established ghettos in some cities and deported Jews from other areas into these ghettos.
- After the invasion of the USSR in June 1941, Special Groups (*Einsatzgruppen*) were sent in to eliminate Communist officials and Jews.

APPLY

APPLY YOUR KNOWLEDGE

a Fill in your timeline of Nazi anti-Semitic policies and actions and complete your graph on the extent of Jewish persecution for the years 1940–41.

b Review your completed timeline and graph of Jewish persecution from 1933 to 1941. Are there are adjustments you would like to make to your graph?

c Looking at your graph, describe the course of persecution. Does it show a gradual increase throughout the years or is it more complex than that? Are there any years where the levels and types of persecution escalate rapidly?

 REVIEW

You began this activity in Chapter 18 and then continued it in Chapter 19, so you may wish to look back to these chapters to help you decide whether you need to make any adjustments to your graph.

APPLY YOUR KNOWLEDGE

Define the following terms and explain how they relate to Nazi anti-Semitic policies of 1940 and 1941:

- *Lebensraum*
- Operation Barbarossa
- Ghetto
- *Einsatzgruppen*
- Deportation
- Red Army

 EXAMINER TIP

Understanding and use of these terms will be helpful for essays on anti-Semitic policies and actions during the war years.

ASSESS THE VALIDITY OF THIS VIEW

 A LEVEL 'The treatment of Jews in the early years of the war (1939–1941) was entirely different from that of the years 1933–1938.' Assess the validity of this view.

a Copy and complete the table below to help you compare the treatment of Jews in the different periods.

Ways in which treatment of Jews in 1939–41 was different from that in 1933–38	Ways in which the treatment of Jews in 1939–41 was similar to that in 1933–38

b Use your completed table to help you answer the exam question above.

REVIEW

Look back to pages 94–95 and 103–104 if you need reminding of the treatment of Jews during 1933–37 and 1940–41.

 EXAMINER TIP

You could also consider different 'types' of Jews in this question. For example, the years 1939–41 brought Jews from other countries under Nazi control. At this stage, there were differences in how these Jews were treated from how German Jews were treated.

SOURCE ANALYSIS

SOURCE A

From the recollections of a Lithuanian policeman involved with the *Einsatzgruppen* in 1941, recorded in an interview for a Sound Archive after 1945. Extracts were later published in a book.

When the Jews were gathered in this large area, they were taken to the pits in which they were laid down and were shot. Some soldiers stood on the bank to shoot, others took the Jews to the pits. We shot them after they had climbed down and lay down, then others would lie on top of the dead and we shot them and so on. At the end bleach was put on the dead bodies. We could not refuse to shoot. If somebody couldn't shoot because they felt ill, the Germans always checked their pulse or temperature. If somebody said, 'I cannot shoot', the Germans ordered, 'Get in line with the others', and that's it. Germans used to take pictures of these shooting procedures. We felt bad and cursed them. We were given Russian guns and rifles. The clothes of the Jews were burnt. They were all shot, mostly in the chest or the head. It could be a thousand or just one or two hundred.

Consider the following questions, then provide a bullet-point outline of the value of these sources to an historian studying the *Einsatzgruppen*:

a Comment on each of the following aspects of provenance in relation to the value of this source for the purpose given:

  • the author
  • the date of the actual source
  • the audience to whom the source was addressed
  • the purpose of the author in providing this source.

b Describe the tone of the source and identify phrases that exemplify this.

c What is the 'emphasis' of the source? Identify the main argument or concern that the author wishes to convey. Can you explain why he might adopt this emphasis?

EXAMINER TIP

All source questions in the exam will contain three sources. You must make sure you consider all aspects of each source.

EXAMINER TIP

This activity is only concerned with analysing the provenance of a source. In the exam you must also analyse the content of the source in terms of ways in which the content is valuable or limited for the historical study given.

21 The impact of war on German society

RECAP

The mood of the German people when war broke out was one of acceptance, but there was no great enthusiasm for war. A principal aim of Nazi policy from the start of the war was to sustain civilian morale and eliminate any weaknesses in the public mood.

The impact of rationing

The Nazis understood that civilian morale had collapsed in the later stages of the First World War because of severe shortages of vital foodstuffs. They were determined to prevent this happening a second time.

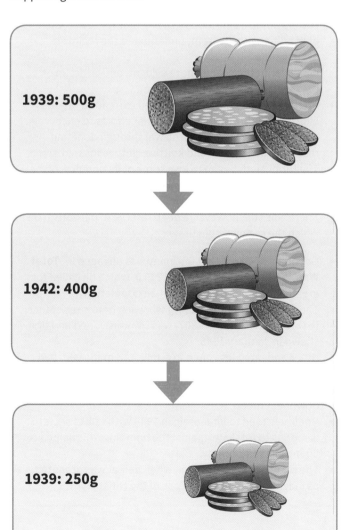

1939: 500g

1942: 400g

1939: 250g

The rationing of meat

- Food rationing was introduced in August 1939, even before war began. Rationing covered bread, meat, butter, margarine, cheese, eggs, canned foods and sugar. Foods that had to be imported by sea from outside Europe, such as bananas, coffee and chocolate, were in short supply.
- Clothing was rationed from November 1939.
- The allocation of food rations was based on age, occupation and race. Manual labourers received more, Jews received less. Pregnant women, nursing mothers and the sick received special allowances.
- The regime was careful not to alienate the civilian population by making them reduce food consumption significantly and, in the first two years of the war, there were adequate food supplies, though shortages of coal, shoes, soap and washing powder did cause discontent at times.
- After the invasion of the Soviet Union in June 1941, imports of food from there were stopped and, in April 1942, food rations were reduced.
- There were further reductions later in the war and food supplies became increasingly precarious by the autumn of 1944. Towards the end of the war, in the spring of 1945, the supply and distribution of food in Nazi Germany completely collapsed and many Germans faced the prospect of starvation.

The impact of propaganda and indoctrination on morale

By 1939, Goebbels had created a sophisticated propaganda system that controlled the flow of information and enabled the regime to spread its own version of events. Speeches, newsreel film, radio broadcasts and the printed media were all deployed to maintain civilian morale by emphasising the successes and minimising the setbacks for German forces. However, as the war progressed and early gains were reversed, the public mood began to change and Goebbels' propaganda became less effective.

The war can be divided into a number of phases, during which civilian morale reflected the ups and downs of the conflict.

Phases of the war	Propaganda and morale
Blitzkrieg, September 1939–June 1941 • The invasion of Poland achieved victory within weeks. • In the spring of 1940, German forces invaded Norway and Denmark, Holland, Belgium and France. All were defeated quickly. • In April 1941 German forces invaded Yugoslavia and Greece and pushed on towards North Africa.	• Quick and easy victories, shown in edited newsreels, gave rise to a feeling of optimism that the war would be over quickly. • Hitler was presented as a military genius who knew better than his generals. • Between January 1940 and June 1941, Hitler made nine major speeches, all of which were broadcast on the radio.
The spreading war, June–December 1941 • Germany invaded the USSR in June 1941 and occupied vast areas of territory. In December the Red Army halted the German advance. • Germany declared war on the USA in December 1941 after its ally, Japan, had attacked the American fleet at Pearl Harbour.	• The invasion of the USSR was presented as a crusade against 'Jewish Bolshevism'. There was a marked increase in anti-Semitic propaganda from this point in the war. • In the early stages of the invasion, as Soviet forces retreated, there was an optimistic public mood. • When German forces were halted outside Moscow in December and reports began to filter back to Germany of the severe winter conditions, the optimistic tone of the propaganda became less effective. • The declaration of war on the USA made clear that the war would not be over soon, as Germans hoped.
The turning of the tide, January 1942–January 1943 • British forces stopped the German and Italian advances in North Africa and defeated a German army at El Alamein in November 1942. • The defeat of an entire German army at Stalingrad in January 1943 marked an important turning point in the war.	• The defeat at Stalingrad was a major setback for Goebbels' propaganda, as he had raised unrealistic expectations of victory. • Letters home from soldiers, giving first-hand accounts of conditions at the front, undermined the regime's propaganda. • War weariness became more evident, and criticism of the regime's propaganda increased. • Attempts to boost morale included extra food rations allocated for Christmas, and further efforts to encourage civilians to 'participate' in the war through donating metals, growing food and knitting clothes for soldiers. • The Hitler Myth began to lose some of its potency as the defeat was largely due to his refusal to allow the German army at Stalingrad to retreat. • There was still, however, a deep reserve of patriotism on which the regime could draw.
'Total War' and the defeat of Germany, February 1943–May 1945 • British and American bombing of German cities caused much destruction and loss of civilian lives. • German forces were retreating in the east. • Italy was invaded and defeated by British and American forces in 1943. • The D-Day landings in France in June 1944 opened up a second front in Western Europe. • Berlin was captured by Soviet forces in April 1945 and Germany surrendered on 8 May.	• Goebbels declared that Germany was engaged in '**Total War**' in a speech in February 1943 in which he called for greater sacrifices from the civilian population. • The propaganda film Kolberg (showing heroic resistance to Napoleon's army in 1807) was commissioned and first shown in January 1945. • Hitler appeared less often in public and made very few speeches, further denting the Hitler Myth. • Heavy bombing and news of defeats in the east led to a downbeat mood. • Goebbels tried to lift morale in 1944 with talk of secret weapons to retaliate against the bombing; this helped to lift morale temporarily. • The final months of the war, when defeat was accepted as inevitable, saw the collapse of the Hitler Myth.

The impact of bombing on morale

From 1942 the British and American air forces mounted a sustained bombing campaign against German cities, industrial areas and ports. The aim of the bombing was to disrupt the production of war materials and to break the will of the civilian population to continue the fighting.

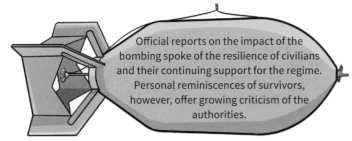

Official reports on the impact of the bombing spoke of the resilience of civilians and their continuing support for the regime. Personal reminiscences of survivors, however, offer growing criticism of the authorities.

Bombing resulted in extensive damage to buildings and high numbers of civilian casualties. Around 410,000 German civilians were killed in air raids and millions were made homeless.

Targets included not only the largest cities, such as Berlin, Hamburg and Cologne, but also small towns.

As raids intensified in 1944–45, civilian morale was further damaged, but people continued to work and open criticism of the regime was rare.

As allied forces closed in on Germany in the last months of the war, and air raids added to the hardships of the civilian population, civilian morale collapsed. Despite this, there were few signs of resistance.

The changing impact of the war on German society

Among the **elites** there was a diverse range of views towards the regime. Many old conservatives shared the Nazis' authoritarian leanings but, especially after 1943, some were concerned that Hitler was leading the country to disaster.

Workers had experienced longer hours since the start of the war, but the 'Total War' measures introduced in 1943 further increased the hours of work and the pressure on wages. There was some evidence of worker resistance to these measures, in the form of increased absenteeism and bad timekeeping, but the regime had a range of measures at its disposal to enforce discipline in the workplace.

Women shouldered many of the burdens of everyday living in the conditions of wartime in their roles as housewives and mothers. Despite the Nazis' ideological objections, the number of women in paid employment increased during the war, especially after the introduction of 'Total War' measures in 1943, although there were still many exemptions from the compulsory conscription of women workers – for pregnant women, those with two or more children, and farmers' wives. In the later stages of the war, women were increasingly used in auxiliary roles in the armed forces to release men for combat duties.

Young people became increasingly subjected to military training and conscription into the armed forces. The age at which men could be conscripted into the forces was reduced from 19 in 1940 to 17 in 1943. Younger teenagers were deployed, through the Hitler Youth, in helping with the harvest and were subjected to increased military training. In the later stages of the war, the age of conscription was reduced to 16 and younger boys were conscripted for civil defence duties in the *Volksturm* (home guard).

SUMMARY

- Nazi propaganda portrayed a German population united behind the Führer in support of the war.
- In reality, there was growing war-weariness brought about by the relentless allied bombing campaign, pressure on living standards and the intensification of war work. This increased in the later stages of the war.
- The Hitler Myth was severely dented by German defeats and Hitler's growing withdrawal from public life.
- Despite these pressures, there was no groundswell of opposition to the regime and the majority of Germans remained staunchly patriotic.

APPLY

APPLY YOUR KNOWLEDGE

Create a line graph charting the course of civilian morale throughout the war years. Include labels at points of your choosing to describe morale at this point and reasons why you have chosen the point.

Civilian morale

1939

1945

Date

EXAMINER TIP

Knowledge and reasons for civilian morale at different points during the war will be useful for any questions on support for the war or how successful the Nazis were at maintaining morale.

REVISION SKILLS

Graphs can be used to portray a range of things over time so you may find them helpful for other topics. Examples include charting the popularity of the Nazis during the 1920s.

APPLY YOUR KNOWLEDGE

a Complete this spider diagram of the propaganda methods used by the Nazis to maintain civilian morale during the war.

Newsreel film from the war front showing military victories

Nazi propaganda methods during the Second World War

b Write a list of reasons why propaganda became less effective as the war continued.

**EXAMINER TIP**

Knowledge of how the Nazis tried to maintain morale and how successful they were will be useful for questions on the use and success of Nazis propaganda during the war.

PLAN YOUR ESSAY

 'Military defeats and increasing war casualties were the major reasons for declining morale amongst Germans during the Second World War.' Assess the validity of this view.

a Create cards of factors that affected civilian morale during the Second World War. On the back of each card, explain how the factor could affect morale positively and/or negatively. You can use the ideas below and/or provide ideas of your own:

Military defeats and war casualties	Allied bombing	Availability of food
Lack of consumer goods	Working conditions and wages	
Living conditions	Increased conscription	

b Arrange your completed cards in a hierarchy formation with the factor that you think most affected civilian morale at the top. Write a paragraph explaining your formation.

c Use your answers to parts **a** and **b** to plan an answer to the exam question above.

EXAMINER TIP

In questions such as these, it is important to take into account differences in people's situations. For example, people in the countryside were generally less affected by bombing and food shortages.

EXAMINER TIP

These factors were not totally independent of each other, and you should account for this in your answer. For example, allied bombing significantly affected living conditions and the availability of food in some German cities.

HOW SIGNIFICANT?

 How significantly did the lives of German women change in the years 1939 to 1945?

a Create a mind-map of the different ways in which women's lives were affected by the war.

b List variations in women's circumstances that would have affected how little or how far their lives changed. For example, older women or younger women exempt from war service conscription.

c Using your answers to parts **a** and **b**, answer the exam question above.

EXAMINER TIP

It is important to consider all the varieties of female experience when answering this question. Age, number of young children, location and other factors would have had an impact on the extent of change that individuals experienced. It is also important to consider things that would have affected all women.

22 The wartime economy and the work of Speer

The mobilisation of the German economy for war

Germany had been preparing for war since the launch of the Four Year Plan in 1936, but the German economy was not fully mobilised for war until 1942. This failure to mobilise fully resulted in shortages of weapons and equipment for the German armed forces.

Hitler had not expected the war to begin in 1939. The Four Year Plan was based on the assumption that a general war would start in 1941 and the emphasis in the early stages of the Plan was on developing Germany's productive capacity, not on the production of armaments

Goering lacked the technical and economic knowledge to do his job effectively; he had poor relations with military leaders and with industrialists, and concentrated on building his own economic empire

Reasons for problems in supplying weapons and equipment for the armed forces

Hitler was so confident that the war would be over quickly that he rejected a 'Total War' effort, which would include the conscription of women into the labour force

The Nazi regime did not establish a clear, unified direction of the war economy; alongside Goering's Office of the Four Year Plan, there were overlapping and competing directions from the Defence, Economy and Armaments Office, The Ministry for Armaments and Munitions, and the Economic Ministry

Different branches of the armed forces demanded highly specialised equipment, built to a high standard; this was expensive and inefficient

The work of Albert Speer

Albert Speer was appointed Minister for Armaments in February 1942, replacing Fritz Todt who had been killed in an air crash. Speer, who had Hitler's full support, set up a Central Planning Agency, which led to impressive results.

The Central Planning Agency coordinated and rationalised the production of armaments through:

- The allocation of labour and materials to armaments factories
- The concentration of production in fewer factories
- The production of a narrower range of standardised products
- The greater use of mass production methods
- Shift working to keep factories running 24 hours a day
- Preventing the military conscription of skilled armaments workers

Production miracle:

- Between 1942 and 1944, German war production trebled; aircraft production increased by 200% between 1941 and 1943, while tank production increased by 250% in the same period
- Productivity per worker in munitions factories increased by 60%

On the other hand, there were still shortages of vital raw materials and the problem of competing agencies was not completely overcome. For example, the SS protected its own interests in building an economic empire through the use of foreign slave labour.

The economic impact of Allied bombing

- From 1942 until the end of the war in 1945, the British and Americans bombed German cities in an effort to disrupt industrial production and damage civilian morale. Speer's efforts to increase production were hampered by the bombing.
- The bombing damaged factories and disrupted supply lines. Factories had to be rebuilt and dispersed and resources were diverted to repair damage to infrastructure.
- In January 1945, the Ministry of Armaments calculated that the bombing had resulted in 35% fewer tanks being produced, 31% fewer aircraft and 42% fewer lorries.
- From January to May 1945 the bombing was intensified, resulting in an actual reduction in the production of armaments.

The mobilisation of the labour force

After war was declared, more men were conscripted into the armed forces. At the same time, there was increased demand for labour in the armaments industries. In order to increase armaments production, labour had to be used more efficiently; the numbers of workers making consumer goods was reduced, while the numbers making munitions increased. However, the full-scale conscription of labour for war work was not implemented in the early stages of the war.

The defeat of German forces at Stalingrad in early 1943 was a profound shock to the Nazi regime and brought about a re-evaluation of policies and priorities. This led to a speech by Joseph Goebbels in February 1943 calling on the German people to support a 'Total War' effort. All businesses deemed non-essential for the war were closed, and more conscription of labour was introduced:

- All men aged 16–65 and all women aged 17–45 had to register for work.
- Small businesses in non-essential trades were closed and their employees transferred to war work.
- A 'comb-through' exercise identified men who could be released from employment and conscripted into the armed forces.

The use of foreign labour

Part of the answer to the shortage of labour for war work was the increased use of foreign labour.

- From 1940 until spring 1942, volunteer foreign workers were recruited from occupied countries in Western Europe.

- After the invasion of the USSR in June 1941 there was an increase in the numbers of prisoners of war (POWs) and Hitler decreed, in October 1941, that Russian POWs could be used as slave labour.
- In March 1942 Hitler appointed Fritz Sauckel to head the Plenipotentiary General Department for Labour Allocation, whose job was to increase the number of foreign workers, which he did by rounding up and transporting 2.8 million forced labourers from Eastern Europe.

By 1944 there were 7 million foreign workers in Germany and another 7 million in occupied countries doing work for the Germans. Concentration camp inmates were also used as slave labour. Foreign labourers made up 25% of the total German labour force. There was a class system of foreign workers, with those from Western Europe at the top, receiving wages similar to those paid to German workers, while forced labourers from the east were paid about half as much. Concentration camp inmates and POWs from the east received no payment and their living conditions were extremely harsh. Malnourishment of slave labourers caused them to be significantly less productive than German workers.

SUMMARY
- In the early years of the war there were labour shortages and inefficiencies which led to shortages of vital equipment.
- After Speer was appointed Minister of Armaments in 1942 the production problems were largely overcome, but Allied bombing hampered Speer's efforts.
- The increased use of foreign labour plugged some of the gaps in the labour supply, but was very inefficient.

APPLY

APPLY YOUR KNOWLEDGE

EXAMINER TIP

Knowledge of methods used to increase the labour force and how these workers were treated will be useful for questions on wartime production.

a Copy and complete the timeline below to show the different methods used to mobilise the labour force at different points of the war.

German labour	Date	Foreign labour
	1939	
	1940	
	1941	
	1942	
	1943	
	1944	
	1945	

b Outline similarities or differences in the ways in which the following workers were treated:

- German workers
- Workers from occupied Western Europe
- Forced labourers from occupied Eastern Europe
- POWs and concentration camp inmates.

IMPROVE AN ANSWER

REVIEW

For more on the impact of Allied bombing see page 109.

Read the paragraph from a student's answer to this question below. Then answer the questions.

 'The main impact of Allied bombing raids on German cities was to reduce industrial production significantly.' Assess the validity of this view.

Answer

Allied bombing raids frequently targeted industrial sites, ports and supply lines. The raids themselves disrupted production as terrified workers had to stop work and take cover. Then the bombs caused damage to many factories, businesses and transport links, some were totally destroyed. Also, workers were killed and injured, so could not work.

a This paragraph needs more explanation of how Allied bombing raids reduced industrial production. It also lacks detail, for example, of specific cities subjected to bombing raids and the degree of destruction. Rewrite the paragraph adding further comment and detail to improve it.

b Write another paragraph analysing a different effect of the bombing raids.

SOURCE ANALYSIS

SOURCE A

From a memorandum issued in April 1942 by Fritz Sauckel. Sauckel was responsible for Labour Allocation. This gives instructions on the use of foreign workers to those in charge of labour conscription in the East.

All prisoners of war, from the territories of the West as well as of the East, who are already situated in Germany, must be completely incorporated into the German armament and nutrition industries. Their production must be brought to the highest possible level. It must be emphasised, however, that an additional tremendous quantity of foreign labour has to be found for the Reich. The greatest pool for that purpose are the occupied territories of the East.

Consequently, it is an immediate necessity to use the human resources of the conquered Soviet territory to the fullest extent. Should we not succeed in obtaining the necessary amount of labour on a voluntary basis, we must immediately institute conscription or forced labour.

All the men must be fed, sheltered and treated in such a way as to exploit them to the highest possible extent at the lowest conceivable degree of expenditure.

a   Copy and complete the table below to help in the assessment of the provenance of this source, in relation to its value to an historian studying the mobilisation of labour for Germany during the Second World War.

The author	
The date the source was written and whether this is significant (use your knowledge of events)	
Who the source is addressing	
Why the source was produced	
The tone of the source	
The emphasis of the source	

b   List the key facts in the content of the source that would be of value to an historian studying the mobilisation of labour for Germany during the Second World War.

EXAMINER TIP

Many students make the mistake of focusing on the content of the source and not giving enough information on how the provenance of the source affects its value. You must consider both.

TO WHAT EXTENT?

 To what extent was Albert Speer responsible for saving the war economy of Nazi Germany?

a   Firstly, consider the situation before Speer became Minister for Armaments. List problems in the war economy, then write a brief summary of how serious these problems were.

b   Secondly, consider the responsibility of Albert Speer by copying and completing the following table.

Speer's policies and actions	Impact of Speer's actions (including limitations)	Other factors that boosted the war economy

c   Using your answers to parts **a** and **b**, answer the exam question above.

EXAMINER TIP

You could take the view that Speer did not 'save' the economy at all, but you would still need to evaluate the situation before and after, and to explain your view.

23 Policies towards Jews and *'Untermenschen'* during wartime

 **RECAP**

In 1942 the Nazi regime implemented its so-called 'Final Solution' to the 'Jewish question', i.e. a systematic attempt to exterminate the Jewish population of occupied Europe. By the end of the war between 5 and 6 million Jews had been murdered. The Nazis also targeted other racial groups which, in their view, were classified as *'Untermenschen'* ('less than human'), including Slav peoples from Eastern Europe, Roma and Sinti, and those they considered 'racial undesirables' – the mentally and physically disabled, homosexuals and members of religious sects.

KEY CHRONOLOGY

The origins of the Final Solution

1933–39		Persecution of the Jews in Germany increases, especially after Reichkristallnacht in November 1938
1941		The invasion of the USSR turns the Second World War into a war of racial annihilation
1941	December	The Nazis realise that their aims cannot be achieved by deporting Jews to Madagascar, or herding them into ghettos in the General Government area of Poland, and that more radical polices were needed

The Wannsee Conference, January 1942

A conference for Nazi officials that was held at a villa on the shores of Lake Wannsee, near Berlin, seems to have been the key moment in the implementation of the systematic murder of the Jews. It was led by Reinhard Heydrich, the most senior man in the SS after Heinrich Himmler. The decision to exterminate Europe's Jews was probably taken at some time in the summer of 1941, after the invasion of the USSR had begun (although some historians would argue that Hitler had always intended extermination). The Wannsee Conference, therefore, was a meeting to inform officials of their roles in the process. After the Conference, the deportations of Jews to designated camps became more systematic, and the mass killings of Jews accelerated.

The 'Final Solution'

As the war turned against Germany in 1942–43, Nazi propaganda became more focused on anti-Semitism. Goebbels and other Nazi leaders made no secret of their aim that the war would result in the destruction of the Jews, although they did not spell out exactly what was happening. The Jewish populations of occupied countries were rounded up and

deported to the death camps in Eastern Europe, usually with the cooperation of the civil authorities in those countries. Only in November 1944, when Soviet armies had advanced deeply into Poland and were getting close to the death camps, did the Nazis begin to close down the camps and try to conceal what they had been doing. Surviving prisoners were sent on forced marches to the west, and the crematoria at Auschwitz were blown up. In January 1945 Soviet forces liberated Auschwitz. Other concentration camps in Germany itself were liberated in the coming months by British and American forces.

The camp system

Concentration camps had existed in Germany itself since 1933. They were brutal places to house political prisoners but they

Chelmno was the first death camp to be established. Victims were first killed in vans pumped with carbon monoxide gas. Later Zyklon B gas was used in all death camps

Belzec, Sobibor and Treblinka were specially constructed as death camps. They were operational in 1942–43. The vast majority of Jews sent there died in the gas chambers

The largest of the camps was at Auschwitz-Birkenau, which became the hub of the extermination programme after 1943. Unlike the other death camps, it was also a vast industrial complex, run by the SS, using slave labour

On arrival at Auschwitz-Birkenau, prisoners would be inspected by the guards; those deemed fit for work were sent to other parts of the camp, while the rest – mainly children, women with small children, the elderly and the sick – were sent straight to the gas chambers

were not designed to exterminate large numbers of people. From the end of 1941, the Nazis built a number of camps in occupied Eastern Europe that were specifically designed to facilitate the mass extermination of Jews. There were six of these death camps – Auschwitz, Chelmno, Majdanek, Belzec, Sobibor and Treblinka.

Jewish resistance

There was widespread Jewish resistance although, in the face of Nazi repression, it was largely smallscale and ultimately ineffective.

- In Eastern Europe, partisan groups established base camps in forests, from where they could mount sabotage raids on German forces. One of these groups was led by the Bielski brothers in Belarus, which attracted 1200 partisans.
- There were revolts in some ghettos, including the ghetto of Bialystok and another larger rising in the Warsaw ghetto in 1943.
- There were organised revolts in the death camps of Sobibor and Treblinka in 1943 and, at Auschwitz-Birkenau in 1944, Jewish prisoners blew up Crematorium 4.

The death marches

From autumn 1944, with German forces in retreat from the Red Army, the Nazi regime organised evacuations and forced marches from the camps in the east, which caused terrible suffering and many deaths. Many died from exposure to harsh winter weather, malnourishment, illness and exhaustion. Many more were shot by guards for being too slow. Estimates of the numbers of deaths range from 250,000 to 400,000.

'Untermenschen' and other victims

Between 5 and 6 million Jews died in the Holocaust but there were many other victims of the Nazis. Like the Jews, Gypsies and Slavs were also classed as 'Untermenschen' and treated accordingly. However, policies towards these groups were inconsistent and evidence of a systematic plan of extermination is fragmentary.

- Most gypsies were rounded up and sent to concentration camps, some to death camps. There was a separate gypsy camp at Auschwitz that housed thousands of men, women and children. Although some were immediately gassed, most died from the terrible conditions in which they lived. About 250,000 gypsies were killed.
- Unlike Western prisoners of war, Soviet POWs were not sent to POW camps but most were sent to concentration camps and some to death camps where they were gassed to death. Over 3 million died.

There were other victims too, such as the many thousands of homosexuals and Jehovah's Witnesses who died in concentration camps.

Responsibility for the Holocaust

Was Hitler responsible?

Fanatical anti-Semitism was always a major motivation for Hitler as Führer.

It was Hitler who set the framework of goals in which his subordinates operated, creating a regime in which the potential for mass killings was always present.

Even though no written order from Hitler to exterminate the Jews has ever been found, leading Nazis operated in a system in which they were 'working towards the Führer' – i.e. trying to interpret and implement his wishes.

Were other Nazi leaders responsible?

The Nazi regime had many overlapping centres of power, and rival Nazi leaders competed for Hitler's approval.

The actual implementation of the Holocaust was the responsibility of the SS, led by Heinrich Himmler and his key subordinate, Reinhard Heydrich.

Other leading Nazis were also involved, including Martin Bormann, Hermann Goering, Adolf Eichmann and Joseph Goebbels.

Were Germans as a whole responsible?

Thousands of lower-level officials, soldiers and police carried out the orders to deport and execute the millions of victims. These included many non-Germans in the occupied territories.

Hitler and his subordinates tried to keep the Holocaust secret but some knowledge of the mass killings in the USSR was widespread in Germany.

Although the German people as a whole were not responsible for the decisions to exterminate the Jews, few were openly critical of the Nazis' actions, and many were directly involved.

SUMMARY

- The conquest of Eastern Europe brought many millions of Jews under Nazi control and created the conditions under which the SS could implement the Holocaust.
- The Wannsee Conference implemented a policy decision that had already been taken.
- Many officials and police from the occupied territories were involved in the transportation and execution of the Jews, but the whole exercise was controlled by the SS, acting on the orders of Heinrich Himmler. He was working within a framework of policy goals created by Hitler.

APPLY

APPLY YOUR KNOWLEDGE

Write definitions for the following terms:

- Holocaust
- 'Final Solution'
- Death marches
- Concentration camp
- Death camp (extermination camp).

EXAMINER TIP

Correct understanding and use of these terms will help you answer questions on the 'Final Solution'.

SOURCE ANALYSIS

SOURCE A

From the personal testimony of Rudolf Reder, published in 1946. Reder, who was one of a handful of survivors of Belzec camp, described the arrival of Jews.

After the victims had been unloaded from the trains, they were gathered in the yard and surrounded by armed SS men and then the commandant delivered a speech. 'Now you're going to the bath house, afterwards you will be sent to work.' That's all.

Everyone was happy, glad that they were going to work. They even clapped. That was the one moment of hope and illusion. For a moment the people felt happy. There was complete calm. In that silence the crowd moved on, men straight into a building on which there was a sign in big letters: 'Bath and inhalation room'.

The women went about twenty metres further on – to a large barrack hut. There they had their heads shaved, both women and girls. They entered, not knowing what for. At the moment when the women were pushed naked, shorn and beaten, like cattle to the slaughter, the men were already dying in the gas chambers. The shaving of the women lasted about two hours, the same time as the murder process in the chambers.

a Write a paragraph on the provenance of this source, in relation to its value for an historian studying the 'Final Solution'. Remember to include an assessment of the following, using your own knowledge of the context to help:

- Who wrote the source and when?
- Who is the audience of the source?
- Why was the source written?
- What is the tone of the source?
- What is the emphasis of the source?

b Write a second paragraph evaluating the content of the source for this study.

EXAMINER TIP

In answering a source question in the exam you should aim to write at least one paragraph on the provenance and another on the content for each of the three sources you are given. Remember to include any limitations to that content.

KEY CONCEPT

Anti-Semitism, Racialism and Social Darwinism are key concepts for the study of modern Germany.

a Create a list of ways in which there were similarities between the treatment of Jews and other persecuted groups in the East (Slavs and Gypsies).

b Create a list of ways in which the treatment of Jews was different from that of other races and groups.

ASSESS THE VALIDITY OF THIS VIEW

A LEVEL 'The war in the East was the reason for the implementation of the "Final Solution".' Assess the validity of this view.

a Write a list or draw a spider diagram of all the factors behind the implementation of the Nazis' 'Final Solution'.

b For each cause identified, assign a value from 1 to 10 indicating how far you feel it was an important cause. For each cause, explain the reason for the value you have assigned.

c Using your answers to parts a and b, answer the exam question above.

REVIEW

For the Nazis' racial ideology, see pages 89–90. You could also consider other anti-Semitic policies before the, 'Final Solution', which you will find on pages 94, 98 and 103.

24 Opposition and resistance in wartime

As defeat loomed and the German people experienced severe hardships in the final years of the war, there was a growing mood of disillusionment with the regime and its propaganda. Despite this, the majority of Germans remained loyal and their main concern was survival. However, a small number of individuals and groups openly opposed the Nazis.

Some individuals, for example, gave refuge to Jews to help them escape deportation to the death camps. Workers who took unauthorised absence from their jobs, or did not work as hard as they were encouraged to do, were expressing dissatisfaction with the regime. In September 1939, after the regime cut wages and bonuses, increased hours and suspended paid holidays, absenteeism increased and many workers refused to work overtime. The regime was so concerned about the subsequent loss of production that it withdrew many of the measures in October.

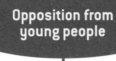
Opposition from young people

Edelweiss Pirates	Swing Youth	White Rose group
• Mostly working-class youths, aged 14–18 • Active in the Rhineland and Ruhr industrial areas • Rejected the regimentation of the Hitler Youth and tried to avoid conscription • In 1944 the Cologne group linked to an underground group that helped army deserters and escaped prisoners of war • Obtained supplies by attacking army depots • Many groups broken up by Gestapo • 13 leaders of Cologne Edelweiss Pirates were publicly hanged in November 1944 to make an example of them	• A form of youthful rebellion that involved unconventional clothes, hairstyles and tastes in music, e.g. listening to American jazz • Swing clubs began in the 1930s, attracting middle- and upper-class young people in major cities, including Hamburg, Berlin, Stuttgart and Frankfurt • Not overtly political but their pleasure-seeking lifestyle offended the moral code of the Nazi regime • In 1941, police began mass arrests of Swing club members; many were sent to concentration camps; repression led some swing youth to become more political in their opposition	• A student movement, based in Munich • Led by Hans and Sophie Scholl and supported by Professor Kurt Huber • Emphasised the importance of individual freedom and personal responsibility • Attacked Nazi treatment of Jews and Slavs • Issued pamphlets in 1942–3 and painted anti-Nazi slogans on walls • Six members executed in 1943

Opposition from students and young people

There was a long tradition among working-class youths to form independent youth groups such as the 'wild cliques', which the Nazis never succeeded in eradicating entirely. Among middle class young people, resistance took the form of unconventional behaviour and, for some, more active opposition.

Opposition from churchmen

- The **Roman Catholic Church** was compromised by its support for many Nazi policies, such as the invasion of the USSR, and by its need to protect its organisation. Only individual churchmen raised their voices in protest against some Nazi policies.
- Bishop Galen spoke out against the euthanasia programme in 1940, which led to a halt to the killings in August 1941.
- Archbishop Frings of Cologne spoke out against the killing of prisoners of war and against the persecution of the Jews. He was placed under surveillance by the Gestapo.
- **The Protestant Confessional Church** in Prussia protested publicly about the treatment of the Jews. One of the leading figures in this church, Dietrich Bonhoeffer, was arrested in 1943 and executed in 1945.

Communist opposition

The Nazi-Soviet Pact of 1939 had compromised Communist resistance, but the invasion of the USSR in 1941 revived Communist resistance. There were two main networks, one involved in spying for the USSR, the other a more independent group that collected information about Nazi atrocities and distributed anti-Nazi propaganda.

In 1941 the KPD had 89 secret cells in Berlin alone, with others in Hamburg, Mannheim and central Germany. These cells were subject to Gestapo infiltration and many were destroyed by the end of 1943, including 22 of the Communist cells in Berlin. Under Gestapo pressure, and with links to Germany's enemy, the KPD resistance had no prospect of attracting mass support.

Army and civilian critics

Among the elites there was much support for the Nazis' anti-Communist and anti-democratic policies. However, many aristocratic army officers and civil servants increasingly came to believe that the Nazi regime was morally repugnant and was leading Germany to disaster.

- The **Kreisau circle** was a diverse group of aristocrats, lawyers, SPD politicians and churchmen. They were united only in their belief in personal freedom and individual responsibility. The group had three meetings at the home of Count Helmut von Moltke in 1942–43, but was broken up by the Gestapo
- In the **army,** there had been some plans to remove Hitler at the time of the Sudetenland crisis in 1938, but the plot was never activated and the conspirators were not discovered.
- In 1943, a group of senior army officers concluded, after the disaster at Stalingrad, that Hitler had to be assassinated to pave the way for a negotiated peace.
- An attempt to explode a bomb in Hitler's aeroplane in March 1943 failed.
- Another attempt to assassinate Hitler was made in July 1944 when a bomb was placed in his headquarters by Colonel Claus von Stauffenberg. The bomb exploded but Hitler survived. The conspirators were arrested, tortured and executed. The army was put under SS control after this, which restricted further opposition.

Overview of the Nazi state by 1945

The unconditional surrender of Nazi Germany in May 1945 brought 12 years of Nazi rule to an end. It had been 12 years of right-wing dictatorship and submission to one man's distorted vision of German greatness. At first, some of Hitler's promises had won favour:

- He helped restore German pride, which had been shattered after the 1914–18 war and the vindictive Treaty of Versailles, giving the German people a new faith in their future.

- He provided political stability, economic recovery and a fair standard of living.

The more sinister side of Nazism was initially overlooked, although the racial fanaticism and the inhumanity with which opponents and outcasts were treated were never widely approved. However, when Hitler plunged Germany into a second and even more deadly war, the dream started to sour. Early victories in 1939–41 gave way to uncertainty, desperation and ultimately, anger.

By 1945, there were few illusions left. The war brought death, misery and physical destruction to the nation. Although German civilians had not felt the impact of war too severely before 1944, thanks to Germany's advanced economy and the spoils of war, the allied carpet-bombing and merciless push from east and west in the final year of fighting had left the country in a state of chaos, shock and disarray; its people were bewildered and demoralised.

There was physical destruction everywhere:

- Towns and communities lay in ruins. Hamburg, Cologne, Düsseldorf, and Dresden were little more than rubble heaps.
- Communications had broken down as roads, railways and bridges had disappeared.
- Industrial plants were smoking or idle; agricultural land was left barren or pock-marked by shells and other war-time debris.

The human costs had also been horrific:

- Around 6.5 million Germans had been killed and many more were unaccounted for; lost on the Soviet-German front.
- In the final months of war, millions of civilians had lost their lives. Half a million or more had perished in the burning cities whilst others, largely in the east, had been killed by the advancing troops.

By 1945 the Nazi regime was something most Germans wanted to put behind them and forget.

SUMMARY

- Despite the dangers, there were groups and individuals who did resist the Nazi regime in a variety of ways.
- The growing certainty of German defeat after 1943 undermined faith in the regime and in Hitler, but there was no groundswell of opposition to the regime.
- Terror and repression intensified during the war.
- There was little common ground between the different resistance groups and individuals.

 APPLY

APPLY YOUR KNOWLEDGE

Create a mind-map of all the different kinds of opposition and resistance to the Nazis in wartime. Include organised groups and individuals.

EXAMINER TIP

Knowledge of who resisted the Nazis and how they did this will be valuable for any questions on resistance and opposition.

SOURCE ANALYSIS

SOURCE A

An extract from the Fifth Broadsheet of the 'White Rose' group, written and distributed secretly to students at Munich University in January 1943.

A Call to All Germans!

Do you and your children want to suffer the same fate that befell the Jews? Do you want to be judged by the same standards as your oppressors? Are we to be forever the nation which is hated and rejected by all mankind? No. Dissociate yourselves from National Socialist gangsterism. Prove by your deeds that you think otherwise. A new war of liberation is about to begin. The better part of the nation will fight on our side. Cast off the cloak of indifference you have wrapped around you. Make the decision before it is too late! Do not believe the National Socialist propaganda which has driven the fear of Bolshevism into your bones. Do not believe that Germany's welfare is linked to the victory of National Socialism for good or ill. A criminal regime cannot achieve a German victory. Separate yourselves in time from everything connected with National Socialism. In the aftermath a terrible but just judgement will be meted out to those who stayed in hiding, who were cowardly and hesitant.

Support the resistance. Distribute the leaflets!

With reference to the source and your understanding of the historical content, assess the value of this source for an historian studying resistance to the Nazi regime. Include:

- As assessment of the authorship, date, audience and purpose of the source.
- The tone and emphasis of the source.
- As assessment of what detail within the source would be valuable and why.

EXAMINER TIP

You will have three sources to assess in an exam question.

REVIEW

If you need more help on assessing the value of sources, look back to the Source Analysis exercises throughout this book.

APPLY YOUR KNOWLEDGE

Why was there so little opposition to Nazi rule? Copy and complete the following table, with reasons in the left column. Then assess to what extent this reason was a factor in 1934–39 and again in 1939–45.

Reason for lack of opposition	1934–39	1939–45

EXAMINER TIP

Reasons for the lack of opposition at different points of Nazi rule will be important for questions on the amount or effectiveness of opposition.

REVIEW

See pages 69–71 for information on pre-war opposition.

APPLY YOUR KNOWLEDGE

Create a chart or spider diagram on the state of Germany in 1945. Arrange your points in the following categories:

- Political
- Economic
- Social

EXAMINER TIP

Knowledge of the state of Germany in 1945 will be useful in answering exam questions which include this topic.

KEY CONCEPT

What sustains a dictatorship is a key concept for the study of modern Germany.

a List three main methods used by the Nazis to sustain their dictatorship in the years 1934–45.
b Explain how these methods changed over time.

HOW SIGNIFICANT?

A LEVEL **How significant was internal German opposition and resistance to the Nazis during the Second World War?**

a Decide what this question means by 'significant'. Write a couple of sentences explaining how you will evaluate significance in your answer.

b Copy and complete the table below for each resistance group with a summary of the activities of each group during the war. Then evaluate the extent of support that group received before giving each a rating according to how significant it was.

Opposition or resistance group	What it did/tried to do?	Extent of the threat	Significance rating out of 10

c Using your answers to parts a and b, answer the exam question above.

EXAMINER TIP

It is a good idea to spend a few minutes really studying the question before you begin planning and then writing your answer. That will help you get to grips with exactly what the question is about so you will not make any silly mistakes and answer a different question!

EXAMINER TIP

In your answer you could consider reasons why opposition and resistance was not more widespread or successful.

Activity answers guidance

The answers provided here are examples, based on the information provided in the Recap sections of this Revision Guide. There may be other factors which are relevant to each question, and you should draw on as much own knowledge as possible to give detailed and precise answers. There are also many ways of answering exam questions (for example, of structuring an essay). However, these suggested answers should provide a good starting point.

Chapter 1

⚙ Apply Your Knowledge

1. 29 September: General Ludendorff suggested the Kaiser made political reforms and requested an armistice.
2. 1 October : The Kaiser appointed Prince Max of Baden Chancellor, and he formed a government.
3. 3 November: Mutiny in the navy spread to the main base in Kiel.
4. 8 November: Bavaria was declared a republic.
5. 9 November: Prince Max said the Kaiser had abdicated. He resigned and made Friedrich Ebert the new leader of Germany.
6. 9 November: General Groener informed the Kaiser that the army no longer supported him so Kaiser Wilhelm II abdicated.
7. 11 November: The armistice was signed.

⚙ Apply Your Knowledge

- **All men and women over 20 had the vote.**

  Strength: very democratic, so everyone had a say in who governed Germany.

- **Proportional representation meant coalition governments were highly likely.**

  Strength *and* weakness: can be seen as both – a strength as this would mean governments that truly represented public opinion so all minority groups, for example, would be represented, but also a negative as it would be more difficult for a government to agree on policy and it permitted extremist parties to win seats and therefore gain a national voice.

- **The armed forces, civil service and judiciary remained unchanged.**

  Weakness: a definite weakness, especially as few leaders of these institutions supported democracy.

- **Electorate could decide important issues through referendums.**

  Strength: very democratic, people would feel involved and consulted in government.

- **No state was allowed to dominate the Reichstag.**

  Strength: all parts of Germany would feel fairly represented.

- **Some human rights were written into the constitution.**

  Strength *and* weakness: can be seen as both – a strength as it should mean these rights were guaranteed, however, the promise of welfare posed an economic burden on the state.

- **President had emergency powers to rule by decree in emergencies.**

  Strength *and* weakness: can be seen as both – possibly a strength as it might restore calm and order in an emergency, but could also be seen as a weakness as it would mean a return to one person making the decisions in some situations.

- **Chancellor and all ministers were responsible to the Reichstag.**

  Strength: would mean the Reichstag had a say in policy.

⚖ Ⓐ How Important?

a **Ways in which the defeat of the Spartacists was important**

- They were a very radical, left-wing group who effectively wanted a republic controlled by workers' and soldiers' councils with nationalisation of all industry – therefore very different to the Weimar Republic.

- They were attracting increasing support from workers through rallies and demos, and already had a presence on most Workers' Councils, which were powerful in some cities.

- The revolt was armed, therefore it did present a real danger to the Weimar government.

- The force used against the revolt (many Spartacists, including the leaders Karl Liebknecht and Rosa Luxembourg were killed) proves that the government, army and Freikorps did consider it a real threat.

Ways in which the defeat of the Spartacists was not important

- They had only a very small membership (c5000) and had many 'enemies' as they were so radical.

- The revolt took place in Berlin only, not across the whole of Germany.

- Although they were armed, the Spartacists lacked the weaponry and military expertise of the Freikorps and army who defeated them.

- Communism was hated and feared by the influential middle classes, who were prepared to support the right-wing tactics to quell the revolt.

Other factors that allowed the Weimar government to be established

- The actions of Ebert and the SPD – in power after the Kaiser's abdication in Nov 1918 but promised, and succeeded in holding elections for a new government.

- The Ebert-Groener Pact was vital as it secured the army's support for the SPD's actions. The army (and Freikorps) defeated the Spartacists and other uprisings that threatened the establishment of the government.

b You should decide on your own ranking of factors.

c Answers need to explain what is meant by 'importance' (for example, how much of a threat the Spartacists posed to the Weimar government) and should examine both ways in which the Spartacists were and were not important as well as examining other factors that were important in the establishment of the Weimar government.

✏ Ⓐⓢ Plan Your Essay

a
- Support: 1, 3, 6
- Challenge: 2, 4, 5

b Supports:

- It was the uprisings in the navy that led to much of the civil unrest.

- Some soldiers had lost respect for their officers and, realising that defeat was inevitable, they deserted their regiments and joined the civil unrest in Germany. Many of these soldiers joined the Workers' and Soldiers' Councils, which effectively governing some towns and cities across Germany.

Challenges:

- Popular action by disgruntled workers led to Workers' and Soldiers' Councils being set up in many towns and cities across Germany. This meant that the Kaiser was not in control of many parts of the country.

- It was the threat of a General Strike in Berlin that prompted the collapse of the Kaiser's government.

c You must reach a judgement and clearly state whether you agree or disagree with the opinion given. You could include each/some of the points given in answers to parts **a** and **b**, but you must give reasons for agreeing or disagreeing and weigh up these factors.

Chapter 2

⚙ Apply Your Knowledge

a · **Reparations**
Many resented having to pay at all, more were horrified by the amount; many were worried about the possible economic problems.

· **Loss of land**
Resented because Germany had not been invaded; reduced the prestige of Germany.

  o **Loss of land in Germany**
  Particularly resented by those who regarded themselves as Germans living in these places; separation of East Prussia from the rest of Germany particularly resented.

  o **Loss of overseas territories**

· **Occupation** of parts of western Germany.

  o **The Rhineland**
  Permanently demilitarised; tension between locals and foreign troops.

  o **The Saarland**
  Free coal given to France, Belgium and Italy, reducing economic income and therefore ability to pay.

· **Military restrictions**
Loss of prestige and reduced ability to defend itself.

  o no airforce

  o severely reduced numbers in navy and army.

· **Dictated peace**
Many resented that Germany had not been involved in the discussions and had little choice but to sign the treaty or be invaded.

· ***Anschluss* forbidden**
Germans and Austrians with links to the other country particularly resented this as they felt Germany and Austria were naturally part of the same country.

· **Forbidden to join League of Nations**
Loss of prestige and standing.

b You need to create a diamond-9 hierarchy from nine reasons and then write a paragraph explaining your hierarchy. One idea might be that the war guilt clause was the most resented because Germans did not believe they were guilty of starting the war, and accepting this clause meant accepting that other countries were entitled to reparations. As quite a few Germans were not bothered about the League of Nations, that might be the reason you place as the least important.

Key Concepts

a
- **Left-wing**: Beliefs that are progressive, based on equality of everyone, and which believe in supporting the poorest in society
- **Right-wing**: Beliefs based on tradition, social hierarchy and economic freedom
- **Nationalism**: Patriotic about your own country; can also mean a more extreme pride which emphasises the superiority of one's own nation
- **Liberalism**: Belief in the value and equality of everyone and an individual's freedom

b Groups more likely to be left-wing are the working classes, while middle and upper classes are more likely to be right-wing.

Improve an Answer

a Answer 1 is better because it is less descriptive (Answer 2 is over-factual and lists the terms of the Treaty, for example), more analytical (Answer 1 has an analysis of responses to the Treaty rather than description of the terms) and, crucially, it gives a clear view and fully addresses the whole question. (Answer 2 doesn't really address the question at all except for a vague attempt in the final sentence, and presents no opinion, instead depending on facts.)

b You should write your own introduction to the exam question.

Chapter 3

Source Analysis

Source 1
- **Author**: Erna von Pustau, daughter of a Hamburg fish merchant; someone 'ordinary' who lived through the period which would add to its value.
- **Date written**: 1947 – over 20 years after the crisis which may have affected her memory, after the Second World War.
- **Who the source is for**: American readers, or perhaps international readers of a history book.
- **Why it was produced**: To inform people of what it was like to live through the hyperinflation crisis. This may mean that information is exaggerated or false, but she tries to be balanced and her ideas on winners and losers correspond to those of many historians.
- **Tone**: One of reflection; trying to make sense of past events.
- **Emphasis**: There were both winners and losers from hyperinflation.

Source 2
- **Author**: Otto Strasser, a radical Nazi; may lessen its value as the Nazis would have wanted to present it as a failure of Weimar government. However it is valuable for showing how the Nazis capitalised on the crisis if this was how they presented it to Germans at the time.
- **Date written**: 1940 – nearly 20 years later, but also when the Nazis were in power. He would therefore want to show how awful life was before Nazi government.
- **Who the source is for**: German readers in the war years.
- **Why it was produced**: As part of this man's recollections of life with Hitler, while Hitler was at the height of his power. He would therefore have wanted to emphasise how dire things were before Hitler came to power.
- **Tone**: One of hopelessness and desperation, using language such as: 'catastrophic', 'ruined', 'immoral', 'ineffective government', 'desperation' and 'future seemed hopeless'.

- **Emphasis**: On the political consequences – anger mounted against government, demonstrations, political violence, etc.

Source 3
- **Author**: Franz Bumm, a civil servant who should have had a good grasp of what was happening as he was President of the Department for Health.
- **Date written**: 1923 – therefore at the time of the crisis itself, which is of value.
- **Who the source is for**: Reichstag politicians – valuable, as he would have wanted to present the truth.
- **Why it was produced**: To inform politicians of the impact, presumably so they could act to improve the situation. This could affect the value, as he may have exaggerated some things, though much of the content is similar to the picture painted by many historians.
- **Tone**: Factual and professional but with some sorrow, e.g. 'shocking decline', 'inadequately' and 'jammed together in the most primitive dwellings'.
- **Emphasis**: On the poor health, living conditions and malnutrition of those most affected by the crisis.

b **Source 1**
- Winners from hyperinflation were big businessmen and peasants and landowners.
- Losers were working class and mostly the middle class.
- Nobody knew the reason for hyperinflation.

Source 2
- Hyperinflation was caused by the defeat of Germany in the First World War (and by implication the Treaty of Versailles).
- Foreigners benefited at the expense of Germans.
- People were angry at the government for failing to deal with the crisis, and political violence was looming.

Source 3
- Rural areas were less affected.
- Worst affected are middle class, widows, pensioners and students.
- Living conditions and malnutrition are increasing.

c Your answer should include the points made in answers **a** and **b**. You must pay equal attention to all three sources.

Apply Your Knowledge

Your flowchart could include the following:
- **1919–23:** The government chose not to raise taxes and/or reduce public expenditure. Instead public spending increased due to social welfare measures.
- **1921:** Reparations payments began – further increasing government spending and debt.
- **1922:** The government stopped paying reparations and tried to negotiate a suspension of payments.
- **January 1923:** French and Belgian forces occupied the Ruhr, taking reparations in the form of goods, meaning tax revenue for Germany was reduced and striking workers were paid by the government, increasing the economic burden and prices. The government again printed more money, further increasing prices.
- By summer 1923 the German mark was worthless.

Assess the Validity of This View

a
- **The Weimar government** (loser)
  People blamed the government for the crisis and its perceived a lack of response in dealing with it (at least, to begin with). This led to an increase in political extremism and violence. However, the government retained power.

- **Students** (both)
  Some 'won', as they rarely had savings or mortgages and could go out and spend anything they were able to earn. Some were more enterprising than older people in using the black market or taking whatever work they could find. 'Losers' were those students who were looking for well-qualified work after their studies as permanent jobs were very hard to find. These may have felt the situation was hopeless.
- **Mortgage holders** (winner)
  Their debts were fixed, so they could afford to pay them off easily as wages rose.
- **Farmers** (both)
  Food prices rose higher and higher but this was only an advantage if they could sell the food. Many could pay off their debts. However, agriculture was a stagnant industry throughout the 1920s.
- **Entrepreneurs** (winner/both)
  Some borrowed then repaid when currency de-valued, others may have lost out through being landlords of fixed-rent properties.
- **Workers** (loser)
  Wages did rise but not as fast as inflation so many suffered, though some fixed renters would have benefited even though prices of food and other consumer goods rocketed.
- **Black marketeers** (winner)
  Could sell goods at undercut prices and still make huge profits.
- **Big businesses** (winner)
  Could borrow and repay – wages for staff didn't rise as quickly as price of goods so profits increased.
- **Pensioners/widows** (loser)
  Had a fixed income, so they were plunged into poverty as prices rose higher and higher.

b You should decide who 'lost' the most. Alternatively, you could give equal weighting and conclude that more than one group of people lost if you do not think there was one group that lost more than another, or you could agree with the question that the Weimar government lost the most.

Chapter 4

Apply Your Knowledge

You should produce a mind-map for this activity. For an example of a mind map, see page 46.

Apply Your Knowledge

- **Coalition government** (a government made up of different political parties because no one party has an outright majority). All governments in this period were coalitions. They were very unstable – there were 10 of them and only one lasted more than a year. It meant that it was very difficult for a government to take decisions or govern effectively.
- **General Strike** (when workers in all, or most, industries stop working, causing severe problems). A general strike in Berlin was organised to help defeat the Kapp Putsch.
- **Paramilitary forces** (military units that are similar to a professional army but are not part of the state's official armed forces). There were several paramilitary groups during this period belonging to extreme right-wing and left-wing groups. Famous examples include the Freikorps and Patriotic Leagues.
- **Putsch** (a coup or violent attempt to overthrow a government). There were two putsches in this period – the Kapp Putsch of March 1920 (led by Freikorps units) and Munich Putsch of November 1923 (led by the Nazi Party).
- **Freikorps** (paramilitary organisations made up of ex-soldiers from the First World War). Freikorps led the Kapp Putsch of March 1920.

- **Patriotic Leagues** (paramilitary organisations, formed from former Freikorps units). Patriotic Leagues were extreme right-wing nationalist paramilitary groups that, between 1919–23, carried out 354 assassinations of left-wing politicians and those who had signed the Versailles Treaty.
- **Assassination** (the murder of someone for political reasons). There were many assassinations by right-wing and left-wing paramilitary organisations of their political opponents in the period 1919–23.

🔍 Key Concept

a. Students need to draw their own copy of the political spectrum shown.

b
- **Far left:**
  Spartacist League: Wanted to incite a communist revolution in Germany; a threat to the establishment of the Republic.

  KPD: Anti the Republic; wanted a communist state and tried to stage revolution in 1921.
- **Left wing**
  USDP: Wanted workers' and soldiers' council to play a role in government so not completely happy with Weimar.
- **Centre left**
  SPD: Committed to the Republic, wanted social welfare reform (links to trade unions).
- **Centre**
  DDP: Middle-class party; supported Weimar Republic.
- **Centre right**
  Centre Party: Strongly linked to the Catholic Church; moderately conservative but supported the Republic.
- **Right -wing**
  DVP: Opposed to the Weimar Republic but did join coalition governments.
- **Far right**
  DNVP: Nationalist, anti-Weimar; one DNVP deputy (Wolfgang Kapp) led a putsch with Freikorps units.

  NSDAP: Wanted to overthrow Weimar government and tried to in 1924; ultra-nationalist, anti-Semitic.

⚖️ 🅰️ How Significant?

a
- **Spartacist League**: Uprising in Berlin, January 1919. Used weapons and violence and tried to persuade the masses to join them. Had some working-class support but mostly city-based. Middle and upper classes were very fearful. Weimar government crushed the revolt brutally using the army and Freikorps. However, the threat didn't disappear – the survivors reformed as the KPD a few months later.
- **KPD**: Led revolts and tried to stage revolutions through various parts of Germany in 1920–21. Supported the strikes during 1923 hyperinflation crisis. Like the SPD, they had some working-class support but were greatly feared by other classes and were mostly city-based. Government didn't even try to crush them – didn't need to, as the threat was pretty low and all attempts at revolution failed early on.
- **Patriotic Leagues**: Assassinated 354 left-wing politicians or those associated with the Treaty of Versailles. Had some support as middle and upper classes greatly feared communism. Government strengthened the law to ban extremist organisations and give harsher punishments, but judges were largely sympathetic to right-wing assassins so unable to suppress the threat.
- **Kapp Putsch**: Kapp, a DNVP deputy, and General Luttitz of the army attempted to overthrow the government in March 1920. A very serious threat as it involved the army, and the

rest of the army refused to suppress it. However, it did not have widespread support from general public. Government could do little to suppress the threat without army's support. Threat of a general strike organised by trade unions helped Putsch to fail.
- **Munich Putsch**: Attempt by Nazi Party to seize power in Munich, march to Berlin and overthrow the government in November 1923. Failed because it had little popular support, nor the support of the police or the army. Government made little direct effort to put down the threat – probably because it didn't see it as very severe. However, right-wing judges were sympathetic to the Nazi cause, and Hitler was only given a short sentence.

b You must decide a score for each based on the level of the threat to the survival of the Weimar Republic. The Kapp Putsch was probably the biggest threat because it involved part of the army and the remainder refused to fire on fellow soldiers.

c You must include analysis of a range of political extremist groups (see answer to **a** above) and the extent of their threat to the government.

⚙️ Apply Your Knowledge

- **Spartacist uprisings**: Successfully dealt with but failed to remove the threat altogether as re-emerged as the KPD. Had to rely on the army and Freikorps, which would later be more of a threat.
- **Assassinations by Patriotic League members**: Strengthened the law to ban extremist organisation and give harsher punishments, but judges were largely sympathetic to right-wing assassins so the problem was not really dealt with.
- **Kapp Putsch**: Had to rely on the lack of popular support, and the threat of General Strike to put down this threat – as the army would not support the government there was little they could do.
- **Munich Putsch**: Debatable whether the government really needed to deal with this threat as it was only small; police effectively dealt with it.
- **Lack of majority governments**: If the moderate, pro-majority parties had worked together more effectively this would have been less of a problem, but they did not, meaning policies and actions were often not carried out.
- **Paying reparations**: Paid initially, but only by printing more money and borrowing more, which led to invasion of the Ruhr and hyperflation.
- **Invasion of the Ruhr**: Passive resistance worsened the problem of inflation and government spending.
- **Hyperinflation**: Took time to deal with it, then the introduction of new currency did stabilise currency and eventually led to growth. However, nothing was done to compensate the millions of people who had lost savings, homes, etc., which left many resenting the government.

⚖️ 🅰️ To What Extent?

a
- Economic suffering led people to support or join extremist parties.
- Lack of effective Weimar governments – coalitions of moderate parties failed to work together to resolve problems, so people turned to more extremist parties.
- Nationalism – belief that Germany hadn't been defeated, etc. by ex-soldiers and others.
- No experience of democracy, so many rejected it as an idea.
- Fear of other extremists – fear of communism drove people to support extreme right-wing groups, etc.
- Some extremists groups were anti-capitalist and many believed capitalism was failing them.

- Hyperinflation shattered middle-class confidence in the government.

b You should add your evaluation to your diagram according to your own decisions.

c In your answer you need to ensure you evaluate the Treaty of Versailles as a factor before going on to consider the roles of other factors. Make sure you clearly state your opinion and follow your argument throughout your essay.

Chapter 5

⚙️ Apply Your Knowledge

- Ended support for passive resistance in the Ruhr (stopped paying striking workers) which reduced spending.
- Stopped printing more and more money – kept tight control over the money being printed to stop inflation rising rapidly.
- Raised taxes on businesses and individuals to help repay debt.
- Reduced salaries of government employees and dismissed some civil servants to reduce spending.
- The Dawes Plan – obtained loans from the USA.

⚙️ Apply Your Knowledge

a Example of a complete Venn diagram with reasons:

Mostly benefited:

Those in debt before hyperinflation

Many business owners – benefited from loans, etc.

Those in 'new' industries – chemicals, cars, aeroplanes, etc.

Mixed fortunes:

Industrial workers – wages rose but unemployment remained high

Middle-class professionals – salaries stayed the same

Mostly lost out:

Government workers – lost job or had salaries reduced

Farmers – many went bankrupt had high debts

Pensioners and widows (anyone on fixed incomes) who had suffered during hyperinflation

Middle classes with savings lost the value of their savings

b Students should summarise their own Venn diagram.

📝 Plan Your Essay

a
- **Work of Stresemann**: As Chancellor he made bringing inflation under control his priority and took several decisions, such as ending passive resistance, which helped bring this about. Also asked the Allies' Reparations Committee to try to find a way to resolve the reparations problem, which led to the Dawes Plan. Stresemann's work as foreign minister helped improved Germany's standing internationally, which also helped economic confidence.
- **Work of Hjalmar Schacht**: Reich Currency Commissioner and head of the Reichsbank, whose idea it was to introduce the Rentenmark, which was such a major part of resolving hyperinflation. Also helped negotiate the Dawes Plan (and later the Young Plan).
- **Dawes Plan**: Charles Dawes and the committee set up to look into Germany's problems with repaying reparations came up with the Dawes Plan, which did stimulate some parts of the German economy and reduced some of the pressure from reparations. It also led to the French leaving the Ruhr.
- **USA**: Loaning 800 million marks to help get the Dawes Plan started.

b
- Economic recovery was not experienced by all businesses.
- Agriculture showed little improvement; many farmers went bust, while others were heavily in debt.
- Salaries for the professions did not increase, so living standards for middle classes did not improve.
- The economic growth was based almost totally on short-terms loans, so it was quite precarious, if the loans were called in, many businesses would collapse.
- Unemployment remained high, and many businesses made savings by reducing their workforce, which made them appear more successful.
- Imports increased more than exports; many businesses were dependent on imports.

c Your essay plan should include the points from parts **a** and **b** above. Make sure you include reasons for and against the opinion and that you come to a judgement.

Assess the Validity of This View

a Ways in which the economy grew 1924–28
- Industrial output grew, largely due to extensive foreign investment.
- Exports increased as more countries were prepared to trade with Germany.
- 'New' industries were established so more companies were created that did well in areas such as cars, aircraft, and chemical and electrical industries (these particularly helped exports increase).
- Some companies made larger profits from becoming more efficient after the crisis of hyperinflation.

Economic problems 1924–28
- Large sectors of the economy became dependent on foreign loans, which meant Germany was very vulnerable to world recessions.
- Imports increased more than exports, so Germany was still buying more from abroad than it was selling.
- Some areas of the economy experienced very little growth or none at all – e.g. agriculture.
- Unemployment remained high compared with other countries.

b Your essay should examine both economic growth and economic problems between 1924 and 1928 and come to a judgement about whether economic growth was an illusion.

Source Analysis

a Red = aspects of economic recovery; blue = areas of less recovery; green = problems in the economy

If we compare the present position with that of four years ago, we see a very great advance in regard to the economic development of the country as a whole.

There has been a far-reaching reorganisation and rationalisation of the industrial system of Germany; the standard of living of the masses of the people has appreciably risen, and in the case of a great part of the working-class has again reached or surpassed the pre-war level.

At the same time there are still considerable branches of the national economy that have had an inadequate share in the general recovery. The position of agriculture, though here and there improvement is apparent, remains on the whole less favourable than that of the rest of the national economy.

Whatever turn the future may take, it is certain that there is a serious temporary shortage of capital.

The difficulties encountered in securing long-term loans have led to a growing reliance on short-term borrowing.

b and c The source claims that 'great advances' had been made in the economic development of Germany: there had been great changes in industry which benefited many people as their standard of living had risen. Many industries did see substantial developments and economic recovery and some workers and business-owners benefited from this. The source does highlight that not all 'branches' of the economy had grown and singles out agriculture as an area which had generally not seen growth. It is certainly true that agriculture had mostly not gained much benefit from the economic recovery. This was partly due to the worldwide agricultural depression. Many farmers had borrowed money and were burdened by high levels of debt, which forced many smaller farmers to sell up. Finally, the source highlights an area of concern: lack of capital, which led to a dependence on short-term loans. Many politicians and economists at the time were aware of the potential danger of this reliance of short-term borrowing on funding economic growth – it made Germany very vulnerable to potential world economic crisis if these loans had to be paid back quickly or the sources of this borrowing dried up.

Chapter 6

Apply Your Knowledge

a
- **Women**: Some women became more socially independent, sexually liberated, etc., but most did not. More women used birth control and the birth rate did decline, so they were having fewer children. Many women became actively involved in politics, especially at local level, and a few became Reichstag deputies, however their influence was limited and no women became ministers or leaders of political parties. There were greater employment opportunities, thanks to the improved economy, and more people were willing to employ women. Many women took advantage of these opportunities, but most still gave up their jobs when they married. Employment opportunities for women were still limited compared with those for men, and there was no equal pay in most occupations. Some women would have enjoyed some aspects of the arts and cultural changes, while others would have disapproved.
- **Pensioners**: Many pensioners had suffered badly from hyperinflation and nothing was done to compensate them for financial losses so most continued to struggle badly financially from 1924–28. Most were horrified by the 'decadence' of Weimar culture and vehemently opposed cultural change.
- **Young people**: Very young people were affected by the changes to elementary schools but older school children experienced little change. Youth employment remained high and would have concerned many, although the unemployment insurance from 1927 would have helped. Unlike older people, many young people supported and enjoyed the cultural changes. Many continued to enjoy youth groups and some joined the new political youth groups.
- **Industrial workers**: Government measures would have benefited them, e.g. accident insurance systems, increased wages, and the growth in power of trade unions meant that many would have felt they had more of a say. Some would have enjoyed some aspects of the arts and cultural changes, while others would have disapproved.
- **Farmers**: Agriculture did not share in the economic growth, so many farmers struggled financially in these years and some lost their farms. Those few that did grow would have

enjoyed the benefits of new machinery. Some would have enjoyed some aspects of the cultural changes (if they could afford to go to them) but more would have been alarmed by them due to farmers' being mostly traditional/conservative. (Rural communities were more hostile and alarmed by the Weimar cultural changes.)
- **The unemployed**: Although jobs were created, unemployment remained high. Many would have been helped by the unemployment insurance from 1927. They were unlikely to be able to enjoy much of the new cultural developments, owing to poverty.
- **The middle classes**: Professionals' salaries did not increase and many would have lost savings due to hyperinflation which were not compensated. Some would have benefited from new employment opportunities, such as skilled positions in the new industries, and some may have started their own small businesses, owing to the improving economic opportunities.
- **Business owners**: Of those that survived hyperinflation (and many went bankrupt in 1924), some benefited from increased trade and foreign investment and would have seen improved profits. Those in the 'new' industries particularly would have done well economically. Like other sectors, some would have enjoyed the cultural changes, while others would not.

b You should position each group on the continuum line according to your own decisions.

Key Concept

- **Social welfare reforms**

'Left': Would have approved of all measures to support those in need, though would have been disappointed by the system not delivering on its promises and things such as 'means testing'.

'Right': While probably approving of continuing support for war veterans and widows, many on the right were alarmed by the cost of social welfare.

- **Increasing power of trade unions**

'Left': Would have approved of this as it gave workers more power and led to increased wages and better conditions.

'Right': Would have worried those concerned about businesses who were suffering due to the changes imposed by unions.

- **'New' women**

'Left': Many would have approved of increasing measures for gender equality in politics and the workplace.

'Right': Many people, especially the right-wing, were alarmed by changes, particularly the increase in birth control and divorce, which they saw as undermining German values.

- **Changes in education**

'Left': Many would have been disappointed that the changes didn't succeed in breaking down the religious and class barriers in secondary education.

'Right': Many would have been worried by attempts to reform what was regarded as a system that worked well. They approved of class barriers.

- **Cultural changes, e.g. night clubs, jazz music**

'Left': Would have been more accepting than those on the right. Many of the famous artists, authors, playwrights, etc. were very left-wing.

'Right': Most on the right were horrified by what was perceived as declining morality and influence from abroad.

- **Expressionist and modern art and design**

'Left': Would have been more accepting than those on the right.

'Right': Many disapproved as they liked traditional forms of art and design.

⚖ Ⓐ To What Extent?

a A social revolution means a fundamental, substantial change in society that usually involves power being given to more or different people and people behaving in different ways. Factors that might contribute to a social revolution are: very weak or very strong governments that either force change or allow it to happen; more people from different backgrounds sharing in political power; more opportunities for different people in work; more or less freedom for cultural changes that cause people to start behaving or thinking differently.

b These are just a few small examples.

- **Aspect of social change**: More people sharing in power.
  - o Examples of some social change: Equal voting rights for men and women led to increased participation by women in national and local politics.
  - o Examples of little or no change: Few Reichstag deputies were women or from the lower classes. No women were ministers or led political parties.
- **Aspect of social change**: More work opportunities.
  - o Examples of some social change: More women worked and took advantage of new opportunities.
  - o Examples of little or no change: Most women gave up work when they got married.
- **Aspect of social change**: Cultural changes causing people to behave or think differently.
  - o Examples of some social change: Some women used birth control and felt free to have more sexual relationships as a result. The birth rate declined.
  - o Examples of little or no change: Most women continued to behave conservatively.

c You need to define what is meant by social revolution before writing about the ways in which society did and did not change.

⚙ Apply Your Knowledge

Art: Expressionism – abstract with vivid colours to express meaning/emotion rather than depict physical reality. Examples: Georg Grosz, Franz Marc, Hannah Höch

Music: Expressionism – conveying meaning and emotion rather than traditional melody and harmony. Examples: Hindemith, Arnold Schoenberg

Literature: Free writing focusing on internal thoughts and emotions rather than physical reality. Example: Thomas Mann

Architecture: Bauhaus school at Dessau – taught students to use different materials such as steel, concrete and glass, and to take account of the function of the building in their designs. Example: William Gropius

Theatre: Experimental plays and musicals incorporated expressionist ideas and used lots of symbolism; topics were overtly political. Examples: Bertolt Brecht, Kurt Weill

Film: Berlin became a centre of world cinema and developed modern camera and lighting techniques. Examples: Billy Wilder, Fritz Lang, Josef von Sternberg

✍ Ⓐˢ Plan Your Essay

a *Points that agree*: Most women continued in their traditional roles as wives and mothers and gave up work on getting married; very few women owned businesses or became prominent in politics, their roles even when they did work remained mostly traditional; religion continued to play a major part in many Germans' lives, e.g. many young people went to church youth groups; although the government tried to break down class barriers through changing the education system, they were largely

unsuccessful; class divisions and those between urban and rural communities remained fairly static.

Points that disagree: The birth rate declined, proving that women's lives were changing as they were having fewer children; the flourishing night clubs in Berlin proved that many younger people (in Berlin at least) were behaving differently; the explosion of art and cultural changes would have affected most people in society (though not all would have approved) as many would, for example, have gone to the cinema; new opportunities and greater social mobility in urban areas.

b Your essay plan needs to include information on both sides and you must reach a judgement on whether you agree or disagree with the quotation in the question.

💡 Key Concept

Many nationalists blamed Jews for the defeat of Germany in the First World War, but a major reason for anti-Semitism was the perceived link between Jews and communism. Many of the middle and upper classes greatly feared communism because of the communist revolution in Russia. Nazi propaganda seized on the fact that some leading Bolsheviks were also Jews to make a link between communism and Judaism. Behind this anti-Semitism was a belief that Jews could not be 'real' Germans because of their differences in customs and culture. Some nationalists feared the assimilation of Jews and extremists, while others, such as the Nazis, saw them as a snake within society, undermining German values. Their high levels of education had enabled them to thrive in professions such as medicine and law and there were also many successful Jewish businessmen and bankers. This success led to jealousy and a suspicion that Jews must be corrupt and that, to do so well, they must be exploiting non-Jews.

Chapter 7

⚙ Apply Your Knowledge

KPD: German Communist Party – Far left – Anti-Weimar Democracy

SPD: Social Democrat Party – Centre left – Pro-Weimar Democracy

DDP: German Democratic Party – Centre/Centre right – Pro-Weimar Democracy

Centre: Catholic zentrum – Centre right – Pro-Weimar Democracy

DVP: German People's Party – Right wing – Pro-Weimar Democracy

DNVP: German National People's Party – Right wing – Anti-Weimar Democracy

NSDAP: German National Socialist Worker's Party – Far right – Anti-Weimar Democracy

💡 Key Concept

a **Far left** – *KPD (Communist Party)*: Wanted totally new political system; not in any coalition government; workers in industrial and port areas.

Centre left – *SPD (Social Democrats)*: Supported and helped establish Weimar system; only once in coalition in these years; supported by industrial workers.

Centre – *DDP (German Democratic Party)*: Supported Weimar system; in all coalitions; supported by academics and professionals but in decline.

Centre right – *Centre Party*: Supported Weimar system but became more right-wing; in all coalitions; broad base of support from all Catholics.

Right-wing – *DVP (German People's Party)*: Supported Weimar system; in all coalitions; most support from industrialists.

Right-wing – *DNVP (German National People's Party)*: Anti-democratic; once in coalition; traditional

support from landowners and elites but increasing support from industrialists and professionals.

Far right – *NSDAP (German National Socialist Worker's Party)*: Anti-Democratic; not in any coalition government; little support but grew in rural areas in the north.

b Based on your understanding and knowledge, create your own information cards.

⚖ Ⓐ To What Extent?

a **Evidence that Germany was politically stable**

- Decrease in politically motivated violence
- Decrease in demonstrations and protests
- No armed uprisings or attempts at revolution by force
- Declining support for extreme left (KPD)
- Limited support for extreme right (Nazis)
- Some right-wing parties started to work with the system – e.g. DNVP was part of a coalition government in 1925
- Election of President Hindenburg shows that even traditionalists were starting to support the idea of a republic

Evidence for political instability

- 9 different coalition governments
- Lack of a majority for most cabinets (only 6 of 23)
- Lack of any long-term programmes or plans to resolve issues due to disagreement within coalitions
- Parties themselves often had factional rivalries that meant a lack of coherent policies
- The elected president held strong anti-democratic views

b Lack of support for extremist parties is seen in the low and declining votes – both the number of Communists and number of the Nazi party Reichstag deputies declined over the period. The Communists did still have a significant number of deputies indicating that their base of support remained solid. However, lack of votes may have meant that supporters chose not to vote at all. People may have agreed with some of the policies of the extremist parties even if they did not vote for them in elections.

c In answering this question remember to give a clear opinion on whether Germany was politically stable and examine the evidence for both sides of the argument.

⚙ Apply Your Knowledge

You should create a mind-map for this activity. See page 46 for an example of a mind-map.

🔍 Ⓐ Source Analysis

a The Weimar political system; opinions on the Weimar political system; effectiveness of Weimar political system; how laws and policies were decided (or not!) in Weimar Germany.

b The tone is mocking and slightly scathing. The author claims to be 'apolitical' but we cannot know if this was truly the case, but as it is in a liberal-leaning publication that would probably have supported democracy, it is likely to be fairly reliable and give an accurate account of what took place.

b Reichstag deputies behave unprofessionally and are an embarrassment to Germany. The political system isn't getting anything done and isn't worth the money spent on the Reichstag building.

Chapter 8

Apply Your Knowledge

a and b Locarno Pact

Date: 1925 (signed in December)
Between: Germany, France, Belgium, Britain, Italy, Czechoslovakia and Poland

Main points:

- Western borders of Germany in 1919 accepted by countries involved.
- Germany agreed to keeping troops out of the Rhineland. France agreed to withdraw its troops.
- Britain and Italy promised aid to Germany, France or Belgium if attacked.
- Germany, France, Belgium, Poland and Czechoslovakia agreed mediation for disputes.
- France, Poland and Czechoslovakia agreed to ensure Germany didn't break the agreement.

Kellogg-Briand Pact

Date: 1928
Between: Drawn up by Germany, France and the USA (many countries signed)

Main points:

- Agreed to renounce the use of offensive wars to resolve disputes.

Treaty of Rapallo

Date: 1922
Between: Germany and the USSR

Main points:

- Trade and economic cooperation to be resumed.
- Diplomatic relations restored.
- Claims for war compensation were dropped.
- Russia agreed to Germany developing weapons and training pilots there.

Treaty of Berlin

Date: 1926
Between: Germany and the USSR

Main points:

- Renewed Treaty of Rapallo.
- Germany agreed to neutrality in any war involving the USSR (as long as the USSR was not the aggressor).

⬆️ Improve an Answer

a Strengths include: Plenty of relevant knowledge; some attempts to qualify 'how far'.
Weaknesses include: It's very descriptive in places, e.g. the first sentence; there's little analysis on how far this shows Stresemann had accepted the Treaty; the final sentence is not good style!

b You need to rewrite the paragraph removing some of the detail and adding in more analysis.

c Your paragraph could include the extent of disarmament or the end of allied occupation.

⚙️ Apply Your Knowledge

a and b Treaty of Rapallo (1922)

Before: Much mistrust between the USSR and Germany. *After*: Improved diplomatic and economic relations.

Dawes Plan (1924)

Before: Allies and Germany distrustful of each other. *After*: Eased the burden of reparations and obtained loans from the USA to stimulate economic growth; improved relations with the Allies by showing Germany would cooperate.

Locarno Pact (1925)

Before: Dawes Plan had helped improve relations but still much mistrust between Britain/France and Germany. *After*: Recognised some of the borders in the Treaty of Versailles and made measures to ensure peaceful resolution of conflict helped improve relations with Britain and France.

Germany joined League of Nations (1926)

Before: Germany was not part of the international scene. *After*: Highlighted that Germany was now accepted and consulted as part of international negotiations and discussions.

Treaty of Berlin (1926)

Before: Ties with the USSR had much improved due to Rapallo. *After*: Cemented ties with the USSR.

Kellogg-Briand Pact (1928)

Before: Improving situation between Germany and the rest of the world. *After*: Helped persuade other countries that Germany wanted to avoid war and promote peaceful resolutions to disputes.

Young Plan (1929)

Before: Fairly good relations. *After*: Further improved relations with the Allies by showing cooperation while also winning Germany some concessions.

⚖️ Ⓐ Assess the Validity of This View

a You should create a mind-map for this activity. Ideas would include: Asking Allies for help in resolving reparations issues; agreeing to restart reparations payments in 1924 (Dawes Plan) which improved relations especially with France, Belgium and Britain; agreeing to keep borders with France and Belgium as agreed at Versailles in Locarno Pact; improving relations with the USSR (Treaty of Berlin); diplomacy of Locarno helped prevent hostile anti-German alliance between Britain and France; signing Kellogg-Briand Pact, 1928; negotiating the Young Plan 1929.

b Ideas would include: Charles Dawes and a committee of financial experts came up with the Dawes Plan rather than Stresemann; Owen Young drew up the Young Plan; Germany's economic recovery meant other countries wanted to trade with Germany again, which also improved relations; diplomats and ministers from countries such as the USSR, Britain, France, etc., who negotiated agreements with Germany, which improved the position; Treaty of Rapallo was done before Stresemann's time; the ways in which Stresemann managed to get around the disarmament agreements angered many other countries (especially France).

c Your answer should analyse the role of Stresemann in the improvement of Germany's international position but you must also analyse the role of other factors and ways in which Germany's international position was not improved.

⚖️ Ⓐ Source Analysis

a *Author*: Gustav Stresemann

Adds to the value because he was Foreign Minister 1924–29, so he was responsible for foreign policy.

Date: September 1925

This would have been during the discussions on the Locarno Pact that would be signed in December 1925 and after the Dawes Plan. This adds to the value as it helps explain some of the policies undertaken. The Dawes Plan began solving the reparations problem as Stresemann suggests in the letter. The Locarno Pact agreed western borders. The writer alludes to discussions at Thoiry and this is particularly useful in showing his attitude: that it was important to improve relations with France before trying to recovery territory in the East.

Audience: The ex-Crown Prince

As a German Nationalist, the ex-Crown Prince would probably have wanted to know what Stresemann's foreign policy plans were. Stresemann may therefore be exaggerating his foreign policy aims, but this seems unlikely as we know Stresemann was essentially a nationalist and wanted the Treaty of Versailles revised.

Purpose: To inform someone of the main aims of foreign policy

This could possibly have been written in response to a request from the former Crown Prince or the letter could have been written just on Stresemann's wishes. As it's a private letter it's likely to be a true representation of Stresemann's wishes.

b Friendly but professional, patriotic and nationalistic – 'our kindred who live under a foreign yoke in foreign lands', 'our eastern frontiers'.

c Protecting Germans and Germany. He's emphasising this as he probably strongly believed it but also because he would have thought that the former Crown Prince would want to hear it.

Chapter 9

⚙️ Apply Your Knowledge

- *Collapse of export trade* – occurred because the Depression was worldwide, so other countries were suffering too and could not afford to buy German goods.
- *Fall in industrial production* – occurred because goods were not being purchased because governments, businesses and individuals (both in Germany and in other countries) could not afford to buy as many German products.
- *Fall in prices of goods* – occurred because companies were forced to drop prices to try to encourage people/businesses/governments to buy their goods.
- *Businesses going bankrupt and closing* – occurred because they could not make profits to buy raw materials and goods they needed, pay workers, etc., and could not borrow from banks, foreign investment, etc.
- *Unemployment* – occurred because businesses closed and others were forced to make redundancies to try to reduce costs.
- *Reductions in wages and working hours* – occurred because businesses tried to reduce costs.
- *Lack of foreign investment* – occurred because other countries were also experiencing a depression.
- *Reduction in German government income* – occurred because businesses were earning less and therefore paying less tax, individuals were earning less and therefore paying less tax, welfare costs dramatically increased.

⚙️ Apply Your Knowledge

- **Increased poverty**
Many became unemployed (around 8 million by 1933) and those who did keep their jobs often suffered wage cuts and/or reduced working hours so their incomes were less. Unemployment benefits became more subject to strict means tests so some didn't qualify and the benefits were for a limited time only.
- **Increased homelessness**
Those homeowners who couldn't pay mortgages (middle classes) and tenants who couldn't pay rent (working classes) were evicted, so homelessness increased. Shanty towns appeared in large cities, e.g. Berlin, where people lived in tents or temporary shelters built from whatever could be found.
- **Increased disease and malnutrition**
Caused by poor living conditions – shanty towns had poor sewage, access to water, no gas or electricity, those living in houses often couldn't afford these amenities – and poor nutrition as people couldn't afford nutritious food. Diseases such as TB and rickets increased. Particularly affected children.
- **Increased middle-class bitterness**
Some middle-class business owners lost their businesses and homes, others, such as some civil servants, were affected by unemployment and

salary reductions. They usually didn't qualify for any state benefits. The middle classes had lost their savings during hyperinflation and were again badly affected by the Depression, so this caused increased bitterness and resentment towards the Weimar government.

- **Increased street violence and violent crime**
  Political demonstrations frequently erupted into violence with the Communist Red Front Fighters' League engaged in street battles with the Nazi SA. Unemployment disproportionately affected young people, which led to more young people committing violent crime and joining criminal gangs (as well as Fighters' League or SA).

- **Increased bitterness towards women workers**
  Anger towards women workers rose as the proportion of women in jobs increased. There was particular bitterness towards married women who had jobs. They were seen as 'double-earners' as their husbands were also earning when many men were unemployed and could not support their families.

Improve an Answer

a Red = economic; blue = political; green = social

Unemployment was not the only devastating social effect of the Great Depression in Germany. Many businesses went bankrupt and industrial production and trade fell sharply. People's incomes rapidly diminished and they became dependent on savings or welfare benefits to survive. The rise in welfare dependents had a huge impact on reducing government income as did the reduction in income tax receipts. Homelessness escalated as people could not afford to pay their mortgages or rents. Malnutrition and diseases caused by poor diets increased as people could not afford good food. People also had less money to spend on goods which further affected the economy and left many businesses struggling to survive. Many people blamed the Weimar government for unemployment and turned to extremist political parties which promised to provide more jobs if elected.

b The paragraph could consider social effects such as increased bitterness and resentment or increased street violence and violent crime. You could also comment on how these social effects were all linked to unemployment.

c Your answer should consider social, financial and political consequences of the Depression as well as examining unemployment in detail. You must follow a convincing argument throughout your essay on whether you agree or disagree with the view in the question.

Apply Your Knowledge

a and b

- Closed banks and took them under government control – eased the immediate crisis but did nothing to resolve underlying problems of businesses not being able to borrow money, etc.

- Reducing unemployment benefits through strict means testing, paying less to young unemployed and providing benefits for fixed periods only – did reduce government spending but caused the collapse of the Grand Coalition and caused much resentment from the unemployed.

- Cut government worker's wages – again reduced government spending but caused resentment and did little to resolve the economic crisis.

- Raised taxes – caused huge resentment of those who still did have jobs and businesses, especially those struggling to survive, though did increase government funds.

- Banning SA – had little impact on reducing street violence; reversing the policy increased street violence again.

Assess the Validity of This View

a See government measures in Apply Your Knowledge answers above. The government could have done the opposite – instead of reducing spending and raising taxes it could have increased spending to try to create employment and improve people's financial situations so they would have spent more money which may have improved the economy. Instead, the government's policies managed to alienate a huge range of people – the unemployed by reducing benefits, government workers by reducing salaries, and those employed or business owners who had to pay higher taxes.

b You should create a mind-map for this activity. As well as the failure of the Weimar government to deal with the impact of the Depression, you could include the following reasons for the rise of extremism:

- Unemployment and poverty led to despair and people to look for an alternative view of the world.

- The actions of extremist parties, especially the Nazis and Communists to try to increase support.

- Democracy had effectively collapsed so it seemed as though it didn't work – people looked for alternatives.

c You should examine a variety of factors responsible for the rise of extremism, as well as the actions of the Weimar government and come to a judgement on whether the government was largely responsible or not.

Chapter 10

Apply Your Knowledge

You should create a mind-map for this activity. For an example of a mind map, see page 46.

Apply Your Knowledge

- **Lower-middle classes**
  Support: Substantial
  Reasons: Most support for the Nazis before 1930 had come from this group and they continued to support them. Supported many Nazis policies, especially anti-communism, anti-Weimar, anti-Semitism and promises of Führerprinzip and nationalism.

- **Farmers**
  Support: Substantial
  Reasons: The Nazis successfully exploited the extent of suffering of farmers due to the Depression and years of low prices. Many farmers would have been attracted by the promise of Führerprinzip and traditional values too.

- **Workers**
  Support: Some
  Reasons: Did attract some support mostly due to promises of 'work and bread' but most workers turned to communism.

- **Industrialists**
  Support: Significant
  Reasons: Some business owners and industrialists turned to the Nazis mostly due to their fears of communism and the appeal of the Führerprinzip and Nazi order and control.

- **The young**
  Support: Significant
  Reasons: Many young people supported the Nazis because this group suffered very high unemployment so liked the Nazis' promise to provide jobs, but also because of the Führerprinzip and nationalism. Many were attracted by the parades, rallies and SA.

- **Housewives**
  Support: Significant
  Reasons: Housewives supported the Nazis because of the Nazis' traditional family values and promises such as 'work and bread'.

- **Catholics**
  Support: Not much
  Reasons: Although the Nazis did attract Catholic support in some areas, most Catholics continued to support the Centre Party which was most in line with Catholic beliefs.

- **Protestants**
  Support: Significant
  Reasons: Variety of reasons including fear of atheist communism and promises of Führerprinzip. Protestants had a greater sense of German nationalism than Catholics who looked to the Pope as a spiritual figurehead, which was against the principle of one all-mighty Führer.

Key Concept

a **Anti-Semitism** – hatred towards and discrimination against Jewish people.

  Social Darwinism – the idea where natural biological selection (the 'survival of the fittest') can be applied to humans so some people and races are weaker than and inferior to others.

  Racialism – the belief that humans are divided into different races and that different races have different characteristics.

b The three terms were at the heart of Nazi racial ideology. This was the belief in racialism where Social Darwinism meant that some races and types of people were inferior to others and could and should be treated accordingly. In Nazi ideology, Jews were considered to be a race and at the very bottom of the racial hierarchy, so anti-Semitism should be a policy of the State.

Apply Your Knowledge

a *Reasons both attracted support*: Failure of non-extremist parties/Weimar politicians to resolve the economic and social problems of the Depression; hatred of Weimar political system; both parties actively recruited unemployed young men for paramilitary organisations; successful propaganda; alternative economic programmes with promises of employment and a better future.

  Reasons Nazis attracted support: Hitler's charisma and personal popularity; use of simple promises and vague policies, e.g. 'work and bread'; focused on attracting support from a wide range of people and areas; nationalist policies; fear of communism.

  Reasons Communists attracted support: Explicitly focused on attracting more support from the working class, especially unemployed; emphasised 'class struggle' and internationalism; attraction of communism over capitalism; targeted former SPD supporters; set up practical help for people, e.g. labour exchanges, reform schools.

b The Communists were, to some extent, victims of their own success as their increasing popularity frightened many people into voting for the Nazi Party because of their promise to destroy communism. The KPD also targeted the 'wrong' people by focusing on the SPD rather than realising the Nazis were the real threat. Probably most importantly however, the KPD focused all its efforts on its existing support base and therefore successfully attracted more working-class support but failed to attract much support from other groups whereas the Nazis targeted a variety of groups and therefore won support from many different types of people.

🔍 🅐 Source Analysis

a Albert Speer was an architect who joined the Nazis in the 1930s. This adds to the source's value because it explains one of his reasons for joining the Nazis – namely, the appeal of Hitler. It was written after the war, therefore the author would probably still have a good memory of events of less than 20 years ago, but as it was written after Nazi defeat, and while in prison, the author may have wanted to plead his own innocence and so overstate Hitler's appeal. As it's an autobiography, it would be written so that Speer could portray his version of events and would be written for an international audience. This could again diminish its value slightly because the author may exaggerate Hitler's appeal to reduce his own culpability and guilt.

b The tone is one of fervour, emphasising Hitler's zeal and passionate speaking: 'tempestuously hailed'; 'wave of enthusiasm'; 'hypnotic persuasiveness'; 'transformed'. These terms all add to the value by indicating the effect that Hitler could have on an audience and why people were drawn to him.

c It is valuable in showing Hitler's ability to persuade and influence people through his speeches, and many other sources give a similar view, although not everyone was convinced. This personal appeal of Hitler is just one aspect of the appeal of Nazism though. There's little in this source on what Hitler actually said, just his style of speaking and the effect this created, though there is some indication that Hitler focused on the 'peril of communism' and 'hopeless unemployment', which demonstrate further reasons for the appeal of Nazism.

⚖️ 🅐 Assess the Validity of This View

a Fear of communism; appeal of Hitler; propaganda targeting different groups with a different message; policies; impact of the Depression; disillusionment with Weimar politicians.

b You must decide what rating to give each factor but you must be able to explain the ratings you have given.

c Your answer should consider the appeal of Hitler, and the fear of communism, and Hitler's ability to play on this fear, before examining other factors that won the Nazis support.

Chapter 11

⚙️ Apply Your Knowledge

1 Hindenburg appoints Brüning Chancellor: March 1930
2 Hindenburg appoints Papen Chancellor: May 1932
3 The Nazis become the largest party in the Reichstag for the first time: July 1932
4 The Nazis lose votes but remain the largest party in the Reichstag: November 1932
5 Hindenburg appoints Schleicher Chancellor: December 1932
6 Hindenburg appoints Hitler Chancellor: January 1933

🔍 🅐 Source Analysis

a Author: Franz von Papen, Chancellor May–Dec 1932, then made Vice Chancellor under Hitler in Jan 1933
 • Historical study 1: Of value because Papen was very involved – conspired with Hitler and others.
 • Historical study 2: Of great value as it's from the man himself, however, may not be trustworthy given that it's from his perspective.
 • Historical study 3: Of some value as Papen would have been an educated observer who played a role in Hitler becoming Chancellor.
 Date: 1952, after the fall of the Nazi regime but still well within living memory
 • Historical studies 1–3: Valuable, as still within fairly recent memory, though Nazi defeat and

discovery of atrocities, etc. may have tainted the view.
 Audience and reason for writing the source: buyers of his memoirs, i.e. members of the public, English-speaking audience if this is a translation. Written partly to defend Papen's policies and reputation
 • Historical study 1: Valuable, as Papen wanted to tell people what had happened, but value is lessened as he wanted to absolve himself of responsibility.
 • Historical study 2: Even though value is reduced as he's writing this to absolve himself of responsibility for Hitler coming to power, it is still very valuable to hear from the man who is central to the historical study.
 • Historical study 3: Lessens the value as it is focused on his own role and things he directly knew about so he could defend himself, so may miss out vital pieces of other information.

b Tone is regretful. The author emphasises that democracy and the constitution were responsible for Hitler becoming Chancellor, and also that nobody, including himself, realised the danger Hitler presented.

c Reduces its value slightly for studies 1, 2 and 3, as it is linked with the audience and the reason Papen wrote the source – wanting to absolve himself of responsibility for making Hitler Chancellor.

⚖️ 🅐 To What Extent?

a • Reichstag election results of 1928: not particularly useful
 • The collapse of the Grand Coalition government in March 1930: very useful
 • Reichstag election results of 1930: very useful
 • The exclusion of the SPD from government meant that no government after 1930 had a majority in the Reichstag: very useful
 • The fall of Brüning's government in May 1932: very useful
 • The Presidential election of 1932: of some use
 • The banning of the SA in April 1932: not particularly useful
 • Reichstag election results of July 1932: very useful
 • Brüning's government took temporary control of the banks to prevent more of them collapsing in 1931: not particularly useful
 • Papen imposed authoritarian rule in Prussia July 1932: of some use
 • Hitler refused to join Papen's government after July 1932 election: very useful
 • Reichstag passed a vote of no confidence in Papen's government: of some use
 • Reichstag election results of November 1932: very useful
 • Schleicher persuades Hindenburg to appoint him Chancellor in December 1932: of some use
 • Schleicher negotiated with Gregor Strasser about the Nazis joining his government: of some use
 • Schleicher's resignation as Chancellor: of some use
 • Papen's negotiations with Hitler in December and January 1933: very useful
 • The Wall Street Crash of October 1929 saw share prices on the New York Stock Exchange drop rapidly and many American companies were badly hit: not particularly useful
 • Papen and Hindenburg believed they would be able to control Hitler once he became Chancellor: very useful
 • Papen and Oskar von Hindenberg persuaded President Hindenberg to appoint Hitler Chancellor: very useful

b Other highly relevant information would relate to the perceived threat from the KPD of armed rising to overthrow the government; Hitler's refusal to be in a coalition unless he was Chancellor; support of businesses for the idea of Hitler leading a coalition government; leader of DVNP agreeing to be in a Hitler-led coalition government; the impact of the Depression on Germany.

c Your answer needs to examine the role of backstairs intrigue as well as other factors in Hitler being appointed Chancellor.

Chapter 12

⚙️ Apply Your Knowledge

You should create a mind-map for this activity.
• Reichstag election on 5 March to gain more votes for Nazis
 – Use of force to intimidate opponents and prevent them campaigning, etc.
• Reichstag Fire, 27 February
 – Led to Decree for Protection of the People and State
 – Used to arrest political opponents (especially communists and socialists)
• Control of the police
 – Ensured SA would go unpunished for their violence
• Winning the support of industrialists
• Winning the support of the army
• Enabling act
 – SA intimidated non-Nazi deputies into voting for the Enabling Act
 – KPD banned
• Violence against political opponents
 – trade unions, SPD and KPD offices, members and newspapers targeted
 – thousands of political opponents put into concentration camps

⚖️ 🅐 How Significant?

a *Factor*: Hindenburg's underestimation of Hitler
 Significance: Significant because it was Hindenburg's belief that he and others would be able to control Hitler, which led to him being appointed Chancellor. You could argue that Hindenburg was pretty insignificant by this stage though, as there was no real alternative by then.
 Factor: Papen and others who conspired to make Hitler Chancellor thinking they could control him
 Significance: The 'backstairs intrigue' was a major factor in making Hitler Chancellor, which enabled him to take actions to establish his power. Papen and others in the cabinet thought they could control Hitler.
 Factor: Nazis' electoral success
 Significance: From the July 1932 Reichstag elections, the Nazis had been the largest party in the Reichstag, which was significant as it meant that, as leader of the Party, Hitler had to be listened to and was in a very strong position. However, even in the March 1933 election when the Nazis used terror to intimidate other parties and prevent them campaigning, the Nazis never held an overall majority in the Reichstag.
 Factor: The failure of other governments in 1932
 Significance: If either Papen's or Schleicher's government (or that of Brüning before them) had been more successful in ruling Germany, particularly in dealing with the effects of the Depression, Hitler and the Nazis would not have had the opportunity to seize power as they did. By the end of January 1933, there were very few choices other than Hitler

for the chancellorship, which enabled the following actions to establish his power.

Factor: The SA's use of violence and terror

Significance: Very important in bringing Hitler to the chancellorship anyway but then played a major role in creating an atmosphere of anarchy and lawlessness after the Reichstag fire (which they may have started) to enable the Decree for the Protection of the People and State, which essentially suspended civil and political rights. Also used terror to intimidate political opponents during election campaigns. Then intimidated non-Nazi Reichstag members into voting for the Enabling Act.

Factor: Gaining support of key institutions

Significance: This was vital, as the army was still a powerful force in Germany and could potentially have removed Hitler from government. This was averted by Hitler meeting army leaders very early after becoming Chancellor to ensure that the army was not threatened

Also important to get key business leaders' approval and the support of the DNVP and Centre Party in agreeing to the Enabling Act.

Factor: Hitler's use of the law

Significance: This played a significant part in consolidating Hitler's power. Firstly, the use of the Reichstag Fire to suspend civil and political rights (the Decree for the Protection of the People and State), therefore making 'terror' legal, then the Enabling Act ensured that Hitler could make all decrees himself without anyone else's approval. The Enabling Act was passed through intimidation but also through making deals with DNVP and Centre Party.

b You need to discuss a range of factors that permitted Hitler's establishment of power by March 1933 (see answers to **a** above) and express your view as to how significant Hindenburg's underestimation of Hitler was. You could decide that he was significant to differing degrees, or that he was not significant at all, as long as you support your view.

🖉 🛡 Plan Your Essay

Agree

- Used violence to intimidate trade unions, liberal newspapers and other political parties.
- Arrested thousands of political opponents and put them in concentration camps; drove others into exile.
- Made it difficult for opposition parties to campaign in the March 1933 Reichstag elections; oversaw voting at the ballot box – ensuring the Nazis did well.
- Intimidated opposition party deputies who took their seats in the Reichstag after the March 1933 elections to ensure they voted for the Enabling Act.

Disagree

- The Reichstag Fire enabled the Nazis to suspend civil and political rights legally (though there is some debate that the SA was involved in starting the fire).
- The Enabling Act – a major part of consolidation of power as it gave Hitler the power to issue decrees without the Reichstag or Hindenburg.
- Hitler won support from the army, industrialists and the DNVP Party, which all helped consolidate his power.

🔍 🛡 Source Analysis

a The tone is one of fear, intimidation and threat of violence.

b The author was an SPD deputy who had been elected to the Reichstag in the elections of March 1933. He would mostly likely have been subjected

to similar intimidation and the threat of violence throughout his election campaign. SPD offices and members had been terrorised by the SA since January 1933 as the left-wing party was not approved of by the Nazis. The Nazis would have known that SPD deputies in the Reichstag would have been very unlikely to vote for the Enabling Act (they were the only party that did not) so they would have been subjected to great intimidation in an effort to force them to vote for the act.

c This source would be of value for an enquiry into how the Nazis established a dictatorship because it shows the different methods of fear and intimidation that non-Nazi members of the Reichstag were subjected to when the Enabling Act, the major piece of legislation that led to dictatorship, was being discussed. The deputy describes being verbally abused, physically intimidated and being made aware of the threat of arrest. The author may well have wanted to emphasize Nazi violence or the threat of it as he would have been opposed to them, so therefore could be exaggerating this. However, unlike other non-Nazi Reichstag deputies, he did not succumb to the intimidation as all members of the SPD voted against the bill. He would therefore not need to exaggerate the violence in order to 'explain' why he had been pressured into approving the bill, although he may have wanted to show his personal strength in resisting such intimidation.

Chapter 13

💡 Key Concept

You should create a mind-map for this activity. For an example of a mind-map, see page 46.

⚙️ Apply Your Knowledge

a A dictatorship is where a country is ruled by one person or party exercising total power and control in an undemocratic way.

b **Creating a one-party state**

Why? To remove an alternative focus for allegiance and prevent political opposition to laws, policies and actions.

How? Through violence and internment in concentration camps; through pressure so other parties 'voluntarily' disbanded, e.g. DNVP; using the law – e.g. the Law against the Formation of New Parties (July 1933) to ensure that no new parties would be created.

Controlling local government

Why? To ensure nationwide control and reduce the likelihood of a federal state rising up against the government.

How? Using the law – e.g. the First and Second Law for the Coordination of Federal States to ensure they were dominated by Nazis; abolition of State assemblies in Law for the Reconstruction of the Reich; abolition of the Reichsrat.

Controlling the civil service

Why? To ensure that policies are efficiently carried out.

How? Non-supporting civil servants forced to resign; Nazi Party officials positioned in all government offices.

Controlling the armed forces

Why? To prevent mutiny and ensure the loyalty of those able to exert control.

How? Army leaders had felt threatened by the SA so removing the leaders of the SA in the Night of the Long Knives was a sign that Hitler valued the army and this encouraged army generals to cooperate with him; merged the offices of Chancellor and President in August 1934; the armed forces swore allegiance to Hitler.

⚙️ Apply Your Knowledge

a and **b** Create and colour-code your own revision timeline.

🖉 🛡 Plan Your Essay

a You should create a mind-map for this activity. It could include:

- SA violence and actions had become an embarrassment to Nazis and other members of the government spoke out against it (Papen and von Blomberg).
- SA lacked a clear role and many members had become restless – Hitler was worried about what they might do next.
- Rohm's ideas contradicted Hitler's own plans – Rohm wanted a 'Second Revolution' where the SA would replace the army and bring a degree of socialism (aiding the working classes).
- It won public support for Hitler and the Nazis as many believed the SA were trying to stage a coup.
- Removing the SA as a threat to the army, won the army's support for Hitler's government.
- It gave Hitler an opportunity to remove other political opponents such as Schleicher and Papen.
- Hitler had grown tired of Rohm and was unsure about his ambitions (rumours of a Rohm conspiracy).

b • Night of the Long Knives (30 June 1934) removed the threat of the SA and other political opponents and won the army's support for the Nazi government.
- Death of Hindenburg (August 1934), which led to Hitler becoming Führer.
- Suppression, persecution and imprisonment of communists, socialists and members of the SPD.
- Banning of the SPD (June 1933) and disbanding of the DNVP (June 1933) and Centre Party (July 1933).
- Law against the Formation of New Parties (July 1933).
- First and Second Laws for Coordination of the Federal States (March and April 1933), reducing power of local government.
- Abolition of state assemblies (Jan 1934) and the Reichsrat (Feb 1934).
- Sacking from the civil service those whose loyalty was doubted.
- Placing Nazi Party officials in government offices to watch over civil servants.
- Concordat with the Catholic Church.

You must number your list in order of how significant each event/policy/legislation was for consolidating Hitler's power. However, it could be argued that the Nazis themselves thought that removing other political parties was the most significant as that was what they tackled first.

c Everyone has a different method for writing essay plans but you must make sure you include analysis of different factors (see answer to part **b** above) as well as an analysis of the Night of the Long Knives (see answer to part **a** above).

⚖️ 🛡 To What Extent?

a There was little overt opposition from within the Nazi Party. However, Rohm and other members of the SA believed the 'revolution' had not gone far enough and that the SA should replace the army as the state militia, which contradicted Hitler's views. Hitler may have been worried that the SA were becoming too powerful, and was also embarrassed by some of their actions. Most importantly, the army itself felt threatened by the SA and Hitler wanted to keep the army on side. Therefore on 30 June 1934, 84 members of the SA were executed and around 1000 arrested during the Night of the Long Knives. This left the SA as a much diminished force that no longer threatened the army or the Nazi Party.

Elimination of opposition outside the Party:

- Offices of trade unions, left-wing parties (the KPD and SPD) and left-wing newspapers were raided and damaged.
- The Reichstag Fire was used as a reason to ban the KPD at the end of Feb 1933.
- The Decree for the Protection of the People and the State (Feb 1933) suspended civil and political rights. Thousands of political opponents (mostly communists and socialists) were 'eliminated' by being put into concentration camps for 're-education'.
- Violence and intimidation was used against members of opposition parties.
- The SPD was banned (June 1933).
- DNVP (27 June 1933) and Centre Party (5 July 1933) voluntarily disbanded as they realised they would be closed down anyway.
- Law against Formation of New Parties (14 July 1933) made forming non-Nazi political parties illegal, ensuring there would be no more formal opposition parties.
- Civil servants who were suspected of being disloyal to the Nazi Party were sacked.
- Elected state assemblies were replaced with Nazi-dominated assemblies.
- State assemblies were later abolished (30 January 1934).
- Reichsrat was abolished (14 Feb 1934).
- Remaining political opponents were killed (e.g. Schleicher) or arrested (e.g. Papen) during the Night of the Long Knives (30 June 1934).

b Eliminating opposition from inside the Party, by killing and arresting members of the SA, was vital in obtaining the support of the German army for Hitler's government. The army was very powerful and was probably the only potential source of opposition that could have overthrown the Nazi government, so obtaining its support was very important. Eliminating the SA opposition also removed other problems, such as their different opinions on what should happen next, and further potential embarrassment caused by their actions.

Eliminating opposition from outside the Party, through violence, intimidation and legislation, ensured that few people were able to speak out against or prevent Nazi policies or actions by July 1934. It prevented organised opposition.

c Answers should analyse the importance of eliminating opposition from both within and outside the Nazi Party.

Chapter 14

Apply Your Knowledge

Genuine support for Nazi policies

- Belief in the Hitler Myth
- Many pleased with Nazi economic policies
- Many supported foreign policy

Propaganda

- Strict control over access to information meant people only read and heard what the Nazis wanted them to
- Presented a positive view of the regime, its leader and policies so many believed in Nazi success

Fear and terror

- Many were terrified of the Gestapo and SD – believed they were everywhere listening and watching – so therefore behaved as they were supposed to

- Use of concentration camps, torture, violence, etc. against opponents of the regime; 'frightened' others so they would not openly resist the regime

Use of the law

- Repressive laws with harsh penalties and an extensive police and legal system to enforce them

Assess the Validity of This View

a Ways in which 'terror' was used to maintain control:

- Torture, violence and imprisonment in concentration camps was used against opponents of the regime to ensure others would be too frightened to resist.
- Fear that the Gestapo and SD were listening and watching their every move was very effective at frightening people into behaving how the Nazis wanted them to.
- Repressive laws with harsh penalties were strictly enforced by the police agencies and the legal system.

Ways in which propaganda was used to maintain control:

- Ensured people could see and read only positive information on Nazi policies and Hitler, which meant many believed them.
- Opposing points of view or opinions were not published, so people did not hear opposing views, which may have influenced them.
- Played on people's existing fears and beliefs, so they were disposed to agree with the message.

b Answers need to include detailed analysis of both terror and propaganda and how they were used to maintain control, but analysis of other factors is not necessary. The essay needs to reach a judgement on the view in the question and support this judgement with further analysis.

Improve an Answer

a Answer 1 is the better answer because it focuses on the question throughout using a combination of detailed description of how the Gestapo worked and analysis of why this was significant. Answer 2 relies on rather vague description rather than analysing the effectiveness of the Gestapo at implementing terror. Also the link to the significance of the Gestapo is very weak 'and shows that they were really significant'.

b Your second paragraph could be on the SS, SD, concentration camps or the legal system.

Apply Your Knowledge

- **Political resistance**: Underground cells of KPD and SPD operated throughout the period, trying to spread opposing propaganda and expose the truth of some Nazi policies. The Gestapo frequently broke up cells but did not manage to successfully get rid of them altogether, however, the cells were not very successful at getting messages out to the public as they wanted to.
- **Worker resistance**: Trade Union offices and members were attacked early on in the regime and Trade Unions were absorbed in the Labour Front. There were some instances of resistance, such as strikes, absenteeism and sabotaging machinery, but nothing more serious. Some workers joined underground communist cells.
- **Resistance by the Churches**: The Confessional Church was created by Protestant pastors who refused to join the official Reich Church. Individual pastors and Catholic priests did sometimes speak out against the regime. The 1933 Concordant meant there was general Catholic compliance with the regime until 1937 when Nazi policies clashed with Catholic ideas and the Nazis extended their control of youth groups and other social movements; the Pope issued 'With Burning Grief'.

- **Resistance by young people**: Some refused to join Nazi youth organisations and wore controversial clothes and listened to banned music. Resistance was therefore not that serious and rarely dealt with very harshly by the Nazis as this was felt unnecessary.
- **Resistance by the elites**: Some civil servants and military officers were disdainful of Nazi methods but did little to actively oppose. Fritsch and Blomberg were both removed from their positions after speaking out against Nazi foreign policy, which strengthened Nazi control of the army.

Chapter 15

Apply Your Knowledge

- **Autarky**: Self-sufficiency or economic independence from trade with other countries

  This was a major long-term aim of Nazi economic policies, especially in the Four Year Plan from 1936, as the Nazis wanted to prepare Germany for war.

- **Rearmament**: Rebuilding supplies of weapons and military vehicles

  This was central to Nazi economic policies. Rearmament began soon after Hitler came to power but increased dramatically from 1936 owing to the Four Year Plan.

- **Autobahns**: Motorways

  Autobahns were built to provide good infrastructure and help reduce unemployment in the early years of Nazi rule. In reality their construction didn't employ many people and they were only used by a few people but they were a visible sign of economic growth.

- **Subsidies**: Money given, usually by the government, to help businesses

  Subsidies were an important part of Schacht's economic policies 1933–36, and they helped businesses struggling during the Depression. They were particularly aimed at helping businesses employ more people.

- **Tariffs**: A tax to be paid to the government on stated types of imports or exports

  The Nazis increased tariffs on imports to help some sectors of the economy (e.g. agriculture) as well as to encourage autarky so people would buy German made products which would increase their production.

- **Mefo Bills**: Credit notes that guaranteed the State would pay a business for work done but offered high interest for deferring on the money for 5 years

  One of Schacht's policies which was used to finance rearmament before the government could afford to pay for it and ensuring it would be kept secret.

Apply Your Knowledge

a and **b** Red = new jobs; blue = other methods used

- From 1933, job-creation schemes, such as building autobahns and houses created some jobs
- After 1936, rearmament created many jobs and by 1939 there were some labour shortages
- Between 1933–36, subsidies were given to some businesses which were used to employ more people
- From 1935, conscription meant most young men were counted as employed
- Reich Labour Service took unemployed young men 'out of the figures' for 6 months
- Married women were persuaded to give up work or dismissed
- Jews and other 'undesirables' were sacked from some jobs
- Figures were inflated through counting some unpaid workers and those on occasional contracts as employed

Assess the Validity

a · **Reduce unemployment**

Nazi claim: 'The Battle for work' won by 1936

Yes, unemployment was genuinely reduced and more people found work, however the propaganda claim was false as the official figures for unemployment were not an accurate reflection of the true picture. People did seem to believe the propaganda claim, though.

· **Revive the economy**

Nazi claim: Image projected of economic prosperity

Schacht's measures did stimulate the economy to some extent, however, there were signs of economic growth before the Nazis came to power; the propaganda contained an element of truth but many Germans experienced falling living standards 1935–36 owing to food shortages and rising prices.

· **Achieve autarky in food and raw materials**

Nazi claim: Autarky was achieved

No to both! Industry did not meet the targets set and imports were still high. Food production increased but not enough to make up for the reduced imports – rationing of some food stuffs in late 1930s.

· **Make Germany ready for war**

Nazi claim: Germany was strong and would win the war

Germany was not ready for war by 1939, and unprepared for a long war. Rearmament had increased massively but targets were not met and some areas were still reliant on imports of raw materials. It caused a massive strain on other parts of the economy. Food production had increased but not enough.

b Your answer would need to explain your view from the start and analyse the aims and achievements of Nazi economic policies as well as Nazi claims about what had been achieved. You could also include the belief of the German people in the success of Nazi economic policies being more important than the reality in some ways.

Apply Your Knowledge

Businesses benefited:

· Suppression of trade unions

· Political stability

· Some given subsidies to help recovery

· Wages were controlled

· Increased trade in early years

· Some took advantage of opportunities of rearmament, autarky, etc.

Businesses did not benefit or lost out:

· Increased state controls on prices, etc.

· Trade reduced in later years

· Shortages of some materials needed by some businesses in later years

· New Nazi enterprises such as Herman Goering Steel Works meant others lost out.

To What Extent?

a **Government spending on public work schemes**

Result: Helped to reduce unemployment but only slightly; did improve economic confidence and gave the impression of prosperity.

Tax concessions

Result: Some people spent more money on consumer goods, which helped with growth.

Subsidies to businesses to employ more people

Result: Helped reduce unemployment and produce more goods, so businesses profited.

Wages and prices were strictly controlled

Result: Prevented hyperinflation; wages did increase for many workers during 1933–36, partly because they were working longer hours; put living standards under pressure as prices rose.

Signing trade deals with foreign countries

Result: Increased trade and therefore profits by some businesses; did not resolve the imbalance of imports and exports – Germany was still reliant on imports. This led to a shortage of foreign exchange.

Creation of Reich Labour Service, 1935

Result: Reduced unemployment because young men had to work for 6 months in farming or construction.

Rearmament

Result: Reduced unemployment; was very expensive (government-financed through Mefo Bills); helped lead to serious shortages of key commodities by 1936.

Increased tariffs on imports

Result: Did help farmers; Germany still imported more than it exported; needed to import a third of raw materials in 1939.

Four Year Plans from 1936 set production targets for businesses

Result: Most targets were not met.

State ownership of some industries

Result: Increased amount of important goods produced, e.g. steel.

b · Worldwide recovery led to a revival of world trade from which Germany benefited.

· Some policies, such as public spending, tax concessions, etc. were begun by previous governments and continued by Schacht. Plus international growth probably meant Germany would have benefited anyway.

· Germany began to experience some economic growth in 1932 before the Nazis came to power, which illustrates that their policies cannot have been totally responsible.

c You could consider what would have needed to have happened for an economic miracle to have taken place, and then weigh up how far this was achieved by giving examples of economic growth and examples of economic problems that remained or developed.

Chapter 16

Apply Your Knowledge

a and **b** – answers to **b** are in brackets

Men: Trained to be soldiers (activities of HJ); physically fit to work (emphasis on PE in schools and activities of HJ); marry Aryan women (taught about racial hygiene in school/youth groups).

Women: Marry Aryan men, ideally soldiers (taught about 'racial hygiene' in schools/youth groups); have lots of children (medals introduced for having larger families); look after the home (German Women's League); raise children to be good citizens (Reich Mothers' Service); not work (especially if married) (loans for women who left work and married an Aryan); not go to university (restrictions placed on % of women on courses); serve the community.

Both: Complete loyalty to the Führer; fit and healthy to produce children; show self-discipline, obedience, etc.; knowledge and agreement with racialism and Social Darwinism (all taught in schools and youth groups).

To What Extent?

a **Ways in which women's lives changed**

· Some professional women lost their jobs.

· Some married women lost their jobs (but only for a time as labour shortages meant women were encouraged back into work by 1939).

· Fewer attended university.

· Some had more children.

· Women's groups were all under Nazi control, so women who attended them would have noticed some changes, e.g. more women 'trained' to raise their children in a certain way.

Ways in which women's lives stayed the same

· Many women already gave up work when they got married, and this continued.

· The majority of women married and became housewives and mothers.

· Most women continued to have only two children.

· Some working-class women continued to take jobs owing to financial necessity (the numbers in work actually increased).

· There had always been organised groups for women to socialise in (formerly Church groups were common; Nazi ones were similar).

b Professional women's lives would have been greatly changed as many lost their jobs. Lives of Jewish women greatly changed due to persecution, and similarly for other minorities, disabled women, etc.

c You should consider ways in which women's lives changed and ways in which they remained the same as before 1933. It is important also to consider variations between different women. You must come to some sort of judgement on the extent of change.

Source Analysis

a **Source A**

· *Authorship*: Social Democratic Party (SPD) members – the political party had been banned by the Nazis and the leaders fled into exile.

· *Effect of authorship*: As the SPD were very anti-Nazi, this may mean the content of the source is one-sided or exaggerated.

· *Date of source*: 1934, so this was during the period of Nazi rule but fairly early on before the full impact of Nazi rule had been felt, therefore written without the benefit of hindsight, which adds to its value.

· *Audience and purpose*: As it was written as a secret report to inform the SPD leadership of what was happening inside Germany, that adds to the value of the source as the authors would have wanted to portray an accurate picture.

· *Tone*: Mocking tone at times ('all that is marvellous', 'a great time without any danger', 'They believe in nothing but their Hitler'); emphasises young people's enthusiasm for Nazism and Hitler.

Source B

· *Authorship*: A leader in the Hitler Youth.

· *Effect of authorship*: Adds to its value as he had experience of what it was like being a member of the HJ.

· *Date of source*: 1982, which may limit its value as it's written quite a long time after the events so the author's memory may not be accurate, but would also have been affected by hindsight and knowledge of Nazi atrocities.

· *Audience and purpose*: As a memoir it would probably have been written with a view to publishing to the general German and international public. This may lessen its value.

- *Tone*: Factual; emphasises monotony and oppression of Hitler Youth.

Source C

- *Authorship*: Hitler
- *Effect of authorship*: As it's written by the Führer this adds to its value as it should convey the leader's opinions.
- *Date of source*: 1932, so before the Nazis took power.
- *Audience and purpose*: The audience was made up of members of the Hitler Youth. Purpose would have been to inspire listeners into continuing to be members of Hitler Youth.
- *Tone*: Passionate, wanting to inspire. Emphasises German nationalism and anything that threatens this: 'ignore social barriers', 'seek and find the German community', 'Let others mock and laugh'.

b Source A

Young people support the Nazis because they feel part of a community and have a good time. Education and knowledge is no longer valued. Many believe they will obtain jobs through persecuting Jews and Communists. Peasants and workers are both enthusiastic because they like being part of the national community and not an undesirable. Young people are at the heart of the Nazi movement and believe strongly in Hitler.

This is supported by other evidence which indicates that young people were among the most enthusiastic supporters of the Nazis and Hitler. However, there were young people who did not join Nazi youth groups and/or rebelled in other ways, such as by listening to jazz music or wearing alternative clothing, so the source presents an unbalanced view. Having said that, this is in 1934 and there is evidence that disillusionment with the Hitler Youth did not really appear until later in the 1930s.

Source B

Hitler Youth was oppressive and boring owing to the constant military drills. This meant that from childhood, people were taught to be tough and obedient without questioning authority. He believes young people put up with this because of their ambitions to impress the leaders and earn rewards and give orders.

Military drill was indeed an important part of the Hitler Youth because the Nazis wanted to train boys to be good soldiers. The other activities mentioned by this person also tie in with what is known about the other activities of the HJ (sport, shooting and singing). However, Hitler Youth groups did take part in other activities, such as camping, hiking and learning about racial hygiene and National Socialist ideology.

Source C

Members of the HJ should do whatever they can to find the German community and hold on to it. Young Germans should be, above everything else, nationalists. Nazi education of young people will benefit all Germans. Every young German dedicates themselves to Nazi ideology and ignores any mocking as they are the future of Germany.

c You need to analyse both the provenance and content of all three sources using your own knowledge.

Chapter 17

🔘 Apply Your Knowledge

a
- **Degenerate**: Someone considered to be immoral or corrupt.
- **Asocial**: Abnormal according to Nazi ideas.
- **Biological outsiders**: Someone whose physical or mental illness or disability meant they could not be part of the 'master race' or *Volksgemeinschaft*.

- *Untermenschen*: 'Sub-human' – racially inferior people.
- **Master race**: The most superior of human races – the Nordic/Aryan race.
- **Euthanasia**: Medical intervention aimed at killing a patient, normally intended to relieve their suffering.
- **Sterilisation**: A medical operation that permanently prevents someone from having children.
- **Deportation**: Expelling someone from a place to somewhere else.

b Roma and Sinti

Attitudes: Gypsies were classed as *Untermenschen* and therefore seen as racially inferior to Aryans.

Policies: Gypsies couldn't be German citizens or marry or have sexual relations with an Aryan (Nuremberg Laws, 1935); were located and classified; after Sept 1939, deported from Germany to Poland.

Tramps and beggars

Attitudes: Tramps and beggars were regarded as lazy asocials who needed punishing and re-educating by Nazi methods.

Policies: Mass round-ups of tramps and beggars from the streets in 1933, 1936 and 1938. Those collected were either forced into work or sent to concentration camps; in 1936 an 'asocial colony' was set up for re-education.

Slavs

Attitudes: Slavs were classed as *Untermenschen* and racially inferior to Aryans, though higher than gypsies.

Policies: Nothing during this period as there were few Slavs in German territory. Ideas of *Lebensraum* were taken by many to mean that Slavs would be affected in the future, though (which they were after war started).

Homosexuals

Attitudes: Homosexuals were classed as asocials and seen as degenerate and perverted.

Policies: As before 1933, homosexuality was banned in Germany. Nazis widened the definition and imposed harsher penalties from 1935. More men were arrested and imprisoned, when released they were sent to concentration camps to 'protect' the public; harshly treated in camps; many 'voluntarily' castrated.

Mentally ill

Attitudes: Considered to be biological outsiders because the Nazis described them as having defects which could be passed on to future generations and pollute the 'master race'.

Policies: From July 1933, sterilisation of people with some mental illness; from 1935 mentally ill pregnant women forced to have abortions.

Aryans

Attitudes: Believed to be the 'master race' and therefore superior to other races. Should be 'protected' from other races.

Policies: From 1935 (Nuremberg Laws), not allowed to marry or have sexual relations with non-Aryans.

Mentally or physically disabled

Attitudes: Considered biological outsiders that threatened racial hygiene and were a strain on the State.

Policies: From July 1933, mentally and physically disabled people were sterilised; from 1935, mentally or physically disabled pregnant women were forced to have abortions; in 1939, mentally and physically disabled children were euthanised – from October this was stepped up in the T4 programme, but was ended in August 1941 due to hostile public opinion.

🔘 Apply Your Knowledge

Create a colour-coded timeline for the four different groups.

🔘 Key Concept

Examples include:

- Compulsory sterilisation and then abortion for some people with mental illnesses and for those with inherited mental and physical disabilities that would reduce the chance of hereditary conditions being passed on and continuing to harm 'racial purity'.

- Euthanasia of mentally and physically disabled children that would stop any possibility of these 'defects' being passed on and continuing to harm 'racial purity'.

- Trying to stop Aryans marrying or having sexual relations with gypsies (and Jews) to ensure what was regarded as mixed-race children would not be born and harm 'racial purity'.

🔍Ⓐ Source Analysis

- The author (Himmler) was a very senior Nazi leader, which adds to its value.

- Date (December 1938) is significant, because in the following September, Gypsies began to be deported to Poland, therefore the 'physical separation' of Gypsies from Germans mentioned in this directive did take place.

- This directive would probably have been issued to the SS.

- Its purpose would be to prepare SS leaders for further laws/orders on how to treat Gypsies.

- The source emphasises that Gypsies are a threat to the German people because of their 'criminality' and 'compulsion to wander'. They are a threat to the 'homogeneity of the German nation' and they must therefore be separated from Germans to stop further mixing of blood (producing mixed-race children).

- The content confirms knowledge that Gypsies were regarded as a 'nuisance' and as 'criminals', and were treated as a separate race based on 'race-biological research'. Nazis were believers in eugenics and Social Darwinism.

- It also suggests there will be different policies for pure and part-Gypsies, as part-Gypsies are thought to be particularly prone to committing crime, though what these policies will be is not indicated.

- The source also says that efforts to make the Gypsies settle have been unsuccessful and hints that more regulations will follow.

⚖️Ⓐ How Significant?

a *'Volksgemeinschaft'* meant 'people's community of the nation'.

- **Roma and Sinti Gypsies**

  Reason: Classed as *Untermenschen* (racially inferior); only those considered racially pure could be part of *Volksgemeinschaft*.

  Nature of persecution: Gypsies couldn't be German citizens or marry or have sexual relations with an Aryan (Nuremberg Laws, 1935); they were located and classified; after Sept 1939, deported from Germany to Poland.

- **Jehovah's Witnesses**

  Reason: Refused allegiance to the Führer or to cooperate with other requirements of being in the *Volksgemeinschaft*.

  Nature of persecution: Many arrested and sent to concentration camps.

- **Asocials (tramps and beggars, homosexuals, criminals, alcoholics, prostitutes, 'work shy')**

  Reason: Behaved unacceptably according to Nazi ideas, therefore would 'pollute' the 'master race'.

Nature of persecution: Mass round-ups of tramps and beggars from the streets in 1933, 1936 and 1938. Those collected either forced into work or sent to concentration camps; in 1936 an 'asocial colony' set up for re-education. Nazis widened the definition of homosexuality and imposed harsher penalties from 1935. More men arrested and imprisoned, when released they were sent to concentration camps to 'protect' the public; harshly treated in camps; many 'voluntarily' castrated; some criminals and work-shy forcibly sterilised and sent to concentration camps for 're-education'.

- **Mentally ill and mentally or physically disabled**

  Reason: Biological outsiders because they had defects that Nazis believed could be passed on to future generations and threaten 'racial hygiene'/pollute the 'master race'.

  Nature of persecution: From July 1933, mentally and physically disabled people were sterilised; from 1935, mentally or physically disabled pregnant women were forced to have abortions; in 1939, mentally and physically disabled children were euthanised – from October this was stepped up in the T4 programme, but was ended in August 1941 due to hostile public opinion.

b • Education in schools – focused on creating new German man and woman, with knowledge of racial ideology, physically fit for becoming soldier/workers or bearing children.

- Only Nazi youth groups allowed after 1936, where education policy/indoctrination continued.

- Policies to encourage women to stop working (especially if/when married), marry Aryans and have many children.

- German Labour Front spread propaganda ideas to workers.

c Answers need to include detailed analysis of the persecution of non-Jewish minorities, including the mentally and physically disabled, mentally ill, those classed as 'asocials' and members of religious sects, in the implementation of *Volksgemeinschaft*. Answers also need to offer detailed analysis of other ways in which *Volksgemeinschaft* was implemented (eg. policies towards young people, women and workers). Policies towards Jews could also be included. Essays must include a judgement, supported by analysis, on the significance of the persecution of non-Jewish minorities against these other factors.

Chapter 18

🔘 Apply Your Knowledge

a **Apr 1933:** Boycott of Jewish shops; Jewish doctors banned from treating Gentiles; Restrictions given on numbers of Jews attending state schools and universities; Jews dismissed from civil service (except for those who had served in WWI); **Oct 1933:** Censorship and control of the press allowed anti-Semitic material. Many Jewish journalists were dismissed; **Aug 1934:** All remaining Jews dismissed from civil service; **Sept 1935:** Nuremberg Laws – Jews classed as subjects not citizens, relations between Jews and Gentiles banned; **Nov 1935:** Definition of 'Jewishness' – anyone who had 3 Jewish grandparents or 2 Jewish grandparents and married to a Jew

b Persecution jumped from mild to moderate from April 1933 where it remained until rising to between moderate and severe in 1935, then dropping back to between mild and moderate in 1936.

🔍 🅰️ To What Extent?

a • **Law for the Restoration of a Professional Civil Service (April 1933)**

  Affected: All Jews who worked in the civil service lost their jobs. To begin with, this did not have a big impact as Jews who'd served in the First World War or who had lost their fathers in the First World War were exempt, but after Hindenburg's death, these Jews lost their jobs too. This had quite a big impact on the Jewish middle class as a large number were civil service employees.

- **Laws to exclude Jews from the professions (1933)**

  Affected: Jewish doctors, lawyers and teachers, but these laws took time to take effect. Some Jews lost their jobs fairly soon but others remained unaffected for quite a while afterwards.

- **Banning Jewish doctors from treating Gentiles (April 1933)**

  Affected: Jewish doctors, but many continued to treat their existing patients as that was what their patients wanted.

- **Law against overcrowding of German schools and universities (April 1933)**

  Affected: Jewish school children and students. Again it took time to completely rid state schools and universities of Jews, so some would have been unaffected for a while.

- **Reich Press Law (October 1933)**

  Affected: Some Jewish journalists and writers lost their jobs.

- **Reich Citizenship Law (1935)**

  Affected: All Jews lost German citizenship so had fewer legal rights. This had a big impact as every Jew was affected.

- **Law for the Protection of German Blood and Honour (1935)**

  Affected: All Jews were now limited to who they could marry/have relationships with and extensions to the law meant that almost any physical contact between Jews and Gentiles was forbidden. This particularly affected Jewish men, who were often prosecuted for this offence on little evidence.

b Socially, Jews were affected because they could not interact with non-Jews as they had before. Young Jews excluded from state schools would have been separated from friends and made to feel isolated. Middle-class Jews were particularly badly affected economically as a large number of these worked in the civil service and professions. This would have had a follow-on effect on Jewish businesses, etc. as Jews had less money to spend or invest. Psychologically these laws would have come as a shock to many Jews. Some would have worried about what would happen next. Increasing numbers of Jews emigrated.

🔘 Apply Your Knowledge

- Jewish civil servants lost their jobs

- Some Jewish doctors would have lost business after they were banned from treating non-Jews (some ignored the ban and patients refused to leave)

- Some Jewish children were forced to leave state schools and universities

- From 1935, all Jews lost German citizenship and became subjects

- Some Jews were attacked e.g. Jewish lawyers during the boycott of Jewish shops

- Many Jewish editors and journalists lost their jobs or could not work

- Jews who were engaged to Gentiles would not have been allowed to marry them after the Nuremberg Laws

- Some Jews would have been left single after their gentile partners left them due to Nazi propaganda and encouragement

- After physical contact between Jews and Gentiles was banned, some Jewish men were sent to concentration camps for violating the law

⚖️ 🅰️ Assess the Validity of This View

a • The Nuremberg Laws applied to all non-Aryans, not just Jews (supports).

- Many communists were sent to concentration camps or fled into exile after the Reichstag Fire (challenges).

- Many local authorities and private businesses discriminated against both Jews and Gypsies (supports).

- Laws were passed to prevent Jews being employed in the civil service or the professions (challenges).

- The SPD party was banned in 1933. Many members were sent to concentration camps (challenges).

- Jehovah's Witnesses were banned as well as persecuted (challenges).

- Many gay men were sent to concentration camps, some were castrated (supports).

- Some Jewish children were removed from state schools by the authorities (challenges).

- Remaining non-Nazi politicians were murdered during the Night of the Long Knives (challenges).

- Disabled people and those suffering from mental illnesses were forcibly sterilised from July 1933 (challenges).

- Jews were attacked on the streets during the boycott of Jewish shops (challenges).

- Early anti-Semitic laws were slow to take effect and were sometimes ignored (supports).

- Some professional middle-class Jews were affected by the Civil Service and similar Laws (challenges).

- Anti-Semitic laws and discrimination could have had a very damaging psychological effect on Jews (challenges).

b Answers must include analysis of Nazi persecution of other groups as well as detailed analysis of Nazi persecution of Jews (use your answer to part **a** to help you with this). Answers must also reach a judgement on the view given in the question, supported by analysis.

Chapter 19

🔘 Apply Your Knowledge

Mar 1938: Austrian Jews lost citizenship, were banned from some public places, lost some property and employment; around 45,000 forced to emigrate; **Apr 1938:** Jews had to register all their property; **Jun/Jul 1938:** Jewish doctors, dentists and lawyers forbidden from treating Aryans (enforced earlier law); **Jul 1938:** Jews banned from more jobs, including travel agents and estate agents; **Sept 1938:** Jews banned from theatres, cinemas, concerts, circuses; **Oct 1938:** Passports of Jews had to be stamped with a J; **Nov 1938:** Jews lost entitlement to welfare; *Reichkristallnacht*, followed by ordering of Jews to pay a fine of 1 billion Reichsmarks for cost of repairs; Aryanisation of Jewish businesses completed; from 13 November Jews only allowed to attend Jewish schools; **Jan 1939:** Jews with 'non-Jewish' names forced to take names of Israel and Sarah

Graph will rise steeply in 1938 to severe and stay there in 1939.

⚖️ 🅰️ To What Extent?

a **How policies and actions changed:**

- Escalation of measures that affected different groups – mostly middle-class Jews affected very early on, then all affected by Nuremberg Laws, etc.
- From 1938, policies began that really started taking Jewish property away, Aryanisation of businesses, etc.
- From November 1938, Reichkristallnacht was the first case of widespread violence towards Jews and destruction of their property.
- As time went on, more promotion of emigration, however possible (by choice and forced).

How policies and actions stayed the same:

- Continued violence and animosity towards Jews throughout.
- Continual attempts to restrict employment opportunities for Jews.
- Encouragement of Aryans to discriminate against Jews in their businesses/leisure interests, etc.
- Anti-Semitic propaganda and scapegoating continued throughout.

b Answers should include detailed analysis of how policies and actions changed and how they stayed the same. There should also be a judgement, supported by analysis on the extent of change.

Apply Your Knowledge

Identification and isolation of Jews

- Passports had to be marked with a 'J'
- Women forced to take the name 'Sarah' and men 'Israel'
- Banning of Jews from public places e.g. theatres, cinemas, concerts, circuses

Economic/financial persecution

- State confiscated Jewish property worth over 5000 marks which began Aryanisation of businesses
- Jews lost entitlement to welfare benefits
- More Jews lost their jobs as salesmen, security guards, travel and estate agents
- Not allowed compensation for Reichkristallnacht destruction

Destruction of property

- Homes, businesses, synagogues and possessions were damaged and destroyed during Reichkristallnacht and Jews could not receive compensation

Physical attacks and arrests

- Thousands arrested and sent to concentration camps after Reichkristallnacht
- 61 killed and thousands injured during Reichkristallacht
- General increase in violence following *Anschluss*

'Encouraging' emigration

- 45,000 Austrian Jews forced to emigrate after *Anschluss* (only allowed/encouraged before)
- Forced emigration of some Jews in Germany from January 1939
- Deportation of Jews from western Poland to General Government area of Poland
- Attempts to deport German and Austrian Jews to General Government but not completed due to numbers involved
- Madagascar Plan – where Jews could be sent to die due to poor conditions – never enacted

Apply Your Knowledge

Factors encouraging Jewish emigration:

- Increasing persecution, humiliation and violence led more Jews to try to emigrate, especially after Reichkristallnacht.
- Professional, well-educated and relatively affluent Jews were more likely to be welcomed by other countries and find work.

- Some foreign countries helped organise schemes to take Jews, e.g. Kindertransport.
- Those Jews who had family in other countries were more likely to want to leave and be able to do so (other countries more likely to accept them, etc.).
- Zionists likely to go to Palestine.
- Forced emigration of Austrian Jews after *Anschluss*, which continued to some extent in the whole of Germany from January 1939.
- Deportation of Jews to General Government area of Poland.

Factors discouraging Jewish emigration:

- Few foreign countries were willing to accept Jewish refugees.
- Policies that hit Jews economically meant they did not have the money to leave – in addition, the Nazis confiscated the wealth when Jews did emigrate.
- Many Jews were strongly attached to Germany and had family, friends, property, etc. that they did not want to leave.
- Jews believed that the persecution could not get any worse – they had been persecuted before and believed it would pass.

Improve an Answer

a The student argues that all anti-Semitic laws and actions can be seen as ways to encourage or force Jews to leave. To counter this argument:

- The Aryanisation of businesses and confiscation of property over 5000 marks meant that some Jews did not have the financial means to emigrate.
- The violence and destruction of Reichkristallnacht was mostly done for its own sake and to punish Jews for being Jews, rather than with a greater aim in mind.
- There were some ideas of where Jews could go, but this was never fully investigated or enacted in any way.

b *Although there were other motives, it can be convincingly argued that a major aim of all anti-Semitic laws and actions in this period were initially to encourage Jews to emigrate and then, to force them to do so.(1) Measures which helped identify Jews(2) and isolate them,(3) damaged Jews economically(4) and hurt them physically(5) can all be seen as actions which were taken to frighten Jews so they would leave Germany. In addition, the range of ideas put forward as to where Jews could be deported to, such as Poland and Madagascar also supports emigration as a main aim of Nazi anti-Semitic policies and actions.(6)*

1 The Central Office for Jewish Emigration forced 45,000 Austrian Jews to emigrate after the *Anschluss* in March 1938. This policy was extended to the rest of Germany from January 1939.

2 From October 1938, all Jews had to have their passports marked with a letter 'J'. From January 1939 all Jewish women were forced to take the additional name of Sarah, and all Jewish males to take the name Israel.

3 By allowing them to attend only Jewish schools from November 1938, forbidding Jewish professionals from treating Aryans and banning Jews from many places of entertainment.

4 Further restricting employment opportunities, confiscating property, Aryanisation of businesses, destruction of property without compensation during Reichkristallnacht.

5 61 Jews were murdered during Reichkristallnacht, thousands were injured and thousands more sent to concentration camps.

6 There were plans to send Jews firstly to the General Government area of Poland, and then to Madagascar. Both plans had the aim of eventually killing Jews through the poor conditions in which they would have to live.

Source Analysis

a Goebbels was informed of the first killing of Reichskristallnacht. Others thought action should be taken before things got worse but Goebbels said it was only one dead Jew and other killings would follow. As there was time to give an order that would have prevented most of the killings, the report deduces that the killings were either intended or at least desirable. Therefore the individuals who carried out the murders could not be punished as they were carrying out the wishes of the Nazis.

b It is valuable as it shows when Goebbels knew about the first killing and that he did not want any action taken to prevent further killings. This ties in with knowledge that Goebbels knew about events and was, at least partly, responsible for them.

c Much information is 'deduced' rather than given in written or spoken orders, in which case the reader is dependent on the deductions of the author of the report. It is also lacking in specific factual detail.

Chapter 20

Apply Your Knowledge

a **Feb 1940:** First Jewish ghetto set up in Lodz; **Oct 1940:** German Jews excluded from wartime rationing; **Jul 1941:** *Einsatzgruppen* killings begin – an estimated 1.3 million Jews are killed by the end of the year; **Dec 1941:** Jews in Germany have to wear Star of David badge

Graph will again rise steeply in 1940 to mid-way between severe and very extreme and then rise again to extreme in 1941.

b Decide whether you need to adjust any part of your graph now you've reached 1941.

c It's unlikely to show a gradual increase throughout the whole period. You may have decided that 1936, for example, was a year when persecution decreased at least slightly (owing to worries about international condemnation, as this was the year of the Berlin Olympics). The following years could be considered to be times when persecution escalated rapidly: 1938 (marked a huge increase in violence as well as increased anti-Semitic legislation); 1940 (when Jews were completely physically segregated from Gentiles in ghettos); 1941 (marked the year when the mass killing of Jews began with the *Einsatzgruppen*). These final two dates were when anti-Semitic policies were applied to the vast areas of Europe that Germany now controlled, so there were many more Jews to deal with.

Apply Your Knowledge

- *Lebensraum*: Literally 'living space', this was the Nazi idea that the Aryan race needed more space. This would be in areas to the east of Germany that were occupied by 'inferior' races. This could be put into practice once the invasion and occupation of countries to the east of Germany took place from 1940.

- **Operation Barbarossa**: The German invasion of the Soviet Union, which started in June 1941.

- **Ghetto**: A part of a city or town occupied by a certain group of people. Nazi ghettos were established all over the Eastern occupied areas and Jews were forced to live in them. They were surrounded by high walls and guarded so people could not escape and only limited supplies were allowed in, to ensure conditions within ghettos were appalling.

- *Einsatzgruppen*: Special groups of paramilitary forces that were under the overall command of the SS. From June 1941, *Einsatzgruppen*, supported by police battalions and local groups, followed the German army into the Soviet Union and murdered millions of Jews, partisans and others.

- **Deportation**: Forcing people to leave a country or region. Jews began to be deported from Germany to the General Government area of Poland from 1940, where they were placed in ghettos. Jews from all over Poland and some parts of the USSR were also deported to ghettos.

- **Red Army**: The army of the Soviet Union. The main remaining opponent to the Nazis in the East from June 1941.

Assess the Validity of This View

a **Ways in which treatment of Jews was entirely different in 1939–41 compared with 1933–38:**

- *Einsatzgruppen* units rounded up and killed huge numbers of Jews as they followed the German Army on their invasion of the USSR. There was no policy of mass killing before this date (although Jews were murdered before this point, of course).

- Ghettoization began in Feb 1940, meaning Jews were totally physically segregated from Gentiles in Poland. Before this date, there had been attempts to segregate Jews economically and socially but they were not physically 'removed' from the rest of the population.

- With relatively small numbers of Jews living in Germany, the Nazis could afford to be cautious in their approach. The Boycott of Jewish shops in 1933 was so unpopular that the attacks on Jews ceased and little was done until the Nuremberg Laws, and even then policies were relaxed during the Olympic games of 1936 and the measures against Jews were only gradually stepped up and applied more vigorously as war approached.

Ways in which there were similarities in the treatment of Jews in 1939–41 and 1933–38

- Although deportation of Jews from one country to another did not occur in huge numbers before the war, some Jews were deported before this date, for example 45,000 Austrian Jews were deported in 1938.

- Anti-Semitic legislation that restricted Jews employment opportunities began in 1933 and continued throughout.

- Although violence and killing of Jews was sporadic and on a much smaller scale before the war, it did occur.

- Confiscation of Jewish wealth, property and businesses occurred before the war years (especially from 1938), although on a smaller scale than once the war began (for those Jews in Poland and the USSR at least).

b Your answer should examine ways in which treatment of Jews was both similar and different before deciding whether treatment can be considered 'entirely different' from the start of the Second World War. You could also include reference to different policies for different Jews. German Jews were not victims of *Einsatzgruppen* squads and although some German Jews were deported to ghettos in Poland, most were not (due to logistical difficulties) whereas the vast majority of Polish Jews, for example, were ghettoised.

Source Analysis

a The author is a Lithuanian policeman who worked with the *Einsatzgruppen*. Local police were often forced (or some willingly participated) to help the *Einsatzgruppen* do their 'work'. This adds to the value of the source, as he would have been an eyewitness and participant in the events. As it is written after Nazi Germany's defeat and when people who collaborated with the Nazis were at risk of being punished, he may be trying to excuse his own behaviour. The source was given in an interview in which the author appears to speak freely and with a vivid sense of recall. Although published later, the flow of the piece might indicate that the events have

been well-remembered and are being 'told straight' – not the result of text amendment and a contrived effort to present a particular case. However, the purpose might also suggest the author is trying to inform people of the activities of the *Einsatzgruppen* while also excusing his part in this.

b The tone is factual but also storytelling with examples of quoted speech.

c The author emphasises that the Lithuanian policeman had no choice, they had to carry out these killings or they themselves would be killed. This could be because he wants to ensure that he is not blamed or punished for his part in the killings. We know that local auxiliary forces were forced to help with *Einsatzgruppen* activities, but we also know that some volunteered or took matters into their own hands.

Chapter 21

Apply Your Knowledge

You need to create your own line graph with labels. It will probably look something like this:

Your line should be high (i.e. high level of morale) through 1939–1941, falling in the late summer/autumn of 1941 as the effect of the Russian campaign kicked in. It might then rise slightly in response to propaganda campaigns, but would slowly fall again through 1942 because of the growing numbers of air-raids. A possible rise might be seen at Christmas 1942, when extra rations were given out to boost morale. A further fall in 1943 would reflect how 'Total War' brought an end to professional sport, non-essential businesses, hairdressers and leisure facilities, and places such as Hamburg saw fire-storms. The lowest point of the line would be in 1944–45, with a possible 'bump' in July 1944, when Goebbels made a final attempt to mobilise Germany. The extreme air raids, bombing, and lack of food and supplies meant a very low level of morale in 1945.

Apply Your Knowledge

a **Propaganda methods:**

- Newsreel film from the war front.

- Frequent speeches given by Hitler by other leaders, e.g. Goebbels in the early years.

- Radio broadcasts.

- Posters.

- Newspaper articles and other printed media.

- Extra rations for special occasions (Christmas 1942).

- Campaigns to involve civilians in the war – knitting clothes, donating metals, growing food, etc.

- Commissioning of the film Kolberg (showing heroic German resistance to Napoleon in 1807), which was first shown January 1945.

b
- Some types of propaganda were drastically reduced – e.g. from February 1943 Hitler appeared and spoke less in public.

- News brought back by soldiers from the front seemed to contradict the official news on the war.

- As war-weariness and bombing took their toll people were less likely and less able to read, watch or listen to propaganda.

Plan Your Essay

a • **Military defeats and war casualties**

Morale was heavily dependent on what was happening in the war. People were worried from a national perspective (wanting their country to win, etc.) but were obviously more worried about their loved ones serving in the forces. As time went on and Germany suffered more

defeats with more men in the forces killed or injured, morale worsened.

- **Allied bombing**

This negatively affected morale on quite a large scale as so many were affected – fear and stress about personal safety and safety of loved ones and sleeplessness from the noise of constant raids, etc., destruction of homes, businesses, roads and transport, services, etc., all made life more difficult and added to other problems such as food shortages and living conditions. Also led to many civilian deaths.

- **Availability of food**

Adequate food supplies meant people were likely to be satisfied, whereas shortages negatively affected morale. Towards the end of the war, food shortages were extreme in some areas and there were instances of starvation. People in the countryside were less likely to suffer food shortages than those in towns or cities.

- **Lack of consumer goods**

Being able to access fuel for heating and cooking, clothing, soap, etc., was important for maintaining morale; lack of these things made life harder and therefore negatively affected morale.

- **Working conditions and wages**

Longer working hours, especially after 1943, and wage freezes negatively affected morale and made people tired and exhausted. More people, especially women, were conscripted into work as the war went on, which many did not like.

- **Living conditions**

Particularly badly affected by bombing when many were made homeless, access to electricity, running water, sewage systems, etc., was poor in the last few months of war, which led to disease and affected morale very badly.

- **Increased conscription**

As more men, and younger men, were conscripted into the forces, and men and women were conscripted into work, this impacted morale directly and indirectly. Some would have welcomed being conscripted, some would have been afraid or disliked it. Relatives would fear for those conscripted into the forces.

b You should arrange your cards in a hierarchy, with the factor that you believe most affected civilian morale at the top, and the factor that you believe least affected civilian morale at the bottom.

c Your plan should include analysis of how military defeats and increasing war casualties led to declining morale, before analysing several other factors that led to morale declining.

How Significant?

a Ideas could include:

- Husbands/brothers/sons being conscripted into the forces meant they would be absent from home, bringing great worry to those left behind. Also meant women had to fill the tasks that men usually did.

- Rationing and shortages of food and other consumables meant that obtaining basic necessities became harder and harder as the war continued. Queuing for food could take hours.

- More and more women were conscripted into war work or the auxiliary forces. This would have been a massive change for many. It also meant practical difficulties such as finding childcare for those who had children.

- Bombing caused huge stress and fear, and the destruction made transport difficult, exacerbated food shortages, made living conditions poorer, etc., even for those whose homes were not hit. Some became homeless, some were injured or became ill.

b Variations in circumstances:

- Older women were less likely to have husbands conscripted into the forces or work so would have had their support around the home; not conscripted themselves into war work. May have volunteered for certain roles. Some may have looked after grandchildren whose mothers had been conscripted into war work.
- Women who already worked in a reserved occupation would have had less change than those who were not working before the war.
- Food shortages were worse in cities so women living in the countryside were likely to have been less affected by trying to feed themselves and their children.
- Women in the countryside were not affected directly by bombing.
- Those women whose husbands were exempt from war service conscription would not have had their husbands absent.
- Wealthier women would have had access to the black market for food and other consumables so were less likely to be affected by shortages.
- Younger women with no children or just one child would have been greatly affected as many would have been conscripted into work and their husbands would have been conscripted too.

c In your answer you should come to a judgement on how significantly women's lives changed. You need to analyse ways in which women's lives changed and how they stayed the same, including reasons why some women's lives were changed more than others.

Chapter 22

⚙ Apply Your Knowledge

a **German labour**

1939: Many workers moved from producing consumer goods to munitions or other war work; concentration camp inmates used as slave labour

1943: All men 16–65 and all women 17–45 had to register for work and some immediately conscripted; all employees working for non-essential small businesses were transferred to war work

1944 and 1945: More conscripted into war work

Foreign labour

1940: Workers recruited from occupied Western countries (until Spring 1942); concentration camp inmates used as slave labour

1941: From October, Russian POWs used as slave labour

1942: March 1942, Plenipotentiary General Dept for Labour Allocation set up to increase number of foreign workers – many were rounded up, transported to Germany and became forced labourers, others became forced labourers within occupied countries

b All workers were expected to work hard and could be punished if they didn't (types of punishment varied from docking pay for German workers to beating slave labourers). Workers from occupied Western Europe were treated similarly to German workers (received similar wages, etc.). Forced labourers from occupied Eastern Europe were paid half what German workers received for the same work. Concentration camp inmates and POWs were treated as slave labourers – receiving no payment and enduring extremely harsh living conditions.

⬆ Ⓐ Improve an Answer

a Allied bombing raids frequently targeted industrial sites, ports and supply lines <u>especially those in the</u>

<u>Rhineland and Ruhr areas. By the end of the war, some cities such as Berlin and Dresden (where 75% of the city was destroyed) had been massively damaged. Industrial production was reduced in several ways.</u> The raids themselves disrupted production as terrified workers had to stop work and take cover. Then the bombs caused damage to many factories <u>and</u> businesses , some were totally destroyed. <u>This meant that production was reduced or sometimes halted completely until they were repaired. As transport links were damaged or destroyed, raw materials or component parts could not be delivered or armaments delivered to where they were needed. Labour was reduced as</u> workers were killed and injured <u>as well as being tired and stressed from the raids and were diverted from production to rebuilding and repairing damaged buildings and infrastructure. This meant there were fewer workers, so fewer goods could be produced. Those workers who did continue in industrial production were tired and stressed from the raids which probably reduced their output.</u>

b Your paragraph could be on any other effect of the bombing raids such as:

- civilian deaths (and the bereavement caused) and injuries
- homelessness, destroyed possessions and poor living conditions
- further reduced food supplies and supplies of other consumer goods
- destruction of roads and other transport links
- destruction of electricity, gas, water supplies.

🔍 Ⓐ Source Analysis

a - **The author**: Fritz Sauckel was appointed head of the department for labour allocation so this adds value to the source as he was 'an insider', responsible for increasing the labour force by finding foreign labour.

- **The date the source was written and whether this is significant (use your knowledge of events)**: April 1942 – only a month after the Department for Labour Allocation had been created and a few months after Albert Speer had began his work coordinating the production of armaments in order to increase the output.

- **Who the source is addressing**: Those in charge of labour conscription in the East – again this adds value to the source, giving instructions on what they should do to 'recruit' additional workers.

- **Why the source was produced**: To give instructions to those in charge of labour conscription in the East, making it a valuable indicator of the chain of command and responsibility.

- **The tone of the source**: Straightforward and serious, making it appear a well-considered memo and therefore likely to represent a genuine opinion.

- **The emphasis of the source**: It was essential to find many more 'tremendous quantity' workers, mostly from occupied countries in the East, and that these people must 'cost' as little as possible, so providing a valuable insight into conditions at the time.

b - All POWs from everywhere should be working for the German war effort and output must be maximised.

- Most labour will have to come from the Eastern occupied countries.

- Conscription or forced labour should be used if enough people don't volunteer.

- All POWs and foreign workers from the East must be exploited 'to the highest possible extent at the lowest conceivable' cost.

⚖ Ⓐ To What Extent?

a Speer became Minister for Armaments in February 1942.

- The Four Year Plan needed longer to run, in order to prepare Germany fully for war, so there were shortages of weapons and military equipment.
- There was no clear direction for the war economy as different departments gave different and competing directions. Huge variety of highly specialised equipment was demanded by different branches of the armed forces.
- Labour shortages were becoming more serious (Hitler refused to conscript women into war work).
- Many small specialised companies contributed to armaments production, most of which was done on a small scale by each firm.

b **Speer's policies and actions**

- Allocation of all labour, equipment and materials to factories was coordinated centrally.
- Fewer factories were used and they concentrated on producing a smaller range of equipment – focused on the essentials.
- Used more mass-production techniques.
- Used more shift working, so factories operated 24 hours a day.
- Skilled armaments workers became exempt from military conscription.

Impact of Speer's actions (including limitations)

- Productivity of all factories and most workers increased.
- Production did massively increase, despite the impact of Allied bombing.
- He did not manage to completely coordinate the economy and there was still some overlap and competition between departments.
- Vital raw materials remaining in short supply.

Other factors that boosted the war economy

- Conscription of more men and particularly women into war work in 1943.
- Increased number of forced and slave labourers from Eastern occupied countries and concentration camps in factories and on farms.
- Workers from other occupied countries, e.g. France, Belgium, Holland.
- Closing down of consumer industries to permit total concentration on war-based industry.
- Wartime propaganda within Germany encouraging long hours and maximum effort.

c You need to state a clear judgement on the extent to which Albert Speer saved the war economy of Nazi Germany. You may of course decide that he failed to save the war economy at all, but this is unlikely. Whichever judgement you reach, you should support it with an analysis of Speer's work and the impact on the war economy. You should also include other factors that improved the economy.

Chapter 23

⚙ Apply Your Knowledge

- **Holocaust**: The term used to describe the mass killing of Jews by various means by the Nazis and their collaborators between 1933 and 1945. It is not usually used for other victims of the Nazis.
- **'Final Solution'**: The plan to exterminate all Jews in Europe.
- **Death marches**: Forced marches of prisoners from death camps and concentration camps over extreme distances that took place as the end of the war approached. They became known as death

marches as so many people died or were killed on them.

- **Concentration camp**: A camp where prisoners were sent as 'punishment'. There were thousands of camps set up throughout occupied Europe and within Germany. Inmates often did forced labour and were treated very harshly. Initially a concentration camp was a camp for the 're-education' of inmates – meaning Nazi indoctrination.
- **Death camp**: A camp where the main aim was to kill all prisoners who arrived there, mostly through gas. There were six death camps.

🔍 🅐 Source Analysis

a The source is written by a death camp survivor, recounting his experiences of Belzec just a few years after the events took place. Therefore, the source provides a valuable insight into what happened at a Nazi death camp. The purpose of the source was probably to inform people about what happened, perhaps even in the hope that people would be held to account for the atrocities witnessed there. The value of the source is heightened because Rudolf Reder was one of only a handful of survivors of Belzec, so there would be perhaps only one other source of information from the same perspective. The tone of the source is one of sorrow. The author emphasises the deceit and brutality of the SS and portrays the Jews as helpless victims of the regime. As this source was written a few years after the events the author is likely to have been affected by knowledge of the extent of the Holocaust, and his personal background would have made him more inclined to show the activities there in the worst possible light. However, the details of the events are similar to many other accounts of other death camps, so it seems unlikely the author is exaggerating this aspect, although he may have been exaggerating that all victims did not know their fate, as other records indicate that many knew what happened at the death camps. This does not really affect the value of the source, as it may be true if he is writing about an early transportation.

b The source gives valuable details of the fate of Jews arriving at Belzec, such as the sign in big letters on the gas chambers of 'Bath and inhalation room', the shaving of heads of women and girls, and time taken for people to die in the gas chambers. It also describes the differing emotions of the victims, who appear terrified and anxious, then happy and relieved, before returning to feelings of anxiety and worry.

💡 Key Concept

a • Mass shootings by *Einsatzgruppen* units killed mostly Jews but Slavs too, especially those suspected of being communist supporters.
- All groups, including Slav POWs were used for slave labour.
- Some Gypsies and some Slav POWs were murdered in death camps, though on a far smaller scale than Jews.
- Members of all groups were sent to concentration camps and many died from the poor conditions and harsh treatment.

b • Only Jews were rounded up and put into ghettos, where many died from harsh conditions.
- There was a plan (the 'Final Solution') for the extermination of all Jews in Europe. While many others suffered, there was never a plan to exterminate the entire group.

⚖️ 🅐 Assess the Validity of This View

a Causes of the 'Final Solution':
- The nature of the war in the East – war against 'lesser races' and 'sub-humans' (Slavs and Jews).

- Anti-Semitic ideology of the Nazis.
- Incremental effect of anti-Semitic policies since 1933 – laws and treatment had increased in severity until exploding into violence during Reichkristallnacht.
- Hitler's extreme anti-Semitism and other leading Nazis wanting to please him.
- Anti-Semitism of Germans and those in occupied countries who, to some extent, colluded with the Nazis or at least were not openly critical of previous anti-Semitic actions.

b There is no correct answer here but you need to spend time considering each cause and the reasons you have rated it as you have.

c You should write a full answer to the exam question, based on the above.

Chapter 24

⚙️ Apply Your Knowledge

You should create a mind-map of opposition and resistance during the war.

🔍 🅐 Source Analysis

This source was written by the White Rose Group, a small opposition group of students based in Munich. It is an extract from the Fifth Broadsheet, which the group created and distributed to try to stir up more open opposition to the Nazi regime and is therefore valuable to historians studying resistance as it is an example of methods that one resistance group used. The date is significant as it was written and distributed as the Second World War had really begun to go badly for Germany as the army were facing imminent defeat at Stalingrad. The White Rose Group may have felt that it was more likely for people to join resistance groups or take part in resistance activities now military defeat was a real possibility.

The tone of the source is passionate to try to persuade people to support resistance and oppose the Nazis. It uses various terms of abuse, such as 'gangsterism' and 'criminal' to emphasise what the group believes is the nature of the Nazi regime. The source also abuses those who choose not to resist the Nazis openly, accusing them of 'indifference' and cowardice. This is valuable as it proves there were Germans who understood the extent of atrocities ('the same fate that befell the Jews') and true nature of the regime. The emphasis of the source is particularly valuable in showing the preoccupations of those involved in resistance because the writers are continually highlighting the future and what the rest of the world will think of Germans who did not resist the Nazis: 'hated and rejected by all mankind'; 'a terrible but just judgment will be meted out'.

💡 Key Concept

a Methods used:
- Popular policies
- Indoctrination and propaganda
- Terror and fear

b These methods changed in their levels over time, particularly during the war years. Especially after military defeat at Stalingrad in January 1943, the Nazis relied more on terror and fear to sustain their rule as genuine popularity diminished and propaganda and indoctrination became less effective.

⚙️ Apply Your Knowledge

- **Support for Nazi policies**

  1934–39: This was an important factor in these years. Economic and foreign policies were popular with many Germans, even those who disagreed with other policies.

  1939–45: Support for Nazi policies remained strong for the first few years even though few Germans were enthusiastic about the war. Support drained away after 1943 as the army began to be driven back and sufferings on the home front really began.

- **The Hitler Myth**

  1934–39: Many believed in the Hitler Myth and that he was the 'saviour' of Germany. Although some Nazis were unpopular and disliked, Hitler retained popularity with many Germans throughout the period.

  1939–45: While the war was going well, the Hitler Myth was improved as many thought he was a military genius. The turning point was defeat at Stalingrad in January 1943 as many blamed Hitler for this. As Hitler appeared in public less and less in the last year of the war, belief in the Hitler Myth almost totally disappeared.

- **Propaganda and censorship**

  1934–39: The Nazis kept a tight control over access to information. Joseph Goebbels was a master of conveying the messages which he wanted to a mass audience. Censorship ensured that very few publications were able to put across a different view.

  1939–45: Propaganda emphasised good news from the front and played down defeats or set-backs which worked until soldier's letters home or other information contradicted the official message. Few people believed the information given to them by the authorities in the last few months of the war.

- **Terror and repression**

  1934–39: With an extensive police system and a legal system stacked against them, open opposition to the regime was dangerous. Many feared concentration camps. Even more feared the Gestapo and SD who 'spied' on the population looking for dissent.

  1939–45: Opposition and hostility to the Nazis became even more dangerous during the war years as the police cracked down on any suspicion of dissent. People even suspected of disloyalty could be killed, rather than imprisoned or sent to a concentration camp as in the pre-war years.

- **War weariness and focus on survival**

  1934–39: Not relevant in these years.

  1939–45: In the last few years of the war, war weariness set in. Germans were suffering from bombings, food shortages, increased working hours, etc. In the final few months of the war especially, there was great suffering for many. Although many were opposed to the Nazis by this time, they were just focusing on survival and accepted that the Nazis would be removed by the Allied powers anyway at some point, as defeat in the war was inevitable.

⚖️ 🅐 How Significant?

a In this case, significance means how much of a threat these groups posed to the Nazis. This could be a direct threat to their power, for example, by attempts at a coup to take over the running of the country, or through more indirect ways that undermined Nazis control and/or support and compliance for their policies. The extent of significance needs to be evaluated through ideas such as how much support each group managed to attract or how serious the type of resistance was.

b · **Edelweiss Pirates**

What it did/tried to do: Rejected the Hitler Youth; tried to avoid conscription; Cologne Edelweiss Pirates helped army deserters and escaped POWs; attacked army depots to get supplies.

Extent of the threat: Only operated in some areas (Rhineland and Ruhr) and only some groups caused problems; most groups broken up by Gestapo; leaders in Cologne publically hanged.

· **Swing Youth**

What it did/tried to do: Young people rebelled against the wishes of the Nazis through clothing, hairstyles and music; not overtly political.

Extent of the threat: In some major cities but as not political, never really challenged the regime itself.

· **White Rose Group**

What it did/tried to do: Issued pamphlets in 1942–43 to raise more opposition to the Nazis, particularly their treatment of Jews; painted anti-Nazi slogans.

Extent of the threat: Very small group in Munich but tried to create more open resistance.

· **Catholic Church**

What it did/tried to do: Only individuals spoke out, e.g. Bishop Galen against euthanasia programme, and Archbishop Frings against killing of POWs and persecution of Jews.

Extent of the threat: As only a few individuals, the threat wasn't great, though some success gained at influencing policy, e.g. end of euthanasia programme.

· **Protestant Confessional Church**

What it did/tried to do: Made public information about the treatment of Jews.

Some leading members continually spoke out against regime, e.g. Dietrich Bonhoffer.

Extent of the threat: On quite a small scale.

· **Communists**

What it did/tried to do: KPD had cells in some German cities.

Extent of the threat: Fairly small-scale owing to imprisonment, killings and exile of many communists before 1939; many cells infiltrated by Gestapo.

· **Kreisau Circle**

What it did/tried to do: Diverse group of elites who met three times to discuss possible ways of resisting.

Extent of the threat: Small-scale and easily broken up by Gestapo.

· **Army**

What it did/tried to do: A pre-war plot to assassinate Hitler wasn't activated. (The land gains Hitler made in the pre-war negotiations with Chamberlain made Hitler incredibly popular in Germany and too difficult to assassinate); after Stalingrad, January 1943, senior officers plotted to assassinate Hitler; two failed attempts – the second was very close to achieving its aim!

Extent of the threat: Had little support from German civilians. Did pose a real threat to the Nazis as the only real opposition to have the means to succeed in deposing the regime.

c Answers should include a detailed analysis of the types of opposition and resistance, giving details of opposition groups and how significant the threat posed by each group was. Answers also need to reach a judgement on the significance of the opposition and resistance, with analysis supporting this judgement.

Glossary

A

Anschluss: (the union) the takeover of Austria by Germany in March 1938

anti-Semitism: hatred and fear of Jews (Semites)

Aryan: the term used by racial theorists, including the Nazis, to describe the race to which non-Jewish Germans belonged

asocials: those who did not conform to Nazi norms including beggars, prostitutes and pacifists, but also the mentally and physically disabled

autarky: economic independence or self-sufficiency

C

Chancellor: the German title for a Prime Minister

communist: a believer in a system based on public ownership of land and industry, where all are equal and people work for the common good

conservative: a person who resists change and tries to preserve social and political institutions in their current state

D

democracy: system of government based on freedom and equality in which power is held either by elected representatives or by the people themselves

E

Einsatzgruppen: 'Special Groups', temporary units made up of police and regular troops commanded by the Gestapo, the SD and the Criminal Police

eugenics: the theory that a race or group of people could be genetically improved through selective breeding

F

Freikorps: a volunteer force setup at the end of 1918 consisting of demobilised junior army officers and NCOs as well as students, adventurers and drifters

G

German Labour Front/DAF (*Deutches Arbeitsfront*): a Nazi-run organisation established in 1933 to coordinate workers into the National Socialist Regime

Gestapo: Secret State Police established by Herman Goering; depended on information supplied by informers

Gleichschaltung: 'forcing into line', the process through which the Nazis attempted to control or 'coordinate' all aspects of German society

K

Kaiser: German Emperor

KdF (*Kraft durch Freude*): 'Strength through Joy', a movement set up by Robert Ley and the DAF to organise workers' leisure times

L

Lebensraum: 'living space', a concept by which Hitler justified his plans to take over territory to the east of Germany

'left': political parties that believe in social, economic and political change

liberalism: favouring individual liberty, free trade, and moderate political and social reform

M

Mittelstand: 'middle rank'; a large but diverse social group including small farmers, small shopkeepers and artisans

N

nationalism: pride in, and loyalty to, one's nation; extreme forms promote the idea of the superiority over others

Nazism: set of political beliefs associated with the NSDAP, including extreme nationalism, belief in the racial superiority of Germans and their right to take the lands of the 'racially inferior'

P

paramilitary: a group of civilians organised into a military style group with uniform and ranks; such groups take on military functions

pogrom: an organised massacre of an ethnic group

propaganda: the systematic spreading of ideas and information in order to influence the thinking and actions of the people at whom it is targeted, often through the use of media such as posters, film, radio and the press

proportional representation: a system of elections in which parties are allocated seats in parliament according to the proportion of votes they receive

putsch: a coup or violent attempt to overthrow a government

R

radicalism: the belief in complete social, economic and political change

Red-Front Fighters' League: the paramilitary arm of the KPD Party; established in 1924, under the leadership of Ernst Thälmann, and engaged in street battles with the SA, the police and other right-wing paramilitary groups

Reichstag: elected lower house of the German parliament

Reichswehr: German Army

'right': politically conservative or reactionary, wishing to slow down the pace of change or to reverse it altogether

S

Slav: a very diverse ethnic group including Czechs, Slovaks, Poles, Russians, Ukrainians, Croats, Serbs and Slovenes

Social Darwinism: the belief that the laws of natural selection, as outlined by Charles Darwin, apply as much to human beings as to plants and animals; 'survival of the fittest'

SS (Schutzstaffel): Hitler's personal bodyguard, created in 1926

Stahlhelm: 'Steel Helmets', a paramilitary organisation of ex-servicemen dedicated to the restoration of the monarchy and the revival of Germany as a military power

Stormtroopers (SA): the paramilitary wing of the Nazi Party, led by Ernst Röhm

T

Total War: a conflict in which a combatant state mobilises its entire population and all of its material resources to participate in the war effort

U

Untermenschen: literally 'subhumans', used by the Nazis to describe those whom they considered to be racially inferior, including Jews, Gypsies and peoples of the Slav race

V

Volksgemeinschaft: the concept of a 'people's community'; it was a key element in Nazi ideology

Top Revision Tips for A Level History

Democracy and Nazism

The History revision tips on this page are based on research reports on History revision and on the latest AQA examiners' reports.

General advice

☐ Make a realistic revision timetable for the months leading up to your exams and plan regular, short sessions for your History revision. Research shows that students who break down their revision into 30- to 60-minute sessions (and take short breaks in between subjects) are more likely to succeed in exams.

☐ Use the **progress checklists** (pages 3–4) to help you track your revision. It will enable you stick to your revision plan.

☐ Eat healthily and make sure you have regular amounts of sleep in the lead-up to your exams. This is obvious, but research shows this can help students perform better in exams.

☐ Make sure your phone and laptop are put away at least an hour before you go to bed. You will experience better quality sleep if you have had time away from the screen before sleeping.

Revising your History knowledge and understanding

☐ Using a variety of revision techniques can help to embed knowledge successfully, so don't just stick to one style. Try different revision methods, such as: flashcards, making charts, diagrams and mind-maps, highlighting your notebooks, colour-coding, re-reading your textbook or summarising your notes, group study, revision podcasts, and working through the activities in this Revision Guide.

☐ Create a timeline with colour-coded sticky notes to make sure you remember important dates relating to the six German Depth Study key concepts (use the **timeline** on page 9 as a starting point).

☐ Make sure you understand key concepts for this topic, such as nationalism, anti-Semitism and Social Darwinism. If you're unsure, attend your school revision sessions and ask your teacher to go through important concepts again.

☐ Identify your weaknesses. Which topics are easy and which are more challenging for you? Give yourself more time to revise the challenging topics.

☐ Answer past paper questions and check the answers (using the AQA mark schemes) to practise applying your knowledge correctly and accurately to exam questions.

Revising your History exam technique

☐ Review the **AQA mark scheme** (page 8) for each exam question, and make sure you understand how you will be marked.

☐ Make sure you revise your skills as well as your knowledge. In particular, ensure you know how to approach the sources question. Practise assessing the value of sources.

☐ Find a memorable way to recall the **How to master your exam skills** steps (pages 6–7) – it will help you plan your answers effectively and quickly.

☐ Ask your teacher for the examiners' reports – you can find out from the reports what the examiners want to see in the papers, and their advice on what not to do.

☐ Time yourself and practise answering past paper questions.

☐ Take mock exams seriously. You can learn from them how to manage your time better under strict exam conditions.

Topics available from *Oxford AQA History for A Level*

Tsarist and Communist Russia 1855–1964
978 019 835467 3

Challenge and Transformation: Britain c1851–1964
978 019 835466 6

The Tudors: England 1485–1603
978 019 835460 4

Stuart Britain and the Crisis of Monarchy 1603–1702
978 019 835462 8

The Making of a Superpower: USA 1865–1975
978 019 835469 7

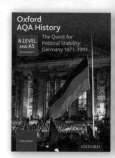

The Quest for Political Stability: Germany 1871–199
978 019 835468 0

The British Empire c1857–1967
978 019 835463 5

Industrialisation and the People: Britain c1783–1885
978 019 835453 6

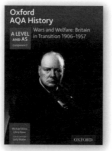

Wars and Welfare: Britain in Transition 1906–1957
978 019 835459 8

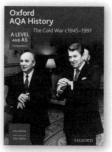

The Cold War c1945–1991
978 019 835461 1

Democracy and Nazism: Germany 1918–1945
978 019 835457 4

Revolution and Dictatorship: Russia 1917–1953
978 019 835458 1

Religious Conflict and the Church in England c1529–c1570
978 019 835471 0

International Relations and Global Conflict c1890–1941
978 019 835454 3

The American Dream: Reality and Illusion 1945–1980
978 019 835455 0

The Making of Modern Britain 1951–2007
978 019 835464 2

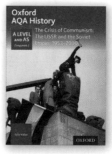

The Crisis of Communism: the USSR and the Soviet Empire 1953–2000
978 019 835465 9

The English Revolution 1625–1660
978 019 835472 7

France in Revolution 1774–1815
978 019 835473 4

The Transformation of China 1936–1997
978 019 835456 7

RECAP · APPLY · REVIEW · SUCCEED

The Tudors: England 1485–1603 Revision Guide
978 019 842140 5

Democracy & Nazism: Germany 1918–1945 Revision Guide
978 019 842142 9

Tsarist & Communist: Russia 1855–1964 Revision Guide
978 019 842144 3

The Making of Modern Britain 1951–2007 Revision Guide
978 019 842146 7

Oxford AQA History for A Level Revision Guides offer step-by-step strategies and the structured revision approach of Recap, Apply and Review to help students achieve exam success.

Also available in eBook format

eBook Available

Order online at **www.oxfordsecondary.co.uk/aqahistory**

OXFORD